RESPONSIBLE FINANCE IN THE WORLD

REALITIES AND CHALLENGES

Cover illustration:
©Freepik.com

ISBN 978-2-7472-2910-4

CONSULTANT for USA:
ESKA Publishing
Paul Lipscomb
3808 SW Dosch Road
Portland, Oregon 97239 – USA
http://www.eska-publishing.com

RESPONSIBLE FINANCE IN THE WORLD

REALITIES AND CHALLENGES

MICHEL ROUX

Foreword: Trust: golden fleece of Finance by Jean-Louis Bancel

ESKA Publishing

Many thanks to Serge MORARD for his involvement in the proofreading of the manuscript in English.

Works by the same author:[1]

Individual works

- "Finance ethical, structures, actors and prospects in France." Review Banks edition, Paris 2005. Mention of honor Turgot Price.
- "Study for the Inter ministerial Delegation for Innovation, Social Experimentation and the Social Economy," Report returned in January 2008.
- "Mutual insurance companies, a developmentally challenged status," ESKA 2009.
- "Co-operative Banks in Europe, Strategies and Challenges," the Essentials of Banking and Finance, Revue Bank Edition, 2009.
- "Retail Banking," Edition ESKA, Paris 2010. Mention of honor Turgot Price.
- "Banking management," Vuibert Editions, Paris 2013.
- "Strategy and governance of the Financial institutions Mutualists," Review banks Edition, 2015.
- "Retail banking Management," Collection Master Degree, Eska editions, February 2017.

Collective works

- "Practical "Relations Company-banks," Francis Lefebvre practical files, Francis Lefebvre edition, 1992.
- "Corporate Governance," under the direction of Jorge MUNOZ, "Impact of corporate social responsibility strategies on the mission and governance of cooperative financial institutions," Rennes University Press, 2006

[1] Michel Roux is Honorary Dean of the University Paris 13–Sorbonne Paris Cité. Banking professional, lawyer.

- "Mutual insurance companies: challenges and prospects for a completely separate model or a full-fledged model in the face of financial, economic and social crises?", 4th edition of the Year of the Financial occupations, works published by the Association of financial economy, March 2009.
- "Debt crisis and financing new growth: A new growth, finance differently, or how to manage paradoxes," The year of financial professions, volume 6, published by the Association for Financial Economics (AEF), Paris 2011, book nominated for the Turgot Prize for the best collective work, honorable mention 2011, category collective work.
- Contribution to a chapter of international collective work: Recent Developments in alternative Finance, chapter; "The Challenges of the Mutual Financial Sphere Statutes to the Test Development," under the direction of Professor William Barnet. Emerald Group Publishing Limited, GB, 2012.
- Year of Financial Professions, How can finance contribute to recovery? Collective work: Financial Professions Center / Bank Review, Chapter; "Finance differently: myth, reality and questions for the financial professions." 2014.
- "Lesson 15," Finance Otherwise, the End of Banks," Emerald Edition, United Kingdom, 2015.
- Year of Financial Professions, "French School of Finance, Myth or Reality": Financial Professions Center / Bank Review, Chapter; "The importance attached to training in Finance," Paris 2016.
- Year of Financial Professions, "What finance in 2030?" Financial Professions Center / Bank Review, Chapter; "What training needs for finance in 2030?" Paris 2018.
- "Mutualism in the 21st century reduces inequalities?", Revue d'Economie Financière, n° 128, 4-2017, Finance et inégalités, February 2018.
- Roux M. and Chneiweiss A., General Delegate of the FFA, co-pilots of the June 2019 issue of the Revue d'Economie Financière, n° 134: "La Finance mutualiste".
- "Les organisations face aux défis technologiques et sociétaux du XXIe siècle", Chapter; "Banque de détail française, fin d'un monopole, fin d'un modèle : des menaces aux possibles !" April 2019.

Summary:

- *Foreword: Trust: New Golden Fleece of Finance*
- *Introduction: Context in general and the quest for meaning in particular*
- *Part 1: Genesis and definitions of responsible finance in the world*
- *Part II: Actors and principal products of responsible finance in the world*
- *Part III: Responsible finance: Utopias or realities, "from sins to works!"*
- *General conclusion: "simply serving the future!"*

Trust: New gold fleece of finance

IN THE ANCIENT TIMES, messengers of gods were periodically sent to the humans devoured by their deadly passions, in order to bring them back to reason. In our modern times, sometimes as tormented as those of the ancient tragedies, the messengers are embodied in the person of some academics who put their science at the service of understanding the evolutions of the World. Michel Roux belongs to this category of descriptors. Once again, he presents us the exploration of sometimes lateral or minority ways about Finance by devoting himself today to the responsible Finance.

Capturing flourishing expressions, impact finance, crowdfunding, corporate social responsibility (CSR), extended social object society (SOSE), etc., the author will help us discover the meaning and scope of all these modern financial techniques.

The first virtue of the book is to clarify the reality of each of these expressions and position it in relation to others. Indeed, the common man is sometimes lost in the avalanche of new formulations. We so often wonder if they only are used for communication or if they bring a real societal added value.

Quite rightly recalling Rabelais' morality, "Science without conscience would be only ruin of the soul," in a second descriptive part Michel Roux presents the actors and the practices of the responsible finance. In the first explanatory part, he presents the causes of the phenomenon and in the second part he makes a judgment on the contributions and the limits of this finance which need to be different.

By reading these two parts, we can better acknowledge the phenomenon over time and understand how the financial and human and societal dimension with the evolution of science and technology.

The reader understands that the world of finance needs to find a compass: trust. More than 30 years ago, the pioneers of solidarity finance started from this observation to build a tool to resist against the drift of unbridled markets, driven by the hubris of unlimited yield, producing market abuses and other frauds, and fueling speculative bubbles whose bursting then produces many economic and social misfortunes.

From this base, thanks to the evolutions of knowledge and to the widening of the awareness of the dangers threatening humanity, responsible finance, without constituting a main stream yet, but a brook becomes a river, advances and widens progressively. It cannot be snubbed any longer. Thanks to Michel Roux for giving it an academic acclaim.

At the end of the reading, we hope that all readers will wish this river to become an ocean so that this message spreads widely in the world of finance *trust, trust again, trust always!*[1]

The myth of the Golden Fleece is initiatory in nature: the trip traveled, with all its dangers, allows Jason to become King Jason. Likewise, after reading Michel Roux's book, the reader will understand that money should only be a tool at the service of humans.

Jean-Louis Bancel

President of Crédit Cooperatif Group.
President of the International Association of Cooperative Banks.
President of the Banking and Finance Coordination Office.
President of CoopFr. & President of Cooperatives Europe.

[1]Conclusion of the good-byes of the Delestraint general, large resistant died to Dachau, his or her comrades in arms in 1940.

Context in general and quest for meaning in particular[1]

"No one has condemned wisdom to poverty (...). While having only contempt for the whole empire of fortune, if I have the choice, I will take what it can offer me better. Happy life, followed by the benefits."

Sénèque, philosopher, playwright, and Roman statesman of the 1st century; born in Cordoba, south of Spain, between 4 av JC and 1 av JC; death April 12th, 65 av. JC,

ALTHOUGH THIS NEW BOOK RELIES ON THE FRENCH EDITION "RESPONSIBLE FINANCE," published in April 2018, it is different in terms of the international level of observation and analysis it brings to responsible finance. Nevertheless, this book follows the structure and organization of the French edition.

Global economy is changing its benchmarks. About 10 years ago, despite the first impacts of financial crisis, the economy of developed countries was still robustly growing. However, the dynamics of the global economy has changed since then, modifying the sources of impulse and modes of adjustment profoundly, especially in the developed countries. These changes are particularly seen in four main domains: international trade (a lesser global growth in passing volume from +6% to less than 3% from 2011, interrupting the virtuous dynamics between exchange and

[1] Some reflections brought up to date and approached in our previous works "Management of the bank of detail," Eska editions, Paris, March 2017; "Strategy and governance of the Financial mutualism institutions," Review banks editions, Paris September 2015 and of an article presented in the letter no. 44 of the French Association of Corporate Governance under the title: University point of view; "Confidence and growth could reappear?"

activity); division of work in the world (sources of productivity, generating the competitive advantage, have moved to Asia); high debt ratio (reduced productivity gains are slowing the income growth and consumption remains dependent on employment); and international politics (*Brexit*, USA, North Korea, near-East unpredictable shifts of equilibrium to China's advantage). Without innovations and improvements in productivity gains, the normalization of monetary policies will be useless.

In the preface of our book *Ethical Finance: Structures, Actors and Perspectives in France*, published by Review Bank Editions, 2005, Professor Olivier Pastré stated, "When I am told about ethical finance, I ask about my ROE (Return on Equity)..." Ethical finance is not (yet) fashionable today. Or rather, it is fashionable in the fleeting and volatile sense that this word can have. Some gargle this word in good faith and in solitude, even though the vast majority of those who have the power to invest consider that this type of investment is, at best, alms.... A lot of progress has been made since these observations, despite the rapid change recorded by the absolute data of socially responsible investment (SRI)[2] and the integration of the concept of corporate social responsibility (CSR).[3] Keeping the recent phenomenon, "Myth or reality," in mind, let us ask a few questions. Have these concepts provided credible alternatives to the speculation and greed of financial systems? Did this "so-called" ethical finance, this CSR, really impact our society and the financial sphere? There are still many hurdles and efforts are to be made for CSR to be appropriated.

Managing paradoxes remains a daily duty. In addition to inequalities of income (only 4 in 10 French people pay income tax), there are inequalities in wealth (1% of the richest French people hold 16% of the total national wealth). In 2001, 75,000 people did not have permanent residences. This number was officially estimated to change to 150,000 by 2018. Almost every politician promised to eradicate this phenomenon (Jospin in 2001,

---

[2]According to Novethic, SRI represented less than €9 billion in outstanding assets in 2005 and nearly €25 billion as at March 31, 2017, as part of its new nomenclature for 122 investment funds whose portfolios are built with strong reliance on Environmental Social Analysis and Issuer Governance. In fact, €9 billion of 2005 are to be compared with the 746 billion of 2015, held by 400 funds, classified as impacts of responsible investment strategy broken down into: very significant impacts of €54 billion; significant impacts of €150 billion; and limited impacts of €542 billion.

[3]Corporate social responsibility (CSR) is company's recognition of social and environmental concerns in their activities and their interactions with other actors, called "stakeholders."

Sarkozy in 2007, Holland in 2012, and Macron in 2017...), but unfortunately, massive arrivals of immigrants; elevated level of the rate of unemployment over the period; and financial crisis were right of these promises. Building 150,000 social housing is a solution considered to end this problem.

At present, 10% of the richest people own 83% of the world's wealth, that is, 1% of the population on our planet owns 50% of its wealth. According to the recent statistics of the United Nations Organization, more than 1 billion human beings live with less than $1 per day; one out of five children does not have access to primary education; nearly 900 million adults are illiterate of which two-thirds are women. More than 1 child out of 10 do not reach five years of age in many developing countries. Moreover, according to British NGO Oxfam's report, published before World Economic Forum (WEF), Davos in 2016, the first eight multibillionaires on the planet hold as much wealth as the poorest half of the world's population. According to the report, inequality has risen as a result of the 2008 financial crisis, particularly in the United States, and has reached a level of concentration unmatched since the end of the 19th century. These fortunate people allow themselves to dream bigger than the States constrained by their debts and the inertia of their laws. In the past, many magnates were interested in the arts and research, but never had their designs reached those formulated by these billionaire philanthropists of Silicon Valley (Colonizing Mars for Elon Musk, the boss of Tesla, killing Death for Oracle's Larry Ellison, eradicating diseases for Mark Zuckerberg, founder of Facebook, etc.). As if these billionaires were trying to settle a debt toward a society that gave them a quick growth in a low income tax framework—a form of social obligation for these new rich Americans, not from a capitalism of heirs, who do not hesitate to enter a new dimension; as one of the superman, without limit and without counter power! Should we rejoice? Do they embody the truth of our time marked by the cult of performance and excess ("Le toujours plus" or "Always more" by François de Closets, published by Grasset, 1982)?

So, why talk about responsible finance? What is it? What could be its impact and performance? Complex fields related to sociocultural practices are preferably deciphered at the ground level. Once deposited in a bank, it is difficult to know what purpose our money is used for. There exist placements which allow an ethical and transparent use of savings. Interdependent savings, socially responsible investment (SRI), ethical investment... are a few such placements. However, one should be careful not to confuse these various fashionable concepts. Interdependent savings and ISR contain a different logic. In addition to the purely financial criterion, that is, interdependent savings, SRI of extra-financial criterion of social or environmental nature makes it possible to finance companies or associations with strong social utility to take part in a durable economy and allows proximity for the companies which do not have access to the financings via traditional circuits. Is it not, too, an oxymoron? It is customary to look at the world of finance in terms of ethics, responsibility, integrated governance, and general interest. In a world dominated by finance, embodied by the terms such as globalization, offshoring, fiscal exodus, and fiscal dumping, can finance and accountability be reconciled? Which method should be adopted and which strategy should be defined?

Nowadays, in an international context of innovation, in all sectors of activity, successive crisis and its consequences amplify the process of change: changes in benchmarks, behaviors, economic paradigms in the face of exacerbated competition, and in a crisis of confidence. There are numerous resistances to change. We are only at the first stage of what psychosociologists call the curve of change, where individuals and institutions successively experience states of denial, loss of bearings, impatience, waiting, and, sometimes anger, before admitting their utility. The denial of reality is what the psychosociologist Léon Festinger (1919–1989)[4] mentions in his book *A Theory of Cognitive Dissonance*, 1957. How do we react? Which solution do we remember? Are we going to sink into an imbalanced future of abundance and inequality?

Recreating a climate of trust is another citizen transition as important as its climate counterpart. The apology to be made, the praise, the plea… of confidence… . Despite these many words that strike the conscience, converting words to action is very complicated. According to the expression commonly used by Alexandre Jardin, there are "the Sayers and the Makers." In these conditions how do we move from words to action to get out of the crisis? We could almost paraphrase the formula of Rabelais prescribing, for the good education of Gargantuan, a solid sport practice and

---

[4]"Cognitive dissonance" refers to the internal tension of the system. This concept was formulated for the first time by psychologist Léon Festinger in his book *A Theory of Cognitive Dissonance* (1957). The theory, qualified as a major of social psychology, the cognitive dissonance, states that when the circumstances bring a person to act in disagreement with his beliefs, this person will experience a state of uncomfortable tension called dissonance, which will subsequently tend to be reduced, for example, by a modification of his beliefs in the sense of the act.

great studies in all subjects to make "a healthy mind in a healthy body." He adds religion as a cherry on the cake, "Because science without conscience is only ruin of the soul." Yes, the soul is in the loop! Therefore, "the economy without trust is ruin… of growth" and in turn of our soul.

Current era encourages us to undertake a quest for meaning and equity. There is a need to find benchmarks for action. For lack of meaning and explanation, any expected change cannot be accepted or integrated by those impacted by its implementation. Citizens are gradually becoming aware of the dangers to which the planet is exposed and especially because of the globalized hyper-consumption that could put their lifestyles under question: direct and indirect pollution, climate change, waste recycling issues, diseases, wastes depletion, and depletion of natural resources. On the other hand, in a society where the news takes the place of a project and the obsession with transparency is exacerbated by a lack of social and economic results, everyone gradually loses confidence: the financial markets doubt in the capacity of policies to deal with globalization other than through debt; Europeans doubt on the necessary solidarity to organize among them. Worse, Western and emerging economies are facing a crisis of suspicion. The crisis of identity of the rich countries, helplessness of the diplomacy on international level, internal crisis of the Muslim world (a confession by many, and not the only one), and culture of hope of the emerging countries stigmatize this observation. You can be the head of the Burmese government and Nobel Peace Prize winner, like Aung San Suu Kyi, and still sorely lack sensitivity and transparency in the evocation and resolution of the Rohingya crisis, the persecuted Muslim minority living in their own country, Burma. We have to face this management of paradoxes.

Commenting on the terrorist insecurity in Europe, in a recent interview entitled "To avoid designating religion as cause of terrorism, one gets lost,"[5] the philosopher, essayist, and novelist Pascal Bruckner urges us to stop using the term Islamo-phobia, which prevents any reflection on the internal problems of Islam (divisions between Shiite and Sunni), in order to combat racism, anti-Semitism, xenophobia, and Islamic terrorism. He also implores us to avoid designating religion as the cause of terrorism with

[5]Pascal Bruckner, who recently published *The Wisdom of Money* (Grasset, 2016) and *An Imaginary Racism* (Grasset, 2017), also stated in this interview that "jihadists strike us not for what we do but for who we are… It is our very existence that is unbearable to them…. It is not Islam phobia that leads to terrorism, but, terrorism that makes Islam hateful and penalizes Muslims moderate," Le Figaro (August 19, 2017).

an explanation, "one gets lost in a multitude of smoking interpretations, such as colonialism, Arab-Muslim humiliation, warming climate change, the Israeli-Palestinian conflict… ."

Majority of political decisions already appear to be outdated, or at least insufficient, including prudential standards, for example, our countries face either exorbitant deficits and or new risks related to energy, digital, and social transitions. In 2008, a financial crash was prevented by partial replacement of highly risky private debt with public debt. Why do we lose confidence and then find it again? These two questions will underpin the framework of the modest reflection we suggest in the context of a struggle against preconceived ideas.

The perpetual pursuit of growth and accumulation of profits, long considered sufficient to give meaning to production, are no longer viable in the long run. We are probably witnessing the end of the myth of eternal growth in a world where the social consequences of digital and climate transitions are uncertain; we will have to learn to broaden our conception of progress. Torn between a digital future close to hell with the diktat platforms or, sometimes, paradise for users who have been able to abandon possession to retain only the service, this transition changes our practices to live, consume, and work—a capitalism that gradually loses its purpose when inequalities are widening. It is a risk of return to economic protectionism.

We live in a world where the unvoiced comments and passions prevail over reason. It is enough to see our topical questions agitated during election time whose pressing priority is not always setting durable periods of transition. It is also appropriate not to politicize everything permanently and not to seek culprits. The ideal solution would be to objectively analyze the facts that are not negotiable and seek applicable options. Certainly, after more than 30 years of immobility and by trying to reconcile everyone, France is now without light and it is seen, too often, the invectives prevail over the search for solutions. The illusion that things are going to get better and the lack of courage of our politicians for major reforms has over-marked our recent past. Antoine Veil said, "After the thirty glorious, there were the thirty sleepy." In a book published by Plon in 2012 entitled *No to 30 painful*, Augustin de Romanet, former head of the Caisse des Depots and Consignations and current boss of the company Paris Airport, speaks of 30 "pitiful" years to describe the period from the late 70s to the early 2000s. Finally, when you run a country, what is most criticized is inaction and renunciation.

The relevant diagnosis was known and established long ago: the priority channels of work, school, and housing are no longer irrigated normally despite the multitude of expensive reforms undertaken, and, in particular, they are closed to the least qualified young people. It is necessary to have French pre-established courses where only the "son of or the former student of..." succeeds his professional career. Nobody should be set for a failure and all beings must have a second chance or may be more. For the poor, it could be sometimes more than a job; it is a project that should be endowed.

Will providence be there to settle everything? No, it can only be a source of frustration and disappointment. The French "rebels" and "resigned claimants" struggle to free themselves from two thoughts that demonize money: their Judeo-Christian education and the imprint left by Marxism. This ideological confinement is harmful; it leads us into rigidity where anything that does not fit into this ideological framework is rejected. French do not like innovations. In France, as elsewhere, people expect acts, from which possible and sometimes unexpected changes in behavior in the modes of citizen expression. We are afraid of change and innovations. It is a pity, we all have unexplored potentialities. It is often easier to sink into denigration that inexorably leads to lack of confidence and daring. It is true that in our history, especially since the Revolution of 1789, it was necessary to wait and reach the extremes (economic difficulties, military defeats...) to enter the leap of the transformation. However, for how long will we remain in conservatism, the preservation of acquired benefits and sometimes in arrogance? Exciting but disturbing! If those who feel affected by reform perceive iniquity, then there will be rejection and sometimes violent rejection. This dimension is extremely sensitive today. When efforts are required, they must be equitably distributed. "To live simply, so that others can simply live" Gandhi proclaimed, which proposes to rethink our social, economic, and financial models and consequently the necessary formation in order to make the skills emerge. We must end the fear of change. As the French writer and painter Wladimir Wolf Gozin (born in 1901) sums up, "To live prudently, without taking risks, is to risk not to live." Along with the energy transition, new behaviors are also needed. The demand for "moralization," by will or force, of economic life has reappeared in the social and political debate far beyond the circle of eternal opponents of capitalism. Invention of writing, at the 4th millennium prior to our era, in Mesopotamia made it possible to save the memories of the past, then came Chinese printing at the starting of the 2nd century after

JC to simplify the use of their ideographic writing. It was sophisticated in Europe in the 15th century by Johannes Gutenberg and facilitated the diffusion of the thought. After the inventions of vapor and electricity in the 19th century and the promises of digital cognitive and artificial intelligence in the beginning of the 21st century, had a large impact on our economy by reducing the costs of access to the culture, health, and energy, but the inequalities worsened (production requires less workforce). After the industrial revolutions, digital revolution changed our existences and our companies, but its effects are very different because the laws of information are different from those of the physical production. What impositions reform the social contract, work contract, and certain statutes? The contractualization is moving. A contract is more flexible than a statute and it adapts better to our world of transitions. We should revisit our design of work and education.

By 2050, 10 billion people will live on this planet and managing the risks of depleting resources (water, in particular) will be necessary; the waste and the explosion of inequalities should stir up this question of organization of work, if one wants to control the relentless struggle between nomads and sedentaries. All these inequalities, transition, and providence call for a change of model. The unforgivable is not so much that France has created nearly a million new unemployed since the end of 2012. First, it produced, and continues to produce, unemployment with an unexpected economic combination of low interest rates, cheap oil, and zero inflation, and then followed this trend for almost 3 years, against the three major European economic models: British liberalism, realism Rhine, and the forced march of the Mediterranean toward competitiveness.

Political, religious, and economic beliefs have long sought to overcome the strict maximization of profit and shift corporate practices toward social (societal) benefits. From mutualism in the 19th century to the creation of the Society for Extended Social Object (SOSE),[6] is a status likely to promote a shared project? The management and governance of companies

[6]According to the works which were undertaken within the framework of a research project with the college of Bernardins and which resulted in the production of a book, The Company with Extended Social Object, a new status for the company under the signature of Segrestin Blanche, Kevin Levillain, Vernac Stéphane, and Hatchuel Armand. This work and book present the principles and motivations of a new management to reconcile the company and society. Starting from the observation that the management criteria were turned to the sole value for the shareholder and discredited the long term, the social ambitions and the environment, it was necessary to test company statutes that are not reducible to the sole Partners' interest.

are questioned. Today, the use and sharing of common goods is trying to prevail in an economy and finance increasingly disintermediated. This process of change accelerates and is reflected in changes: benchmarks, behaviors, economic paradigms in the face of exacerbated competition, and a crisis of confidence. The digital revolution, the energy transition, and the profusion of regulatory standards invite innovation. The crisis in all of the social democracy calls for reinventing new tools, new business models, new social protections in a world hit by the digital economy and eager to respond to the ecological imperative. At the same time, the search for a way out of the crisis gives back to solidarity, a hope of development to the companies of people who develop other logics of enterprise (report to the territory, link with the stakeholders...).

If we want to be interested in acts and not in words, there is an urgent need to adapt the forms of wage labor to the new conditions of the digital economy. Agility, flexibility, ability to adapt to the new paradigms that assail us, simplification of our codes and conventions are required if we want to remove the obstacles to employment. In question, too, this development of cognitive artificial intelligence that would make 85% of the current jobs would not exist by 2030 according to a serious Californian think tank "The Institute of the Future" where the only way to adapt will be mobility and ability to quickly acquire new knowledge. With a question of this significance, where will this artificial intelligence be placed: replacing trades, creating new jobs, or reinforcing employees? Our leaders often remain convinced that this economy of the 21st century operates in successive cycles and that after the rain will come the good weather, in short, the providence! This form of myopia is accompanied by a lack of overview and a stalemate on long-term consequences. Times are changing and we have fallen into a form of dictatorship of urgency.

Internet bubble, Kerviel affair, subprime crisis, tax havens, conflicts of interest, payments of significant sanctions for illegal conduct, malpractices in sports, moral hazard problems (e.g., some financial actors who can take excessive risk with other people's money because they know they will be helped if their own difficulties lead to a general risk), ethical and financial regulation issues of companies and financial institutions are debatable. Despite the historical and institutional developments, the introduction of rules of conduct, the creation of compliance officers, and ethics officers' jobs in banks and companies, these excesses could not be prevented. Why? The established rules of ethics could nevertheless answer, at least in their content, to an ethical requirement of the agents. These rules fit even in the practices, but, they are often used, even thwarted, or diluted in the modalities of competition and in the search of reputation. Finally, the main challenge of compliance for business and finance professionals is that of the survival of their activities, which they are also responsible for controlling.

For a better understanding of this financial sphere, let us consider the economic situation in an international environment. In the beginning of 2018, the economic situation, both in euro zone in the United States and in China, confirms the continuation of a cycle of world growth well synchronized. On the political level, the principal events remain in Europe: the contained crisis in Catalonia does not seem to affect the financial markets; the unexpected result of the German elections always complicates the formation of a government coalition; the negotiations of Brexit continue. Rest of the world was marked by the reduction plan of taxes presented by the American Congress and the permanent risks of generalization of conflicts related to the dramatic situations of countries like Syria and Yemen, not counting the provocations of the North Korea. Zone by zone, the economic situation is as follows:

- The United States: 11 months after the elections, at the end of December 2017, US President Donald Trump celebrated the first major reform of its mandate which has been the adoption by the Congress of the greatest fall of taxes for 31 years. Intended measures to support employment and investment. The gross domestic product is above 2% and monthly job creations are above 2,000,000. Only uncertainties are the accumulation of rumors and court cases concerning the President's entourage.
- Europe: The economic figures of the euro zone and the indicators of the economic climate continue to rise upward and are diffused well at the labor market whose average unemployment rate is lower than 8.8%. In spite of a monthly reduction with 30 billions of its plan of acquisitions of new assets, European Central Bank maintained its position until December 2018.
- Emergent countries: The economic situation of the large countries, starting with China, remains satisfactory. The outputs of recession are confirmed in Russia and Brazil. The 19th Congress of the Chinese Communist party consolidated the executive team in October 2017, which affirmed its determination to control the necessary transition toward a little weaker but better quality growth with,

in particular, the concern of reducing pollution and to slow down the excessive recourse to the credit.

What role does responsible finance play to restore confidence in our economy? Can individuals who want the ethics to prevail in the practice of their financial affairs do so? Does the individual exercise of virtue suffice to bring about the general functioning of finance? Does not the systemic logic of the operation of the latter tend, on the contrary, to impose a loss of ethical sense of individual and collective behavior? Are some business and governance models more conductive to developing responsible practices?

Without establishing an exhaustive list of the salient facts for our society, the subject of the debt cannot be ousted. This debt has become the key to the global economy today. About 10 years after the 2007 crisis, we do not even talk about forgetfulness but euphoria. Within the framework of the 10th World Forum Convergences[7] "Together, let us innovate for a world Zero Exclusion, Zero Carbon, Zero Poverty!" held on September 4 and 5, 2017 at the Brongniart Palace, Paris, Jean-Louis Bancel always thought *"that the bankers could make a useful use of finance."* However, at the time of the 10th edition of the World forum Convergences, the president of the Cooperative Credit did not hesitate to underline a paradox: *"10 years after the tsunami of the financial crisis, of many questions are posed in the banking environment, obviously populated the financial ones whose memory is connected with that of a goldfish... ."* That is not a problem; Jean-Louis Bancel shares with Convergences *"a co-operative vision of the world,"* consistent "to put himself together to become the Master of his destiny. A logic shared by the whole of the cooperative banks and mutualisms, strongly anchored on their territory, who have a privilege over the financing of local companies and development of an economy with strong social appreciation.

While global debt was only $142 trillion in 2007, it now accounts for 327% of global gross domestic product with a record $217 trillion. On the financial markets, the Dow Jones benchmark rose above 22,000 in 2017, a triple since 2009, and Nasdaq (the technology index) just quadrupled to over 6,500 points raised by the valuation of GAFA who engage in a race

---

[7] Impetus in 2008, Convergences is a platform of reflection, mobilization and plea. Convergences promotes the development objectives durable (ODD) and the fight against poverty, exclusion, and climate changes in the countries developed as in the developing countries. Composed of more than 200 organizations resulting from all the sectors, Association acts to cause the reflection and the action, to diffuse good practices and to support the coconstruction of partnerships innovating strong societal impact.

of who will reach the $1 trillion worth of valuation on the stock market. This is the course that has just crossed Apple, in the year 2017, and with an amount of $1,275 billion, it is, also, the year of the record of dividends distributed in the world.

In the absence of temporary inflationary risk, the languor of the French and European recovery, despite the abovementioned buoyant winds, is under the influence of the credit myth that creates value. Do central banks drag us into toxic monetary policies? How far can they "run the printing press" in the absence of real controls? "Failure to the crisis, fault of the debt?" For years, the international macroeconomic environment has lived under the illusion of a factitious growth maintained by low interest rates. Cheap and easy money stopped the normal cycle of the business, while allowing nonprofitable companies to continue. Would debt replace creativity? Abundant flows of liquidity maintained the regular rise in the markets. The latter, under the "wait and see eye" of the central banks, replaced the States. In order to constrain inflation, which seems more of a fear than a reality today, the common answer that central banks have come up with is called monetary normalization. The central banks are quite conscious that the amount of the debt is insupportable in long term—a real dilemma that only inflation and recession can solve. To stop the madness of a one-dimensional system, the margin is narrow. The solutions for real productivity gains are probably the tax reforms and reorientation of public investment toward education and training—a sick ecosystem of debt where the markets are dependent on the rates. Growth is on the rise, but inflation remains to be seen. For rates to rise, we need economic growth and inflation. Global growth prospects are good but inflation forecasts are more uncertain.

In Greek, "*krisis*" (crisis) means screen or sieve. So, a crisis can be beneficial, an occasion to call itself into question. "Trust is an invisible institution that governs economic development," said Kenneth Joseph Arrow (American economist, coincumbent, with John Hicks, 1972 Nobel Prize in Economics). So, how to reclaim this confidence, a necessary condition for a way out of the crisis? Among ethics, good governance, and integrity, what about the trust in organizations? How to provide, under these conditions, effective support in the face of accelerating pace of technological, social, and economic changes affecting our societies. With new technologies, smart grids, and renewable energies, the world is changing paradigms. How to accompany these transitions? How to release the energies to come out of 30 years of inefficiency?

By the way, what is responsible finance? There is, probably, as many definition as authors who approach this subject, hence the need to explain its origins to decipher the workings and evolutions to make sure that the first intentions of the pioneers of this movement have not been diverted into a world where financial innovation continues to generate differentiation to create more margins. Responsible finance is a generic term that covers many investment vehicles.

At the beginning of the 21st century, its main areas were ethical funds (excluding sectors of arms, alcohol, tobacco, etc.); sustainable development funds (taking into account environmental criteria); sharing funds (supporting the world of humanitarian or charity associations); and solidarity savings funds (focusing on the development of local economies, integration, employment, and microcredit). This was yesterday, and although we are moving into uncertainty, now the field of responsible finance is an even broader and more innovative concept that covers, always, more domains, which can be summed up by the combination of practices aimed at reconciling performance with social, environmental, or societal impacts. Responsible finance has undergone changes to deal with emerging issues, such as inequalities, migration, resource use, climate, and so on, by relying on available technologies such as digital and social networks.

In addition to labeled or unlisted funds[8] (including these extra-financial criteria in investment decisions), without establishing an exhaustive, a few tools to SRI and solidarity finance can be quoted, such as crowd funding which is a fundraising tool operated via an Internet platform allowing a group of contributors to collectively choose to directly finance the tracked projects or peer to peer lending of loans between individuals; green bonds, a term translated as an environmental obligation linked to a bond issue launched by a company, an international organization…; changes in traditional shareholder engagement where shareholders will put pressure on companies to influence their policy

[8]Several forms of labeling coexist alongside the SRI label, for example, for investment funds that respect the commitments of socially responsible investment; there are other labels, such as the Ecological and Energy Transition for Climate (TEEC) of the Ministry of the Environment, or the Finansol label, issued by the agency of the same name. To facilitate the selection of socially responsible assets, there are also stock market indexes that include companies that implement concrete actions for sustainable development. They are managed by rating agencies such as SAM, Vigeo, or Eiris, the latter two having merged in January 2016. Among the most important indices are: Footsie4good, Euronext-Vigeo, and the Dow Jones Sustainability Index (DJSI).

toward responsible finance. This can take several directions, such as asking a bank to no longer invest in fossil fuel or tobacco-related assets, or asking a company to study its impact on the environment and presenting a plan to improve the environment. The impacts can be, from now on, companies can be granted by the State an approval "Social enterprise of social utility" (ESUS)[9]; socially responsible real estate funds, which may take the form of SCPI (Civil Real Estate Investment Company); or OPCI (Real Estate Investment Trust).

These include companies selected on the basis of energy performance criteria; social use (HLM which stands for moderate rent housing, premises rented to associations of public interest...); the new actors of alternative financing among returns, risks, and solidarities associated with a reflection on digital governance. Integrating free software is the first step on this new path. Innovations of responsible finance are the services of climate, revolution of impact investing (investment in unlisted companies that are socially innovative, commercially competitive, and with high ROI). All these main topics will be approached from three aspects: genesis, regulation, and perspectives.

Many questions and uncertainties about the evolution of society remain and, as part of this book, our reflections will try to integrate some of them which seem fundamental to us to reinforce our theme and shape our future.

Among these questions, the enumeration of which is probably only provisional and not definitive, we will retain four: (a) the necessary strengthening of the economic culture so as not always to criticize finance despite its wanderings; (b) Has the financial sphere learned from previous crises? (what are the risks of new bubbles? Are toxic products eradicated? What becomes of shadow finance?...); (c) The growing judiciarization of business; (d) the eruption of digital "*neobanks*," banks whose products and offers are accessible only by mobile application that implicitly impacts the business model of traditional banks (after the branch, online banking, here is the mobile bank...). Let us quickly take up these different questions.

---

[9]In order to obtain this ESUS approval, companies must therefore act in one or more areas of the social and solidarity economy and meet many criteria (the average of the 5 highest salaries does not exceed 7 times the SMIC; high cannot exceed 10 times the SMIC, leaders are elected by employees or members, at least 30% of employees have contracts for integration or professionalization, or are recognized workers with disabilities ...). In France SMIC = Minimum Growth Salary.

a. Economic culture and pedagogy

In the preamble, if we want to make finance more responsible, it may be appropriate to stop beating it. Like business, finance needs to be rehabilitated. One may not like rent, not be fascinated by individual property and capital, but, a business needs finance. As the fair and nonconfiscatory tax, finance must be at the service of the general interest as it is a tool for the firm. There is certainly a reality that cannot be denied, which is partly linked to the crisis. It is true, bankers, sometimes, sought to avoid regulations to play with tax havens and have not hesitated to take the consequent wages (in Europe more than 3,000 bankers, according to the ECB, perceive more than €1 million a year). Faced with these findings that could be multiplied, it is simple to make finance a single enemy. It is a very convenient caricature in a tense political context. This simplification prevents us from asking the right question: how can the bank finance the economy in a better way? However, in the subprime crisis, French banks still showed their resilience. By focusing attention only on their slippages, we forget that most of the business and profitability of banks come from retail activities, the bank of individuals and SMEs (an activity that accounted for 67% of the product Net Banking for the main French banks in 2016).

This is not to deny the facts but this reminder makes a perfect transition with the evocation of a report for pedagogical purposes (although dating late 2013, but still relevant) entitled precisely, "Responsible finance." This document decrypts the functioning of finance, focusing particularly on the notion of responsibility, in a still complex financial world that has changed since the crisis of 2008. This opus, the result of the work of a commission that brought together various stakeholders of the business world (business leaders, journalists, academics, etc.) under the aegis of the Foundation Responsible growth,[10] raises questions without recommendation. Its main objective is to raise awareness of the issues of finance.

According to Eric Delannoy, Weave Consulting and Vice-Chairman of the Editorial Board of this report

---

[10]Under the auspices of the Institut de France, the Croissance Plus Foundation, created in 2010 by former presidents of the Croissance Plus association, brings together business leaders of all sizes, representatives of social entrepreneurship, trade union, university, journalism, and economic research. A place of open and apolitical debate, it aims to educate the general public on the market economy. One of his first initiatives is to work toward bringing the world of education closer to that of the company.

Establishing responsible finance involves reconciling two parameters: effective financing of the economy and measured risk-taking. According to him, the aims of the report can be summed up in three points. First, the rehabilitation of risk, otherwise there is no growth possible, but assuming possible negative consequences. The debate then focuses, in particular, on the solvency of banks. The report then stops on the role of the regulator. A role back on the scene thanks to the crisis. The report wonders if certain measures (such as the Financial Transaction Tax) are not counterproductive. Finally, the report discusses the ethical behavior of financial players and the authors suggest to act in this respect on corporate governance.

A long-term job to pursue because the critics of finance will not fail to raise the nagging question: have the financiers learned all the lessons of the crisis? Too many examples and recent topics in the news comfort the doubts often for lack of explanation and transparency in the communication.

b. Has the financial sphere learned from previous crises?

To answer this question, three explanations hold our attention: Are there any risks of new bubbles? Are toxic products eradicated? What becomes shadow finance?

- Are there any risks of new bubbles?
  As already mentioned earlier about the evolution of the world debt and the enthusiasm of the financial markets, we do not even speak of forgetting anymore but the euphoria of financial markets that in 10 years they would become the illusion of a form of security.[11] François Vidal, Deputy Director of the newspaper's editors, Les Echos, doubts this, despite the substantial progress made in prevention and regulation under the auspices of the Basel Committee in order to preserve the soundness and solvency of banks. European banks, and more specifically French banks, have done quite well under "stress tests"

[11]On August 7, 2017, on the website of the newspaper Les Echos (www.lesechos.fr Ideas—Debates, Editors & Analyzes), François Vidal, Deputy Director of the editorial team, was asked in an article entitled, *Finance: The Illusion of Security*, how to know if finance is no longer a weapon of mass destruction? How to be sure that the next financial crisis will not bring the world economy back into turmoil?

(exercise of simulating extreme but plausible economic and financial conditions in order to study the consequences on banks).

The European banking union has strengthened the sector. This is supported by the evidence of the sixth Spanish bank (Banco Popular) that narrowly escaped bankruptcy, thanks to its acquisition for a symbolic euro by the Santander group whose spell was settled in 24 hours. We are far from the scenarios of the collapse of Lehman Brothers or Dexia with their potential risk of domino effect. The return of such scenarios is more than unlikely, but has the financial risk completely disappeared? With the planned end of accommodative monetary policies, aimed at lowering interest rates, and under the combined effect of diverging views in the rules put in place on both sides of the Atlantic with President Trump's will of deregulating (diverging interests on the level of own funds) uncertainty could increase. With the uncertainty governed by central bankers, a difference from 2007, would the latter have sufficient financial resources to cope? But, is the world still safe?

- Are toxic products being eradicated?

With respect to toxic products (investment instruments that are difficult to sell and whose illiquidity leads to a sharp depreciation of balance sheets, or even bankruptcy, of the financial institutions that hold them), it is estimated that despite more than $320 billion fines[12] their circulation was not stopped. The new capital requirements and low rates that have reduced banks' margins can explain this. The latter then increased the use of securitization. Although difficult to quantify, outstanding subprime or toxic assets amount to more than $3 trillion worldwide. The subprime mortgages that had been slipped into financial investments just prior to the last financial crisis were bundled together and sold as "securities" to investors and raised serious concerns in the United States. Are not we talking about new American bubbles? Thus, subprime car loans ($179 billion of outstandings at the end of 2016 according to the Federal government) and US student loans are the most worrisome, as that is where most late payments accumulate. Loans to households with very low

[12]Among the recent sanctions, the United Kingdom's Royal Bank of Scotland (RBS) announced on Wednesday, July 12, 2017, that it would pay $5.5 billion (€4.8 billion) to the US regulator FHFA (Federal Housing Finance Agency) for issuing $32 billion (€28 billion) of financial securities related to doubtful home loans before the financial crisis of 2007.

credit ratings ("deep" subprime mortgages) have also exploded and now account for 33% of securitized loans, compared to 5% in 2010. Finally, as in 2008, "synthetic" securitizations, which consist of transferring only the risk (and not the property of the credit), multiply. China is also raising growing concerns because banks resort to mounting complex securitizations to offload toxic assets. About 30 of them would constitute $2,000 billion of this type of debt—an amount multiplied by 6 in 4 years.

- Shadow finance

Finally, the third explanation is the accelerated development of shadow finance (shadow banking). It includes all companies that provide banking services (credit, wealth management, etc.) but which are not regulated as such. These include hedge funds, crowd funding platforms and wealth management companies. This shadow finance has grown. According to Fed. in 2007 finance outside the prudential rules weighed $50 trillion, whereas today it would represent more than double. As banking regulations grew, in 2017, they accounted for more than a quarter of global finance.

Ultimately, it seems difficult for some of these examples to subscribe to the promises of Cultural Revolution of the profession toward a more responsible finance. Banks are still listed on the stock exchange and are still subject to the criterion of profitability and the legally possible in a regulatory framework with gaps and trying to catch up with technology. The law is still lagging behind new technologies. As the citizens of the world call for a change in the rules of the game and claim this quest for meaning, their banks continue their "business."

c. The growing judiciarization of business

For journalist Laurent Thevenin, Les Echos, "The cost of litigation for large banks continues to climb" (article posted online on August 17, 2017). Based on CCP Research Foundation figures for 20 of the world's largest banks, amounts paid or provisioned reached $264 billion in 2012–2016. This amount, which covers payments and provisions for fines or compensation to poorly treated customers in particular, is 5.2% higher than that accumulated over the previous period from 2011 to 2015. According to a familiar saying, no one is supposed to ignore the law. It is clear that in the face of the exuberance of laws and regulations, in response to an issue to be addressed, companies are confronted with an increasingly complex management of legal and regulatory risks. Reputational risk management is essential to minimize the risk of corporate noncompliance, avoid litigation of any kind, to prevent it rather than undergo it, and then manage it if it is unavoidable. Although the national legal risks, now largely European, are more easily identifiable, the internationalization of companies requires them to consider the local legal and regulatory constraints based on their activities, but also from now on the reality of the extraterritorial effects of foreign laws, particularly American laws in view of the proactivity of US justice.

In his editorial of economic newspaper "*Les Echos*" dated February 28, 2018, titled "Banks: the colossal bill of the crisis," Guillaume Maujean did not hesitate to speak about American "diktat" on the world finance by evoking the sum of $345 billion in fines, penalties, and amicable transactions that banks had to pay to US states and Wall Street regulators. The journalist recalls the paradox. It is US that engendered the most important financial crisis that imposes its legal views and arrogated $300 billion of the $345 billion for the period of 2009–2017. Europe is recovering only $22 billion. Also, in the same edition of February 28, 2018, journalist Edward Lederer confirms the point with the data from a study by the Boston Consulting Group which emphasizes that it is the North American banks that have paid the highest price, with a total of $220 billion penalties over the period. European banks logically shared the balance (one-third of the total), with $125 billion mainly paid to US bank regulators. The memory remains clear for BNP Paribas who paid nearly $9 billion for breach of embargo. Deutsche Bank was not spared either, fined with $7.2 billion for its role in the subprime.

Faced with the risks of associated litigation and questioning of their reputation, companies can only integrate this risk in their corporate governance.[13]

[13]Readers are referred to the article by Sylvie Frontezac, lawyer Jeantet, published in the Letter No. 50 of the French Association of Government of the Enterprise (AFGE) under the title, "Towards a generalization of programs of compliance." We report here the conclusion of the article, "compliance programs are thus being generalized to all companies, banking and non-banking. The implementation of an effective program requires a regulatory watch to allow management of all risks, guide activities by protecting the reputation of the company. The reality of US sanctions and the actual exposure of European companies to the extraneity of American justice should encourage them to integrate the reality of this reputational risk in their corporate governance."

Another example of this growing judiciarization is in climate reporting. An Australian NGO, Environmental Justice Network, lodged a complaint in early August against the largest Australian bank, Commonwealth Bank, for failing to properly inform investors of financial risks related to climate change in its annual report. According to the NGO, by not providing information on climate change risks in its 2016 annual report, the bank "does not give a fair and truthful view of its financial position and its performance." Moreover, in the financing of fossil fuels, according to a report quoted by Novethic in June 2017, financing by the 37 largest global banks fell below the $90 billion mark in 2016, according to the latest report "Banking on Climate Change" published by Rainforest Action Network, Banktrack, Sierra Club, and Oil Change International. They went from $111 billion to $87 billion, a decrease of 22% year-on-year. This is the first time that this funding has decreased. The trend is even stronger for the French banks that pledged against coal during the COP21. On the other hand, their investments in oil sands and shale gas infrastructures across the Atlantic are increasing, despite increasing pressure from civil society. However, "This is all the hypocrisy of French banks! They continue to indirectly finance what they refuse to directly finance," responds Lucie Pinson, a member of the Friends of the Earth Association.[14] Credit Agricole continues to fund companies that are behind two power plant extension projects in Indonesia. French banks have made several commitments that go in the right direction on corporate finance but not far enough to avoid prosecution.

In the margins of judiciarization, our society also knows another danger. We live in the dogma of the transparency (earlier, the moral order was carried by the religion, maintained by the society!). It can cause vocations of denouncements and gradually our state becomes that of suspicion, where the legal order is replaced by the justice of the media and social networks.

Does this mean that this wave of judiciarization will stop? On the contrary, it runs the risk of taking a long-term view with the new, very

[14]Created in 1970, the Federation of Friends of the Earth France is an association for the protection of man and the environment, under the 1901 law and is approved for the protection of the environment. It is independent of all economic, political, and religious powers and is the world's leading environmental network Friends of the Earth International, present in 77 countries.

structuring regulations, whether they are transparency on the markets or the protection of personal data of consumers presented by the European regulators.

d. The digital "neobanks"

Banks whose products and offers are accessible only by mobile application implicitly impact the business model of traditional banks (after the bank branch, online banking, here is the mobile bank...). Banks that exacerbate competition with traditional banks are strong on twitter but sometimes fall behind on the promises of digital. Are these neobanks totally disruptive? These amplify the business model of the bank of the future. But, questions remain on various topics, such as the security of data, complexity of interest rate models that has a certain cost—questions that we will have the opportunity to address during the review of responsible finance issues.

Why this book?

We would like to decipher this innovative but complex topic of responsible finance in the world. In addition to drawing the contours of a better life together as part of a better funded economy, this very ambitious book would like to take a look on finance without concessions and awaken the consciences by explaining the workings and developments possible toward responsible finance. To understand this area, identify its challenges (race to size, transparency, selectivity, performance, security, etc.), and anticipate possible changes in the medium term, we will be careful not to use prospective methods using the past and the exploration of possible futures (anticipation) for the benefit of decision-making and action, hence the development of long-term policies and strategies. Certainly, the future is to be built as an expression of will and responsibility, but we should not forget that our society has entered a form of dictatorship of urgency where cult of speed and worship of the moment are imposed. The "all at once" is the ambient consumerism; it is this super activity chosen or undergone that affects us all. Has the urgency become the symptom of hyper modernity? Should we succumb or resist? How to understand this subject of responsible finance: by technique, politics, or morality? Would the quest for meaning and search for sensations be the revenge of a prisoner's urgency? Sometimes the weight of time or the illusion of erasing it, produces a relation to self, marked by excess, and a relation to others becomes ephemeral! Internet, globalization, and money are not enough to explain the changes we are experiencing. They participate in the development of our ecosystem and resonate between them to amplify the urgency.

An "otherwise" finance impacts the business models of credit institutions. In summary, and to justify the structure of the book, its purpose is to show that finance can contribute in a sustainable way to the common good only if we succeed in introducing more responsibility both in theory and practice. This requires a profound paradigm shift, a humanization of finance both personally and institutionally. It will be a question of presenting the origin of the current evolution of the socially responsible investment toward a responsible finance. Will these new frontiers serve the performance? Then, to identify the products and the actors and finally, the challenges that this responsible finance will face in this context of globalization of our economies.

After these warnings, as we have already pointed out, we live in a chaotic and uncertain period where the aggressions are multiplying on all sides (we make the conventional war to our enemies and the economic war to our friends). We must be wary of those who do not want to see, hear, or know this irenic vision.[15] If at all, it is very good to proscribe. Therefore, perhaps, here came (not the time of the cathedrals as the song says in the musical ND of Paris) the time of a new management for a finance otherwise and more responsible!

The book is structured in three parts to feed the reflection and the deciphering of this nebula that constitutes the responsible finance in the world. Through these three parts, two main objectives are pursued by this book: (1) making people understand how the human and societal dimensions in the financial field interact with the evolution of science and technology; (2) make it clear that the world of finance needs to find meaning again. Confidence is the lever.

[15]By irenic vision we mean the fact of wanting to reconcile ideologies or events that are difficult.

Part I: Genesis and definitions of responsible finance in the world

If desirable, is the transition from responsibility in finance to responsible finance, nevertheless, possible? And if so, how?

Regulatory (CRD 4,[16] BRRD,[17] TLAC,[18]...) and technological (Big Data and digital wave) changes have upset the economic model of large universal banks in particular and financial players in general, not only in customer relations and their ability to finance them, but also in the refinancing and management of their own liabilities. There has been the period of quantitative easing, an exceptional access which should be limited in the long term, so they will see an increase in other more traditional sources of financing, especially market financing and customer deposits. However, to be traditional, these sources of financing are nonetheless experiencing significant changes related to the definition of resolution plans, the new bail-in regime, and the resolution ratios (TLAC and MREL) involving a new hierarchy of claims and thereby the revision of the structure of their liabilities.

Today, there are other risks such as the emergence of new players in financial services, for example, aggregators and payment initiators, who already fear greater volatility of deposits in bank balance sheets, when is not a decrease in favor of more easily advised and realized investments, or even a capture by the first neobanks. Beyond the accusations of green washing responsibility is a theme that is gradually rooted in a scattered order with concepts whose domains and definitions are not homogeneous and universal.

After the precept of "consume differently" there seems to be another development of "fund differently" in response to the quest for meaning. How can finance support the promotion of a responsible economy? A question that already provides partial answers (green bonds,

[16]The Capital Requirements Directive (CRD IV) package, consisting of a directive and a European regulation, gradually implements Basel III in Europe from January 1, 2014 until 2019. The purpose of these texts is to protect the saver, the borrower, and the prevention of banking and financial crises.

[17]Bank Recovery and Resolution Directive (BRRD): This reform of the bank creditors' hierarchy, transposed into French law by order in August 2015, strengthens the stability of the banking system and the security of depositors.

[18]TLAC is the acronym for Total Loss Absorbing Capacity, which is the ability of an institution to face its debts.

extra-financial criteria, impact measurements...) that must be presented, understood, and analyzed. In addition to the origin of this terminology of responsible finance and its many definitions, the book aims to situate it in relation to the concepts close to ethical finance, microcredit, sharing finance, participatory finance, solidarity savings... Responsible finance is a broader concept than ethical finance, too often limited to socially responsible investment and sustainable development. There are many questions between morality and performance, between myth and reality!

Part II: Actors and principal products of responsible finance in the world

This book is more focused on new tools and new players and their perspectives in responsible finance. A panorama of burning news that seeks to understand and enrich the debate, it is the goal of this book to try to meet this challenge. Responsible finance, we do not really know what it is and we know even less, a priori, what it can serve. The concepts socially responsible investment, sustainable finance, solidary savings, share finance, microcredit, green bonds, crowd funding, and so on, most of them recent, fall under one heading or another of responsible finance. In a world where financial innovation persists in creating differentiation in order to create more leeway, the first imperative is to try to define it and draw up an accurate map.

After "Brexit," compared to other continental European cities, Paris is a major financial center in terms of size and economic weight and is likely to welcome new players in responsible finance. Similarly, France's exponential growth in the Fintech industry represents a decisive attraction for international investors in the innovations in financial technology, digital technology, and new products of responsible finance.

However, new paradigms are needed: social and solidarity economy, circular economy, governance rating, green financing... The integration of green and sustainable financing is a major issue addressed by international finance. Investors are disengaging from coal and fossil fuels. At the same time, the green bond market is developing both in France and internationally. It is necessary to understand and decipher these new products and actors. Are they able to influence future investment strategies?

Part III: Responsible finance: utopias or realities, "from sins to works!"

If the impacts of a more responsible finance on the image and the notoriety of the firm are recognized, including those on its durability and differentiation compared to the competitors, the lack of legibility on the creation of future value, acceleration transitions, lack of time, resistance to change, risk aversion, unstable rules and laws, and investment strategy paths are still long to integrate and apply these new perceptions of sources innovations and productivity gains.

Responsible finance applies to all areas of finance. If it is to be promoted even better among socioeconomic actors by integrating their specificities, it is also necessary for traditional and new funders. As a financier, it appears necessary to have a complete arsenal for financing the life cycle of companies as well as those of the social and solidary economy. So far, the latter have relied almost exclusively on conventional credit or the contribution, too often reduced, of members and shareholders. New tools, facilitated by the ESS Act (known as the Hamon Law), must be studied and made available. The concept of own funds or quasi-equity should be promoted. New debt instruments (subordinated, medium-long-term debt, short-term debt, trade finance, factoring, etc.) or dedicated instruments such as the issue of securities or traditional debt, loan funds, equity funds capital risk should be used. Features that can be complemented by dedicated guarantee schemes include regional or sectoral guarantee funds, mobilization of national public funds (future investments, access to social housing…), or European banks (EIB, EIF, Bank of the Council from Europe…).

What are the recommendations to become sustainable, responsible, and profitable? The purpose of this book is to provide a point of progress on how economic and financial actors, in general, can better integrate the objectives of a more responsible finance into their priorities. This transition to transparent appropriation of finance dedicated to economic development is a necessity and must not sink into threatening green washing. Despite the multiplicity of tools and rules, responsible finance, by its approach and traceability of its performances, appears as the only likely phenomenon to accompany the financing of the multiple transitions that reach us.

Genesis and definitions of responsible finance in the world

"It is a sad thing to think that nature France, he tells peaks and that mankind does not listen to it."

Victor Hugo (1802–1885), poet, playwright, committed French politician

IN THE PREAMBLE TO THIS FIRST PART, dedicated to genesis, definitions, and regulatory frameworks of responsible finance, let us recall some generalities and specificities of the vocabulary of professionals in the sector to better understand the context of the action. A vocabulary is the source of incomprehension when it accompanies the drifts and the cupidity of the system. Thus, to escape tax heaviness, the financier speaks of "tax optimization"; his counterpart, a specialist in financial law and regulation, talks about "sales of unsuitable contracts" for fraudulent activities and "regulatory arbitrage" to qualify discrepancies between national regulations. As business is business, the only preoccupations are the criteria of profitability and whether is it legally possible. In his book, *Dive in troubled water Explosive Investigation Among Bankers*, Joris Luyendijk,[1] considers that "the cliché of the evil and immoral banker does not make sense… . For bankers, the keyword is 'Amorality,' which they clearly distinguish from immorality. However, the amoral decision evades the question of good and evil and focuses solely on whether an action is authorized or not.

[1]Work published by Plon in 2016, translated by Lorraine De Plunkett.

The word 'ethics' is pronounced only in association with 'professional,' and evokes an almost absolute obedience to the hierarchy."

We share this finding of opacity and intentional complexity to generate profit margins, but how far can we go? To prolong the reflection, in their book published by PUF in February 2016, *Financial Markets, Without Faith or Law*? David Allouche and Isabelle Prigent agreed that we should stop criticizing finance. According to Allouche and Prigent,

> *Those who persist in maintaining debates around morality are condemned to bring only coercive and unrealistic responses. In France, the rejection of the markets is due to a lack of knowledge of their activity and to the fact that the majority of French are savers but very few investors, perhaps waiting for the fulfillment of the promises of the candidate whose finance was the enemy ... .*

For them, after explaining their usefulness, it is not a question of limiting the role of the markets but reinforcing the weight of the long-term actors to make funds converge toward an actor of the economy and being able to formulate a project and prove its validity. In these conditions, we have following questions in our book: Is a more responsible approach possible? What portions constitute "social and solidarity" savings, "crowdfunding," or financial patriotism? What should we worry about when we have the opportunity to invest?

Talking about responsible finance, we have often been tempted to use the expression "to make it finance the real economy." But, is there an unreal economy? So, what role is devolved to finance and banks, the two adjectives closely interpenetrating? It is common to separate this financial sphere from the real economy, as if the financial world was "unreal" and operated independently of other sectors of the economy. It is not so!

According to the latest report of the French Banking Federation (trade union of the profession) in 2016, the financial sector in France participates, as the other sectors, in economic life by its added value (a contribution of 2.7% to the value added total in France), its number of jobs (2.3% of private employment with 370,000 employees), and its €2,203 billion in loans to the economy (of which €927 billion in business loans and €914 billion of outstanding real estate loans). However, finance is not an industry like any other. It plays an absolutely vital role in providing the economy with the capital it needs to function by allocating savings resources to productive uses. There will be no economy without finance, no developed economy can exist without developed finance. This financing of the economy is mainly done by the banks and by the financial markets. It is therefore essential to recall, briefly, their intermediary role.

In the generic sense, the term *bank* is usually used to describe companies with different functions, statuses, or activities (public limited companies, cooperatives, merchant banks, network banks, etc.). Banks play a specific role in creating and managing the currency, the means of payment that allow economic agents (households, businesses, and local authorities) to dispose of the money in their accounts using checks, bank cards, transfers, and automatic withdrawals. They finance the needs of the economy by granting loans, either from the deposits entrusted to them or by borrowing from the markets. This role of intermediary transforming the often short maturity savings into long-term credit is essential for the functioning of the economy. In order to manage their loan portfolio and help financing their clients, banks are required to carry out market transactions.

Another role that banks have to play is to protect the savings their customers entrust to them, for which they have developed the system of covering the risks. In the working of a bank, it is necessary to distinguish the risks that they take for themselves as a part of their own account activity, the risks which they carry on their assessments, within the framework of their intermediary activity, and those that they may bring, by their advices and their products, to their customers. More precisely, the bank of detail or network is the one that employs 80% of the manpower in this profession as opposed to the bank of financing and investment, which is the most affected by the crisis and which occupies less than 10% of employment. The latter, specialized in financial engineering, asset management, and derivatives, has been severely tested during crises both internationally and in France.

It has probably forgotten the risk control by myopia and/or greed, and worse, it has outsourced them. Absorbed by the profit race, it must now strengthen the control of its market and counterparty risks. It may be a time to rediscover the fundamentals of the core business of banking intermediation[2] to better understand the risks and better serve the

[2]Receiving deposits, granting credit, and managing payment means are enough to understand that credit institutions are intermediaries who do the processing. The function of intermediation is the operation of linking nonfinancial agents (NFAs) with funding capacity to other NFAs with a financing need. The Banque de France is more willing to talk about financial intermediation, in the broad sense, and it analyzes this intermediation rate, which

economy. However, four French banking groups are among the top nine in Europe (source *The Banker*) attesting to their solidity.

The retail bank is an inseparable partner of the everyday life of every citizen and a factor of integration into society. Perceptions of income, settlement of household expenses, support for personal and professional projects, or wealth creation, all these are the reasons for using the services of the retail bank. According to French law, a bank is one of the legal categories of credit institution (Article L.511-1 of the French Monetary and Financial Code). Banks are credit institutions that hold the monopoly of granting bank transactions as defined by law.

In France, Article L.311-1 of the Monetary and Financial Code provides the following definition, "Bank operations include the receipt of public funds, credit transactions and payment banking services." To approach Community law, the concept of the reception of funds by the public, known since the banking law of January 24, 1984, was replaced by that of "receipt of repayable funds from the public." This can be attributed to the order no. 2013-544 of June 27, 2013 regarding credit institutions and finance companies.

Although relatively unnoticed, this change in terminology may not be trivial. At the same time, at the end of this "monopoly," exacerbated competition is developing in areas as diverse as collaborative consumption, complementary currencies, participatory finance, and parallel banking systems, under the weight of new regulatory constraints so complex that they create more doubt on the purpose of the reforms undertaken. If some banks have a share of responsibility in the crisis, they are, perhaps, a little fast—the object of a denunciation of the political class who does not always know how it works. Debates over the necessary banking reform have drifted into a general debate that could turn away from realities and turn against the banks that the economy needs. "*Criticize the*

measures the share taken by resident financial institutions (central banks, credit and similar institutions, securitization funds, UCITS, investment insurance, and other financial intermediaries, excluding financial auxiliaries) in the outstanding amounts of financing available to resident NFAs. The intermediation rate, in the strict sense, corresponds to the share of the only credits granted by these financial institutions in the total financing of NFAs. The intermediation rate, in the broad sense, takes into account, in addition to these credits, the securities issued by the NFAs and held by the financial institutions. For example and to emphasize the importance of the evolution of these rates, the financial intermediation rate in the strict sense was, respectively, 55% in 1995; 43% in 2000; and 40% in 2010. The broad financial intermediation rate increased from 75% in 1995; 70% in 2000; and 55% in 2010. This last decrease results, in part, from an increase in outstanding securities issued by NFAs faster than that of the share held by financial institutions.

bankers but do not destroy the banks!"[3] In his article, Professor Raghuram Rajan states, "*The public discourse is, seldom, nuanced. More decided and strident is the opinion, the more it is able to capture the attention of the public, to be repeated and to frame the terms of the debate.*"

The financial "crisis" of 2008–2009 accentuated the challenge of growing importance of market finance in our economies of "commodified" universal bank model, and more generally of economic activities considered too capital-intensive as a whole. In this context, cooperative banks, occupying a dominant position in French retail banking and often close to the traditional social economy by their status, have been subjected to strong criticism to an extent where their founding values are sometimes questioned, especially the existence of significant differences between their model and the one on which the capital form of commercial banks rests.

The impoverishment of the middle classes and the use of loans as substitutes for wage increases, securitization, subprime, circumvention of regulations, weak regulation, and lack of credibility of rating agencies represent the main facilitating elements (without constituting an exhaustive list of explanatory factors) of the financial crisis that began in 2007.[4] In this context of uncertainty, banks must rediscover the virtues of the core businesses, that is, intermediation trades. Since 1980s, their "business *models*" have tried to innovate on the financial markets in order to create better margins and meet the macroeconomics requirements of what Henri Bourguignat[5] called the "three-D" rule for "deregulation,"[6] "decompartmentalization,"[7] and "disintermediation."[8] European banks have followed,

---

[3]This was the title of a column published in *Les Echos* (April 4, 2013, p. 10) by Raghuram Rajan, senior advisor of the Ministry of Finance, India and professor of Finance at the Booth School of Business, University of Chicago.

[4]For a precise analysis of the financial crisis, the reader can refer to the issues of Documents and Debates: of the Banque de France: Number 2 published in February 2009 and Number 3 published in January 2010.

[5]Henri Bourguinat, Professor of Economics at Bordeaux IV University, is the author of the "3D rule" or "3D theory" (deregulation, disintermediation, and decompartmentalization), presented in his book *International Finance*, University Presses of France, Paris, 1992.

[6]Deregulation is the removal of regulations and controlling the prices of banking services to allow smoother financial flows. It started in the United States before being adapted by the rest of the world. Apart from harmonization of financial systems and removal of transfer fees, major innovations in this area are related to decompartmentalization.

[7]Decompartmentalization represents the separation of activities between retail and investment banking for speculative purposes without exposing the customer deposits to risk.

[8]Disintermediation is the direct access of companies to finance by issuing securities rather than debt to institutional players.

to a lesser extent, their American counterparts in this financialization of the economy with the earthquake that we are deploring today and the mistrust against them. The amount of losses banks underwent during years 2007, 2008, and partially 2009, raise concerns about the legitimacy of the economic model on which the market activity is based. The business of intermediation is brought up to date because it generates, admittedly, a low net banking income (it is the difference between the products and the bank operating expenses. It is not a turnover but is akin to the added value of industrial and commercial companies in the analysis of the intermediate management balances), and ensures a recurrence of results based on the margin, and not on the added value, which are less volatile and fluctuating than those obtained based on market activities. Activity of the retail banks is likely to restore the confidence, which cannot be decreed but deserves to be maintained.

Financial markets, sometimes in association with banks, also play a key role in a country's competitiveness and wealth. Owing to increasingly sophisticated tools, they manage the risks and allocation of savings. However, the multiplication of financial crises makes it difficult to question the social utility part of its development. Financial markets are places where investors who have money and businesses meet the local and federal governments that need them to invest or finance. The financial instruments (stocks, bonds, etc.) that materialize this financing are traded in these markets. Other more complex instruments (notably products called "derivatives" because they are used as a reference to the previous instruments) are also traded in these markets, either for risk-hedging purposes (to avoid the risk of penalizing price variation) or for risk-taking purposes (seeking a profit related to a change in the value of the instrument), often called "speculation." In addition to banks, financial market players are different types of investors: individuals, pension funds, SICAVs or mutual funds, insurers, private equity or venture capital funds, arbitrageurs, hedge funds, some of which have a speculative vocation and others do not.

Based on their culture and economic developments, division of roles between banks and markets varies in different countries. In the United States, where markets have grown more and for longer than in Europe, other financial players have emerged, about 30% of corporate financing needs are covered by banks. In Europe, and particularly in France, the percentages are almost reversed.

Financing a modern economy requires significant capital, as different economic agents, such as households, businesses, and public administrations, have different financing needs depending on their economic activities. As a field of study, finance has traditionally been divided into two specialties: corporate finance and market finance. Although partially overlapping, these two specialties have different orientations. Corporate finance focuses on business financing and investment choices, whereas market finance studies financial markets, especially, what determines asset prices and how investors compose and manage their asset portfolio (stocks, bonds, derivatives, etc.). This price mechanism makes it possible to evaluate the investment opportunities that security issuers seek to finance, while considering the risks they entail. The approaches used in market finance are both empirical and theoretical. The problem is how to connect lenders and borrowers efficiently. This hypothesis (linked to the behavior of the agents and necessity of having predictive information) discussed and questionable efficiency implies that the prices on the financial markets reflect all available information. For example, if a particular set of information available at a given moment, the price of a security is equal to its "fundamental value" and future price movements (adjusted for risk) are as likely to be upward as downward. The pricing of assets follows random, unpredictable processes because its variation depends on new information which itself is unpredictable.

To a large extent economic growth depends on the effectiveness of its financing. The possibility of obtaining minimum cost credits is essential for business development, but this should not be at the expense of financial stability. History also tells us that long periods of financial stability, without financial bubbles, did exist, as was the case between 1945 and 1965 during the period of economic expansion, called the "glorious thirties." Another period of financial runaway was between 1980 and 2000, since this period has experienced unparalleled global growth. However, historically, the financial system has always had periods of euphoria, where the possibilities of gain erase the perception of risk, followed by periods of collapse where risk aversion becomes acute. Financial crises are as old as finance, since the "tulipomania" in Holland in the 17th century; bankruptcy of John Law in France in the 18th century; or the American crises of the 19th and early 20th century that led to the creation of the Federal Reserve (Fed), the US central bank, and the Securities Exchange Commission (Sec), the stock market regulator in the United States. In France, until the end of the 1970s, the economy could be described as a debt economy, that is, the share of intermediated financing was much higher than that of the direct financing.

Moreover, because of the credit framework until 1987 and exchange control, completed in 1990, the system was not much open to the outside. Therefore, bank credit was the only way to finance the economy, and it was exercised in the context of a weak competition among financial institutions. During 1980s, France gradually switched to a more regulated financial system by fixing the interest rates freely on the markets, inspired by the Anglo-Saxon model, and leading to a financial market economy, which was essential because of liberalization of capital movements (notably with the single European market). For finance to contribute to our goal of responsible growth, effective financing of the economy needs to be combined with "measured" risk-taking, which may not eliminate all crisis but will make them less frequent and less painful.

Responsible finance is part of a long-term development approach that requires creating a new articulation between the economy and the human. How was it born? How is it different from its precursors linked to the more limited fields of SRI and solidary finance? Will it be more convincing and relevant in developing a new financing model for our economy? These are the questions dealt with in this first part, about its genesis, its conceptualization, and its evolution in a new regulatory framework.

In our book *Responsible Finance*, we spoke of a 1,000-year-old mistrust of money and the diversities in cultural social behavior from one country to another. For human beings, money has always been a source of tension and discomfort. Difficulties abound and go far beyond language. It is even said that the French, more than other people, would be even more disturbed by this word, not daring to call it by its name. Earning money would be unhealthy and one would even talk more about receiving a salary or fees. Pascal Bruckner in his essay[9] draws a parallel between the United States and France.

> *the American credo, Greed is good is opposed to the French cult of pleasure. The United States is obsessed with marital disloyalty when France, horrified by the triumph of materialism, shows towards the errors of the flesh a tolerance that has become a way of life.*" In France, he tells us, money is taboo: "*what the French reject is, first, the unequal distribution of income. But they are also suspicious of the success, always suspicious and result, according to them, connivance. But today, when the money-king is being blasted, it is rather the rare money which predominates ...*

[9]"The Wisdom of Money," essai grasset, Paris 2016.

And there is[...] with us a formal condemnation of the wealth provided that we can enjoy of its advantages ...

We are not only uncomfortable talking about money, often quick to denounce provocative accumulation or misuse. Yet, it testifies to the mode of organization of the life of a society. It can shape the human relations, positively or negatively, depending on the way we use it. We recall that, from origins to religious activism, a millennial mistrust of finance, shared by religions, politicians, and philosophers, characterizes its path. From the 8th century BC, the Babylonians implemented a legislative device, the Hammurabi Codex to severely regulate the activity of traders and bankers. Kautilya stresses since 4th century BC in India that financial transactions must be scrupulously scrutinized by the state, so that money lenders who practice usury can be punished. This mistrust can be found among the Greeks and, later, among the Romans. Majority of Western religions also condemn the practice of interests. Judaism, Christianity and Islam justify, identically, their rejection, supplemented by religious considerations to proper confession. The fundamental prohibition of usury in Jewish law goes back to Deuteronomy, whose injunctions take the form of the commandment, "You will not give your brother interest." The tribal conception of duty, however, extends the solidarity to the members of the confession, only for certain interpretations, which explains the role played by the Jews in the financial activity of the middle ages.[10]

Indeed, traders are aware of their need for financing that allows their development, but the rate of usury is prohibited to Christians. Thomas Aquinas extends the prohibition of financial speculation to all capital gains made without transformation, "The man who buys a good to sell it unchanged is like the merchants who were driven from the temple of God." In his condemnation of the act of commerce, Aquinas, one of the greatest Christian theologians, is unaware of value added in space and time through the distribution of goods, investments, and costs of opportunity. Since then, the church has shown its reservation against this judgment of St. Thomas. However, it is written in the New Testament that Jesus said, "It is easier for a camel to go through the needle hole than for a rich man to enter the Kingdom of God" (Mark 10, 25). This

[10] Jacques Le Goff's *The Exchange and Life, Economy and Religion in the Middle Ages*, 2004, plural collection, Hachette literatures.

sentence made it difficult for Christians to relate to money. We also specify that critics are also very strong in the political and philosophical field from Aristotle to Marx, and from the Trotskyite parties to current anti-globalization movements. The refusal of the legitimacy of the interest rate is for Aristotle based on the sterility of money: it is not small and the interest is an unnatural reproduction of money by money (it can be explained as the opportunity cost and the necessary financing of development and innovations). But, Aristotle is resolutely modern and quite current in his questions about the moral legitimacy of the fortunes procured without effort, the damage produced by the pursuit of gain through monopoly, the increase of inequalities, or the exploitation of the weakness of needy people. These challenges will be repeated and amplified by Marxist criticism in the 19th century ("The Capital" of Marx).

We see too many protest movements nowadays. Anti-globalization organizations, for example, are obviously opposed to the consequences of an international financial market. For many, the Tobin tax on capital flows would be a solution to prevent speculation which according to them is purely financial and totally disconnected from the market economy. The Vatican,[11] though it has long accepted the liberal system, still condemns the effects of "excessive liberalism." Meanwhile, the bishops of France warn against the excesses of globalization.[12]

Finance is necessary to the capitalist system and is therefore gradually accepted. The development of commercial capitalism, which some authors date around 16th century, is at the origin of the gradual reconsideration of ancient judgments. In particular, Calvin makes a distinction between consumers lending, which must remain free, and lending to the enterprise, which may legitimately give rise to specific remuneration while contributing to the production of new wealth. Max Weber (1864–1920, German economist and sociologist considered as one of the

[11] Read the homily of the inauguration mass of Pope Benedict XVI's pontificate, broadcast on April 24, 2005, liturgical date: 5 PA.

[12] According to "Benchmarks in a global economy," published on April 28, 2005 by the social commission, in the eyes of bishops, globalization must be considered positively, on the imperative condition that humans remain at the center of the economic system. The Social Commission of Bishops analyzes this requirement in three areas: finance, growth, and social justice. The document warns about the race for short-term profitability, concentration, very easy access to debt, or the drift of certain remunerations. The Church suggests certain ways to deal with these new abuses: ethical funds, elaboration of a right that apprehends the company as a community of people, a more equitable distribution of profits, etc.

founders of sociology) shows how the Protestant ethic could be satisfied with the "spirit" of capitalism; Protestantism has completely upset the appreciation of economic activity. Protestant ethics make economic success moral and encourage material success. Therefore, the search for profit is indeed available in the liberal theory. Adam Smith introduces the notion of "invisible hand." Economic development is based on the pursuit of profit and its maximization. The concern for of all organizational interests is also favorable to the general interest, but it is often expressed in different ways. This section offers a perspective on the origins of "virtuous" finance. In addition to the fact that the two individual terms in our "responsible finance" are not irreconcilable, how could it guarantee the smooth functioning of a modern finance and how does it contribute to the construction of a new space for reflecting the governance of an "otherwise" finance? Before mentioning the genesis of responsible finance, let us briefly discuss a history of banking and insurance in both their capital and mutual forms.

Some international questions about the banking model

Following the global financial crisis of 2007–2010 (subprime crisis, falling financial values, and declining economic growth) and the debt crisis in the euro area (fear of insolvency of sovereign debt for the euro area), it appeared that the banks had to resort to public financial aid. This has led to a need for greater control and regulation through the Volcker Rule in the United States, the Vickers Report in the United Kingdom, the French Banking Separation Law (Law No. 2013-672 of July 26, 2013 on Separation and Regulation of Activities Banking), and the draft regulation following the Liikanen report in Germany and Europe. The question of separating the market activities (trading own or third party accounts) from other banking activities (deposits, loans, and strategic and financial advice, etc.) has thus again become essential in the eyes of governments and regulators, for better protection of customer deposits and state aid. However, the establishment of this separation of activities is not uniform at the global level and could introduce a distortion of competition.

In the United Kingdom, the Vickers report calls for more equity and short-term liquidity for retail banks. It even proposes to isolate these "retail" activities in subsidiaries, thus going beyond the Basel III recommendations. However, given the banking lobbying of the United Kingdom, the implementation of these recommendations may not to be finalized before 2019.

In the United States, the Volcker rule is limited to protecting savers by limiting the investments of deposit banks in risky activities, such as trading for its own account, hedge funds, or private equity funds.

This reform is much more restrictive than a pure separation of the deposit bank as envisaged by the bank separation laws recently put in place by France and Germany. This model (Bank Structural Reform, BSR), which was also to be adopted at European level, was withdrawn on October 27, 2017 from the European Commission's 2018 work program.

It had a risk of distortion of significant competition, because European banks could no longer enjoy the benefits of " universal bank" model, as we know it, including allowing access to deposits of customers, which is a much cheaper funding resource than using the market. This would lead to increased indebtedness of European banks, which would thus reduce their profitability and competitiveness against foreign banks.

However, this distortion must be put into perspective for the moment, considering the smaller number of banks ultimately impacted in France, or even in Europe, given the thresholds. Especially since the reorganization of the banking system in the United States will reduce the profitability of US financial institutions, a cost that US banks will have to compensate, just like foreign banks working in the United States, also impacted: it is therefore a complex and costly reform, which adds to all global banking regulations and could benefit local banks in Europe and Asia.

Although national legislation in Europe and draft European regulation aim to limit excessive risk-taking and limit the size of the balance sheets resulting from financing and investment activities, these measures are in practice difficult to maintain. Increased debt financing may be difficult to reconcile with the already stringent Basel III prudential regulation. Therefore, if we take the French case, still considered the most restrictive, only two banks out of the ten concerned, BNP Paribas and Societe Generale, perform their activities on their own by creating occasional Opera Trading Capital and Descartes Trading. The other institutions concerned preferred to stop certain trading activities in order to avoid the cost of such a spin-off. Especially, since these subsidiaries represent just less than 1% of the activities of BNP Paribas and Societe Generale respective investment, and financial bank, these are as much to say a drop of water. The universal banking model is not in question.

Moreover, even though the bank separation is not so impacting, it also does not allow tightening the banking activities. Indeed, what will happen if the subsidiary that manages proprietary speculation goes bankrupt and causes heavy losses for the parent company? In the past, two of the four main French groups, BPCE and Crédit Agricole, have already isolated their market activities in their respective subsidiaries, Natixis and Cacib, had to come to their rescue, respectively, in 2008 and 2011. Insulation is not a quick fix.

Finally, banking risk is not only inherent to market activities. Recent counter-examples are numerous. The real-estate credit business has been a major source of risk: in Spain, the fall in property prices and insolvency of borrowers have made banks virtually bankrupt; in the United States, the subprime crisis is a mortgage crisis that has affected the markets thanks to sophisticated securitization mechanisms. These mechanisms had allowed banks to take out the risk from their balance sheet (at least in appearance).

In the context of financial globalization, the separation of banking activities may never be effective. In practice, the reform of the banking system requires coordination between the states, since the big national banks have subsidiaries abroad, which can escape this new regulation. For the moment, the ideal is that each business manages its own results, without cross-subsidy. Each of them is assigned its objectives and no financial compensation is made from one activity to another. Lastly, despite increasing digitalization, the retail service requires a real closeness to a dense network of agencies that require substantial real estate investment and staffing.

Banking and insurance, an old story!

The origin of *the bank* goes back to Babylon, to the second millennium BC. At that time, the loan on goods (especially cereals) was already practiced in the precincts of the temples. With the appearance of money, around the 7th century BCE, money lending and deposit operations developed by the end of the 5th century AD. With the crusades (the first one took place in 1095), trade accelerated and banks, mainly Italian (the first bank was created in Venice in 1151), participated by facilitating purchases and sales of precious objects, cereals, spices and metals. From the 12th century, exchanges started between the Europe and the

East. Existence of major trade routes in northern Europe, and trade fairs facilitated the use of the payment letters reducing insecurity related to manipulations of change.

The Renaissance (between the 14th and 16th century) saw the emergence of large international institutions: the Fugger in Germany, the Medici, Alberti, or Strozzi in Florence, and several other Genoese, Venetian, and Milanese families founded banks. The cities of London and Amsterdam became important financial centers by the 17th century.

In its full industrial revolution (steam, steel, electricity, etc.) 19th century witnessed the development of the modern banks supported by more intense use of the fiduciary money, the scriptural money (the check in 1864), and titles. Middle of the 19th century saw the creation of major retailers such as: Société Générale and Crédit Lyonnais in France, Deutsche Bank in Germany, and Barclays Bank in Great Britain. In the 20th century, the state strengthened its authority over banks and imposed regular controls. In 1945, France nationalized (the state then became the owner) a number of banks, including the Bank of France. Starting from the 1960s, banks have been experiencing a new boom. Gradually, French families are "banked" and a real race to open the windows begins, especially following the Matignon agreements in 1968, under the effect of a monthly salary and their mandatory payments in an account. At the same time, banking groups are growing, diversifying, and becoming more international. The beginning of the 21st century saw the rise of electronic banking and new payment instruments. After the remote banking, it is the neobanks (use of mobiles in the current management of accounts and payment methods; 29 contactless payments per second were recorded in 2016) that impact the profitability of bank branches. According to 2009 records, for the first time, a net balance in the number of bank branches created closures (In France, the number of bank branches has decreased by 5% since 2008 and has just over 30,000 branches at the end of 2018. 55 branches per 100,000 inhabitants. Germany also reached 30,000 counters, but with 10,000 points of sale less secure during the same period).

Despite its importance in the economic and social lives, it is necessary here to consolidate the history of banking and insurance by the parallel emergence of the too often misunderstood *mutualism* and its integration into French society during the 19th century. This panorama, without being exhaustive, takes up the general historical context of the establishment of mutualism, and then the main specificities attached to the historical evolutions of cooperative banks and mutual insurances.

Mutualism is not an instinctive movement; it can be likened to a structured and spontaneous form of life in a society backed by mutual aid. Since antiquity, examples of the first fruits of mutuality forms can be found in collective ranching in Babylon; brotherhoods of burial of antiquity; and later, with the fellow builders of Middle Ages cathedrals. The beginnings of the cooperative movement are to be sought in the United Kingdom in the aftermath of the Napoleonic wars with the contribution of Robert Owen (1771–1858), who, as early as 1817, emphasizes that "misery results in competition between man and machine and the only way to remedy it is collective action and the subordination of the machine." William King (May 1, 1828) publishes his first thoughts in "The Cooperator" and encourages the poorest to open their own supply store.

The sources of inspiration of the cooperative and mutualism movements of the 19th century are complex and come from many utopian and theoretical experiments aimed at promoting the virtues of a solidarity ideal. Among the main sources, and at the risk of omitting them, let us mention: (1) the solidarities originated from confraternities, confessional or professional, and companionship; (2) some, including Walras, saw the advent of workers in the ownership of capital through savings; (3) others, Christian democrats combine solidarity and charity (Raiffeisen); (4) the socialist and communist utopia of Proudhon and Saint-Simon were at the origin of the modern social economy; (5) According to Leon Bourgeois (1851–1925), French politician and sculptor, radical parliamentarian of the Third Republic, first president of the League of Nations, winner of the Nobel Peace Prize in 1920, the institutions of the mutualist economy could constitute a middle way between capitalism and socialism, between liberalism and statism (state control). Mutualism is the political and historical movement that has led to the creation of mutual or cooperative forms of association in the fields of insurance, banking, construction, education, and in general all forms of production or trade. The adjective mutual refers, more precisely, to the reciprocal character of a right or an obligation. The mutual society is similar to the cooperative society in terms of nonprofit association such that its clients (and sometimes its employees) are at the same time its associates.

In a revolutionary France marked by liberal concerns and governed by the Le Chapelier's law of June 1791 (repealed in 1884) which proscribed the coalitions of employers and especially workers in order to avoid all wage demands, many citizens plunged into misery and joined forces to create the first solidarity organizations. Thus, "The Soum of the Shroud," was one of the first mutual aid societies to ensure that the dead are not thrown without a shroud to the mass grave.

In France, mutualism is the citizen, political, and historical movement that led to the creation of mutualism or cooperative forms of association in the fields of insurance, banking, construction, education, and in general of all forms of production or commerce. The adjective mutual refers, more precisely, to the reciprocal character of a right or an obligation. All these actors belong to the world of social and solidarity economy (ESS), a broader concept than mutualism. ESS refers to a set of enterprises organized in the form of cooperatives, mutual, associations, or foundations, whose internal functioning and activities are based on a principle of solidarity and social utility. The ESS employs 2.39 million workers in France, about 12.7% of private employment, according to the 2015 employment report published by Research and Solidarity in June 2016. The largest workforce is involved in areas of social action, financial and insurance activities, education and health. The July 31, 2014 law related to ESS supports and secures this sector. In its article 1, this law particularly opens the field of ESS to commercial companies respecting its principles.

Between values and performances, the model of the cooperative bank was invented in Europe, and more precisely in Germany in the 19th century, with the initiatives of Frédéric-Guillaume Raiffeisen and Hermann Schulze-Delitzsch. Raiffeisen created the first credit union operating on a model based on the unlimited liability of members, the volunteer work of directors, and a limited geographical constituency. The model developed by Schulze-Delitzsch is characterized by an extensive geographical reach, remuneration of directors, and possibility of paying dividends to members. Mutuals and cooperatives are collective forms of enterprise (in the event of a cessation of activity, available assets are not shared among the members, since they do not own them individually and the general assembly is sovereign, i.e., one person = one vote), it is, however, necessary to mark the differences between the two: mutual companies, unlike the cooperatives, have no social capital, and the funds come from the contributions of their members. These contributions are generally fixed and essentially constitute the funds for mutual funds'. By definition, a bank is not mutual, it has a social capital. We can speak of mutualism "mind" banking, with reference to the mutualism philosophy.

How did we move from the first credit unions to cooperative banks in France? In 1863, Jean-Pierre Beluze created the "Crédit au travail," a bank of cooperatives, which inspired the Caja Laboral Popular,

Mondragon, Spain. Etienne Cabet founded the "Société de credit au travail" in 1863. At the same time a savings bank for the workers, a credit society between members, and a bank of credit and discount were created. For their part, Léon Walras and Léon Say participated in the creation, in January 1865, of the "Caisse d'escompte des associations populaires," the purpose of which was to make advances to companies and groups known as the "Credit, Production and Marketing Association," constituted on the basis of mutual guarantee or joint and several liability. However, these initiatives borrowed from a certain utopia quickly proved fruitless and died down in 1868. However, the idea of credit being accessible to all remained present in society, especially as banks, in conjunction with economic development, were investing in large industries, particularly in international trade and settlements, and were not at all concerned with the local situation. In France, the Raiffeisen and Schulze-Delitzsch models resulted in the emergence of to two types of institutions, respectively: Mutual Credit (1882, Creation in Alsace of the first credit union of Crédit Mutuel, based on the Raiffeisen model) and Banques Populaires (1893, creation in Angers of the first popular Bank by Ludovic de Besse).

The 19th-century France, a country of farmers, was already experiencing a structural adjustment of the financing circuits of its agriculture. This situation led to the emergence of the third major French cooperative actor, that is, Crédit Agricole (November 5, 1894 law that authorizes the constitution of local Credit Banks between members of agricultural unions, which engage their responsibilities according to the principle of mutualism). In 1999, the Caisse d'épargne assumed the status of cooperative bank and in 2009 Caisse Nationale des Caisses d'Epargne and Banque Fédérale des Banques Populaires were merged.

As a reminder, the International Cooperative Alliance counts 750,000 cooperatives and 100 million jobs worldwide. In Europe, 160,000 cooperative enterprises employ 5.6 million people and have 123 million members. France ranks third with 21,000 cooperatives and 750,000 jobs. Their turnover amounts to €257 billion. Every second person is a member of one or more cooperatives.

From insurance to health and provident: between corporatist protections, complexity of services and race in keeping with mutual insurance companies

How to ward off the misdeeds of chance and provident, go from assistance to the foresight of the 19th century? To understand the rise of mutualism in the 20th century can be, in short, a brief progression in the history of insurance. A typology of the companies which constitute the global sphere of the insurance can be realized according to the legal regime and their control.

It is commonly accepted that the world of French insurance is made up of three major subsets and all these actors do not intervene on all insurance markets, and the partitions have tendency to gradually fade. Insurance companies, (commercial companies or mutual insurance companies) governed by the insurance code; mutual companies governed by the mutuality or the rural code; and, finally, the provident institutions governed by the Social Security Code may also carry out insurance operations. We will endeavor to present a brief history of these three subsets.

Insurances companies

As for the history of the bank, it is almost 2,000 years before our era the beginnings of some form of insurance appeared. The Babylonians first develop a system called "ready to the big adventure" (cover the sea risks). This rule is even incorporated into the Hammurabi Code, the ground law of the Babylonian civilization. While the loan to big adventure spreads throughout ancient times, at the first millennium BC, the concept of metallization was created in Rhodos: the merchants whose goods arrive at destination compensate those whose cargo was lost on the way. A little later, Greeks and Romans introduced a form of life insurance of a special kind: a group of individuals contribute for a while. This sum was then set aside until it was finally given to the last survivor of the group. In 1063 AD, it was in the Venice that the first insurance contracts were born.

After 1830, the pauperism that followed the rise of large-scale industry was so dramatic that it was widely treated and relayed by classical literature (Victor Hugo, Eugène Sue). Paradoxically, if the French revolution had been able to throw suspicion on for-profit provident enterprises, it did not spare the nascent mutuality either through one or more fraternities. It is the birth of the welfare state and the Declaration of Human Rights of 1793 proclaiming, "Society owes their livelihood to unhappy citizens ... ." In 2016, 93 insurance companies realized €32 billion of turnover in a core business represented by the individual and collective insurance (death, incapacity, disability, and health risks).

Mutual insurance companies

From a professional segmentation (agriculture, fishing, building, crafts) to a geographical segmentation (Poitevins, Manceaux, Savoyards ...) mutual insurance companies gained shape at the beginning of the 20th century. The important, if not decisive, weight of the departments of Center West raises the question of why this region played a leading role in setting up the cradle of the mutual insurance company. Do not we talk about "Mutuelles de Niort?" In 1910, in the region under the aegis of the cattle dealers, anxious to protect themselves against the accidents or the diseases, the first insurance mutual was created in Loulay (Charente Inferieure), the heart of the dairy zone.

From 1934, mutual insurance companies were set up at the initiative of socioprofessional groups (national education staff for Mutual Insurance Automobile Teachers of France, MAAIF, later on MAIF; MAAF for craftsmen; MACIF for industry and commerce). Their growth accelerated by the surge of mutuals without intermediaries following the World War II, while the commercial insurance sector dominated by nationalized companies was under the influence of general agents.

Since the beginning of the 19th century, groups of individuals who wanted to establish the conditions for taking control of their and their families protection against illness, disability, old age, and death created the first mutual aid societies. At first, these companies were corporatists in the same district or same city, which caused an apprehension among the political authorities that they will disturb the social order. However, in 1852, Napoleon III legalized these companies for better control and ensured their development at the same time.

At the end of the WWI, France faced a demographic challenge that it had to meet. At the same time, while returning to France, the departments of Alsace and Lorraine brought along the social insurance created by Bismarck in the German Empire, and thus the principle of a compulsory system of social protection was developed. It was only by 1930 the first compulsory schemes in the industrial companies were established, followed by the creation of the Social Security in 1945 which ensured integral benefits and at the same time a reform of the code of mutuality instituting the prevention of the social risks and their consequences. In order to comply with the European directives, a new code of mutuality was adopted in 2002. It imposed more stringent financial security rules and at the same time an age limit ratio for the boards of directors. It also forced mutual companies to separate social (clinics, pharmacy, optics, dental, etc.), pension, and sickness activities. This resulted in the merger of many mutual companies. In 2016, around 488 of them had €18 billion in turnover (contributions). Today, they cover 38 million protected people and employ 55,000 workers.

Provident institutions

The 19th century industrial revolution produced decisive changes in society. Traditional self-help structures, family, village, parish, were no longer sufficient to meet the protection needs of employees. New structures were born, committees, desks, federations, unions, institutions, whose vocation was to ensure the risks of accidents at work, retirement, sickness, and maternity by solidarity mechanisms. Gradually, these structures evolved in line with national social legislation and were consolidated to strengthen and offer a better guarantee to policyholders and beneficiaries.

Thus, the provident institutions were created legally under the Social Security Code, unlike the mutual companies governed by the Mutuality Code or insurance companies, covered by the Insurance Code. A pension or supplementary pension institution is defined as a private legal entity with a nonprofit purpose, administered by the social partners. In 2016, there were 41 net sales for €13 billion, and a cumulative net income of €100 million in 2016 (+4%). Turnover has increased in health, but declined in case of retirement.

Between solidarity and usury: SRI and the genesis of responsible finance

The history of solidary finance is merged with the financial sphere and the concept of usury. In his article "Solidary finance: history and relevance," published in the "Encyclopedia of Sustainable Development,"[13]

[13] No. 103, November 2009, Récollets Editions.

Jacques Dughera reminds us that solidary finance, forerunner of socially responsible investment and therefore responsible finance, is nothing more than a fair exchange between a saver and the one who needs to borrow. He says:

> *But rather than remain in the act of charity by the gift, solidarity finance establishes a creditor/debtor relationship that does not turn the debtor into assistance and the creditor into despot. From the end of the middle Ages, some Recollect and Franciscan monks prefer to lend rather than give. In 1637, to allow access to credit for the largest number of Parisians, Louis XIII authorizes the creation of Mont-de-piété. It is obviously with the development of capitalism and the consequent rise of inequalities, that the currency (and the money that takes its place) will have all its meaning. But whereas for most contemporaries of the birth of capitalism, the search for profit becomes an objective in itself going up to pay a rent on the money lent (the interest), for Proudhon (1809–1865) and a part of the ancestors of solidarity finance, it is above all a matter of bridging the gap between men, all men, without interest and without remuneration from the saver.*

This was the project of people's bank developed by Proudhon in 1849 in Besançon after the official filing of statutes before notary. His project was based on the idea of a "bank of exchange" or "bank of the people" which must make it possible to realize a true economic democracy thanks to the mutual and free credit which gives the possibility to the workers to own the capital which they lack to get rid of the owners. This bank must be based on three essential principles: free credit through a gradual elimination of the interest rate; elimination of the gold-based currency replaced by a "swap" without the cash redemption condition; the generalization of the bill of exchange payable on sight for goods or services. It was when mutualism came into existence that we have just discussed above.

Regarding Mont-de-piété in Europe, it was an Italian monk, Bartolomé de Terni, who had the first idea to fight wear and misery associated with the mount-of-piety, found in Perugia in 1462. Despite several attempts and after the failure of the most serious one supported by Richelieu, in 1637, who had authorized doctor Theophrastus Renaudot—founder of the Gazette de France—to open a pledging office in Paris, it was not until Necker and Lieutenant-General Lenoir saw the concept of Mont-de-piété reappear. It is by the letters patent of Louis XVI of December 9, 1777 that a Mont-de-piété of Paris[14] reappeared in February 1778 to relieve the discreet miseries of the humble and precious. The "Monts-de-piété" established in the great French regional metropolises will always remain as an excellent barometer of the state of our society between passions, setbacks, hopes, and disillusions. Although they have a pawnbroker monopoly, these institutions have striven to fully exercise the banking profession by diversifying their activities and offering solidary savings, microcredit, and debt rescheduling for individuals.

If solidary finance inscribed its history at the heart of that of solidarity and usury, already present in the Middle Age, it really took off at the end of the 19th century with the development of capitalism and inequalities it generated. The digging of these at the end of the 20th century renewed its forms and we strived to understand how did we progressively move from solidarity to ethical finance, and then, perhaps to responsible finance. Is it only a question of semantics? In order to bring some elements of answer, let us strive to observe the way of thinking and the perspective of some major theoretical steps widely discussed in our aforementioned book dedicated to ethical finance. How did we go from an industrial logic to a financial logic to try to reach a more responsible logic of finance where the creditor/debtor relationship would no longer turn the debtor into an assisted and the creditor into a despot? After the precept of the "consume differently" why not evolve, too, toward that of "finance differently" where responsible finance would be an alternative to conventional financing without pretending to become an alternative finance that would supplant and erase all links with them.

The dysfunctions observed in the management of certain multinationals, in this period of transition between the end of the 20th century and the beginning of the 21st century, as well as the stock market disorders that followed, were at the origin of an abundant literature on the theme of responsible governance. Among the most significant analyses, we will retain three[15] to support our argument.

[14]According to the biographer Eric Deschodt, author of, *History of the Mont-de-piété*, edition of the search for noon, November 1993, after 7 years and once Richelieu disappeared, a decree of Parliament summoned Théophraste de Renaudot to close his pawnshop on the grounds "That by making the banker, the latter compromised the dignity of the medical art!" In truth, usury had powerful supporters and it will continue to develop during the Great and Century and the Enlightenment.

[15]Three works referred to bibliographical: (1)Pastré (O.) &aVigier (M.), *Confused Capitalism*," Discovery Edition, 2003: (2) Perez (R.), "Governance of the Company," *Collection*

For Olivier Pastré and Michel Vigier, what differentiates Enron from previous scandals (Maxwell, Credit Lyonnais) are the finest financialization and deregulation pushed to its extreme. These authors believe that nineteenth-century capitalism rationalized production, achieved high productivity gains, and accelerated technical progress, but it stubbornly struggled on a market opportunity. The crises of overproduction (including the crisis of 1882 in France and then 1929) were stopping the economic machine at regular intervals. To overcome this contradiction, Henry Ford invented the "five-dollar day" at the beginning of the 1920s. To sell an automobile production, it is necessary to find solvent customers. Ford said, "Why not make my workers my first customers? It is enough to increase their wages significantly; their orders will allow me, by the extension of my production capacities and the realization of economies of scale, to lower my prices and thus to have access to a larger solvent clientele." And so on. This reasoning was theorized at the macroeconomic level by John M. Keynes and later concretized by Franklin D. Roosevelt, President of the United States. The employee was thus placed at the heart of the economic regulation system not only as the sole labor force, but as a pillar of both supply and demand. In this context, inflation has advantages; it allows to maintain an illusion, supposedly virtuous, on the exact value of the products manufactured. It also pushes for consumption (poorly paid savings is a poor alternative) and it cancels the cost of debt. The problem is that this regulatory system is structurally inflationary. The raise in real interest rates initiated by governments in the 1980s had the merit of purging the system. The population saved again because the rates become really remunerative and the explosion of service trades acted as a new industrialization (but as these trades are based on the intangible, they are difficult to count and regulate). According to the same authors, it was not the merchant banks that were the first to design the financial innovations, products, and administered rate oblige, but, "it is the State that defines the framework, without realizing that once these energies are released, the control of regulation, and especially the financial one, would be more and more difficult to assume. How to make private what was public while financing budget deficits without harming the saver again important?" The 90s will confirm this heavy trend generated by companies, namely the primacy of financial logic over industrial logic within a capital system marked

Reference Mark, Discovery Edition, 2003; and (3) Aglietta (M.) & Rebérioux (A.), *Drifts of Financial Capitalism*, Albin Michel, 2004.

by the general decline in the rate of profit. For Olivier Pastré and Michel Vigier

> *The objective was to reduce the need for capital by using the leverage effect of indebtedness and thus to make shareholders happy in the short term; traditional capitalist construction consists of using the company's balance sheet to create and then finance the development of its activity.*

The American, European, and Japanese financial systems have massively pushed the companies to multiply the financial operations by arguing about the globalization and especially the revolution of the new economy. Would we witness a strong comeback of the "new economy"? In case of France, the event is obvious. After confusing turnover and results, parallel growth of mobile technology with that of the Internet, while only the second was a real new technology, it should be admitted that the fundamentals of the "net" (practical aspect, flow considerable information, price comparisons ..., time savings) continued with the positive evolution of household equipment rates. New purchasing behaviors are born. It seems that a "new economy" is reborn with a new management and without obsession with an almost immediate introduction on the stock market of "young shoots." Will bankers appreciate the disruption of the uses of virgin land brought by more discreet and mature businesses and will they finance? What could our elders have said at the end of the 19th century when they discovered the fairy electricity, Graham Bell's phone, the deployment of the railroad, rubber processing, vaccination, Panama and its resounding bankruptcy?

Olivier Pastré and Michel Vigier, in their book *The Disoriented Capitalism*, note that "The annual endowment of the company to pension funds is calculated from assumptions on the performance of existing assets, facing the needs of pensioners current and future. During the 1990s, many US companies used annual asset return assumptions of up to 11% based on stock market growth. The rise in the stock market thus finances American pensions without any financial effort from their employers."

The stock option policy prompted the owners of the firm to abandon operational management to their senior managers. They focused on their financial strategy, including the external growth imposed by the stock markets to justify ever higher stock prices. "The function of social plans has expanded. Until 1990, under the pressure of bad results, people were fired when the survival of the company was at stake. Today, we dismiss as a preventive measure to improve profitability and increase dividends paid to shareholders"; we are far from ethics!

Roland Perez, in his book *The Governance of the Company*, breaks down into an organizational approach which shifts from an industrial logic to a financial logic. To do this, it relies on the evolutions observed in the balance of power between the actors and explains the consequences of the supremacy of the financial investors. After taking power in the company of managers, at the expense of business leaders, he noted, for a second time, the preponderance of shareholders on managers. For Roland Perez, the entrepreneur is considered the provider of equity, by committing his personal funds, he assumes only the risk. By using external money, we enter the era of managers. Adam Smith, one of the founding fathers of political economy expressed his feeling about the first "*managers.*"

> *The directors of these sorts of companies are the managers of the money of others rather than their money; we cannot expect that they bring this exact and careful vigilance that associates often bring in the handling of their funds.*

According to Roland Perez, this is how industrialization developed at the beginning of the last century

> *The development of the big industry, made possible by the creation of companies using public savings, was from the mid-nineteenth century in Europe as in the United States bringing a separation increasingly marked between the leaders of these large units and a dispersed shareholding.*

However, the shareholders did not hold power in the company. During the period of the 30 glorious years (1945–1974), it was a managerial vision that prevailed, oriented mainly toward growth objectives. According to Roland Perez, the shareholder is considered to be one of the firm's suppliers "This conception of the managerial firm has been very successful, particularly as we understand it, among the senior executives of large joint-stock companies." In a country like France, the importance of which is reflected in the state of the economy, it was able to reinforce the idea that the management of big companies, whatever their status, participated in some ways in public service, and as a result, financial markets should not play a major role. It is in the face of the success of the managerial approaches of the firm that left the shareholders that the theory of the agency was developed in the 1970s.

The theory of the agency whose major contributors are C. Jensen and William H. Meckling (1976) and which according to Roland Perez is "based on different currents of thought have built a new paradigm that we could call that of organizational finance." The firm is no longer represented through the entrepreneur, as in its canonical form, but as a node of contracts. The various stakeholders (providers of capital, employees, customers, and suppliers) are linked in this node of contracts, thanks to this legal fiction that the commercial law can authorize creating "legal persons" who are in fact companies. Two categories of stakeholders play a major role: shareholders "because their property rights are exercised only as a last resort" and managers "because they have information privileged by their position in the organization." Roland Perez then explains that "the scope of the theory of the agency is the questioning of the traditional status of the firm by the managerial theory."

In this respect, the theory of the agency was the counter-offensive weapon used by ultra-liberal economists to legitimize their vision of a firm wholly owned by its shareholders, without further consideration. It can be observed that the period during which this theory was forged and spread corresponds to a modification of the long-term trends of the American economy with a relative decline in growth rates posing in more acute terms than before the trade-offs between profitability and growth. Thus, in parallel with a slowdown in economic growth, financial players are gaining momentum and, as they become more professional, they will be able to act and have a stronger influence on the behavior of the managers of the firms, leading them to favor the introduction of short-term strategies. For Roland Perez, "*The fundamental circuit for any economy, which goes from the saver to the investment classically, associates the image of the household saver to the entrepreneur investor.*" This growing institutionalization of the savings-management circuit has the effect of changing the nature of the relationship between the company and its shareholders. As soon as they are not present directly, but through the savings funds, the relationship between them becomes "professionals"; those of the company and those of the fund or funds concerned. How will companies react to this new situation? Still according to Roland Perez,

- "By bending their strategic choices, sometimes by reversing them in relation to the past.

- By modifying their structures, their organizations, their incentive and control processes, that is their management system. But, especially by "staging" the representation of their performance and making communication on it a management objects."

Michel Aglietta, similar to the previous authors, locates the origins of this dogma of the financial capital ("the company directed in the only interest of its shareholders" or dogma of "the value for the shareholder") in the Seventies owing to the rising inflation. The leading causes of its appearance are found in a critic of the Fordism with its irremovable owners and with the consequent overheads blocking the development of capitalism. This movement was reinforced at the end of the 80s in the United States with the coding of the first charters of governance under the influence of the lawyers and the pension funds. According to Michel Aglietta,

> "the problem, it is that the shareholders, far from finding power, on the contrary lost some! The inspecting devices forged by the charters of governance, for example the stock-options, were easily diverted thanks to financial montages invented by the investment banks. Assemblies intended to enrich an elite including the owners and the intermediaries by the chain of financial information, the cabinets of audit at the credit rating agencies".... "Gold in the Nineties, the stock exchange euphoria created collusion between the officers of the company and the shareholders, in a process of mutual enrichment. Whereas before the leaders sought to maximize the long-term growth of their company, they privileged the short-term maximization of its stock exchange courts, which is different! With all the more of spirit which their remuneration were directly indexed on the quoted value of the company and with as much less control on behalf of the shareholders than those were filled by the flight of the indices."

The governance crisis and these fraudulent bankruptcies combined with the financial crisis marked by the bursting of the stock market bubble transformed the nature of the risk.

The financial sphere is moving from a global risk to a multiplication of basic, interdependent and spread risks in an increasing number of markets and investors, resulting in sustained volatility and increased uncertainties. Firms' balance sheets are bursting with financial assets at the expense of industrial assets. Very quickly, the regulators will try to intervene (Sarbanes-Oxley law in the United States in July 2002, on financial security in France) by regulating the different professions of the financial information chain without directly attacking the substance of the problem and the type of disseminated information.

Michel Aglietta summarizes these measures as follows: "It simply amounts to wanting to moralize the system, without calling into question the perverse logic of the dictatorship of the stock market price.[16] Of course, we must first put in cause the theory of the almighty shareholder. The company must be redesigned not as an object of property, but as an entity coordinating a plurality of skills animated by a collective interest." With the corollary: a true board of directors' "mediator" of all stakeholder interests of the firm and a collective savings more focused on long-term prospects to reduce market volatility.

All of these first studies underline the complexity of the subject and especially the fact that the value for the shareholder has become an essential reference at a time when this financial capital could appear less strategic than the human capital. With these governance concerns, the dishonest ones were probably only catalysts of the crisis, the responsibilities are, perhaps, to find out the excessive and unrealistic weight of the financial performance at any cost because no device is saved from embezzlement. The inflection of these behaviors is always done by relying on the preponderant role of the shareholder, thus marking the prevalence of the financial component in the mode of governance.

Another important consideration, prior to the analysis of the latest theoretical developments in economic thought, is to remember that this field has been invaded for over 40 years by mathematicians who wanted to transfer the tools of "hard science (as, chemistry, physics)" to "finance." In economics, human behavior can hardly be reduced to equations. These theoretical transpositions remain interesting and can be useful in predictive models (health economics, demography ...). However, if they participate in the development of reference frameworks, they cannot shield the financier from the effort of reflection that leads him to take into account all economic and social realities—a good transition, to address social responsibility and impact investing.

The theoretical approach and currents of thought of ethical finance constitute an emerging field in which the work evolves in a rather

[16]Title of the interview given to the newspaper *L'Expansion* dated November 23, 2004 ("The Dictatorship of the Stock Market Leads to Disaster") about the release of the book: *Dérives du Capitalisme Financier*. Interview by: Emmanuel Lechypre and Franck Dedieu.

inconsistent way. They are largely marked by Anglo-Saxon literature. However, it is possible to identify three main orientations: the study of the performance of ethical funds, the nature and use of extra-financial information, and finally the analysis of investor behavior. There are many weaknesses in explaining the theoretical underpinnings and relying on underlying approaches that are more about social responsibility or environmental dimension. As early as the 1960s, there were many American research on the theme of social responsibility with the current of the "Business Ethics": the company is a moral agent that exists "thanks to society, that it has a power, that it uses resources and that in return she has homework"[17](Bowen 1953, Davis 1960, Frederick 1960, McGuire 1960, Davis and Bolstrom 1966, Walton 1967, Corinne Gendron 2000 for Quebec).[18] In France, it was not until the 1970s that this current was embodied in the one known as "Business and society research" with the Sudreau report on the reform of the company privileging the conditions and the working relations. In the 1990s, in France, the current of Business Ethics was relayed by the circle of Business Ethics which transposed the reflection of the moral behavior of the manager to the company, hence the idea already evoked the "agent moral."

In terms of currents of thought, "if the notion of ethical investment has its origins in the Quakers in the eighteenth century in the United States, it is at the beginning of the twentieth century, more precisely in the late 20s, that it is manifest in a more institutional way with the creation of the first collective investment fund that obliges itself to follow ethical investment rules." The movement for ethical investment already took off in the United States in the fight against South African apartheid. It was initially based on a logic of exclusion developed by religious congregations and is then oriented toward positive selection criteria to take into account issues related to civil society.[19] In terms of a pioneering study on the

[17]For more details, refer to the book cited in reference: Corporate social responsibility, understanding, writing the annual report, Igalens (J.) & Joras (M.), Personal collection, ANDP, Paris, 2002.

[18]Frederick (W.C.) "The Growing Concern Over Business Responsibility," *California Management Review*, 1960, pp. 54-61; McGuire (J.W.) *Business and Society*, McGraw-Hill, New York, 1963; Davis (K.) & Bolstrom (R.L.) *Business and its Environment*, McGraw-Hill, New York, 1966; Walton (C.C.) *Corporate Social Responsibilities*, Wadsworth, Belmont, CA, 1967; Gendron (C.) "Social Issues and Representations of the Company," *Review of Mauss*, Biannual, 2000, p.15.

[19]Taken from the working paper of Frédérique Déjean, CREFIGE, Paris Dauphine University, 2002, entitled: "Socially responsible investment: A review of the literature."

performance of ethical funds, let us mention Luther, Matako, and Corner (1992),[20] whose contributions consist in highlighting the complexity of the links between societal and financial performances. For these authors, the contribution of financial performance under the ethical component is difficult to establish, especially in the case of international investment. Comparative studies are made difficult by their nonexistence. Virtually only the "Ethical Investment Research Service"[21] tries to characterize all ethical funds. Indeed, a collective investment fund is considered ethical if its portfolio contains at least one selected value on extra-financial criterion. A second category of studies dealing with the use of societal information in the choice of investments raises the same issue as before, namely the persistent conflict between societal performance and financial performance. Does investment decision-making privilege ethics or finance?

Patten (1990),[22] after a synthesis of what exists in research based on the theory of decision, lists three possibilities: (1) the two criteria are equally important; (2) societal information is a substitute for financial information and improving the image of a firm can condition future profits; (3) societal information is a way to prevent possible violations of the law. In 1999, these results were contradicted by Teoh, Welch, and Wazzan,[23] who highlighted the importance given to information according to the time horizon of decision. The third and last category of topics is the beliefs of investors: Who are they? Do they present notable differentiation criteria compared to conventional finance actors and do they have rational behavior? They express rationality consistent with their belief without always succumbing to shareholder activism.[24]

---

[20] Luther (R.G.), Matako (J.) & Corner (D.C.) "The Investment Performance of the United Kingdom's Ethical Unit Trusts," *Accounting, Auditing and Accountability Journal*, vol. 5, no. 4, 1992, pp. 57–70.

[21] Association created in the 1980s by churches and charitable organizations in the United Kingdom to promote corporate social responsibility (CSR).

[22] Patten (D.) "The Market Response to Social Responsibility Disclosures: The Case of the Sullivan Principles Signings," *Accounting, Organizations and Society*, vol. 15, no. 6, 1990, pp. 575–587.

[23] Teoh (S.), Welch (I.) & Wazzan (C.P.), "The Effect of Socially Activist Investment Policies on the Financial Markets: Evidence from the South Africa Boycott," *Journal of Business*, vol. 72, no. 1, 1999, pp. 35–89.

[24] Several studies by Lewis (A.) & Mackenzie (C.) address these topics, in particular: "Morals, Money, Ethical Investing and Economic Psychology, *Human Relations*, vol. 53, no. 2, 2000, pp. 179–191.

Even a little distant from directly financial concerns, this section cannot ignore the problematic stakeholders relaunched by Freeman RE[25] in 1984, which will renew the theoretical justifications for the existence of a social responsibility of the company by formalizing the idea that it can no longer ignore the existence of groups affected by its activities. Who are the "stakeholders," the stakeholders affected by the activity of the company? To answer this question, theoretical research opposes, there are generally two approaches. One more restrictive and of a "contractualist" nature, the stakeholders have a contractual or quasi-contractual relationship with the firm, these are employees, customers, suppliers, public authorities; and the other, more general and of an "institutionalist" nature, is all individuals, institutions, environment, natural resources, fauna and flora. For the legitimacy of the concept of social responsibility or in addition to its scope, this brings us back to the debate about accountability for performance.

More recently, since the end of the 20th century, multidimensional crises denounced a model in which finance is seen as an end and not as a means. The 2007 crisis is probably just the tip of a deeper iceberg. It is not just a crisis of indebtedness; it is a model crisis of a hyper-financialized capitalism model. Moreover, this has, been called financial, turned into a protean crisis. Economists then criticized standard financial theory because it does not take into account the social dimensions of finance. They defend an institutionalist approach that relies on the use of an historical perspective, the consideration of norms and conventions, and the embedding of finance in social relations.

The anchoring of finance as an institution offers a particular framework of analysis, that of the theory of natural resources of Elinor Ostrom (American economist and political scientist, 1933–2012) on the Commons,[26] then goods and information services. Regarding this last point, we refer the reader to Benjamin Coriat's book *The Return of the Commons, the Crisis of the Ideology Owner*, published by LLL, liberate Edition, 2015.

[25] Freeman (R.E.) *Strategic Management: Stakeholder Approach*, Pitman, Boston, 1984.

[26] A common is a system that wants to be as open as possible with at the center one or more shared resources (natural or intangible), managed collectively by a community, it establishes rules and governance in order to preserve and perpetuate this resource while having the right to use it. The commons thus question the question of property. Thus, currently we have two types of property: public property and private property, the commons are a third way to explore. Elinor Ostrom received a Nobel Prize in Economics for her work on the commons.

At the same time, the relationship between two companies has become ambivalent. Firms with technical progress produce goods and services to meet the needs of economies, but they can be sources of concern because of the risks they generate as predators of natural resources and, sometimes, carry social inequalities. The social responsibility of the company will then gradually become the ambiguous expression of this dual relationship. To explain this evolution, some theorists will not hesitate to talk about "disembeddedness" (liberal perception of the economy where social responsibility has no place to be, efficiency being ensured by the self-regulation of markets) and embedding (the inseparable economy of social organization). Very quickly, the vision of the general interest will oppose the liberal perception to adopt an exploded approach of the social responsibility of the company: On one hand, an individualistic company striving to satisfy the expectations of the stakeholders[27] (or "Stakeholders," a theory that challenges the primacy of the shareholder in the governance of the firm) and on the other, a company more sensitive to the global issues of society. Stakeholder theory strives to bridge the gap between business and civil society through apparent re-embedding.[28] Michel Capron and Françoise Quairel-Lanoizelée, underline the political vision underlying the theory of the stakeholders fearing that it develops in a deletion of the role of the State and, without frame, of democratic deliberation. They do not hesitate to say that it is based on "an exploded view of society ... leaving behind a whole set of relationships and interactions between stakeholders." According to these authors, "It is impossible to consider an exhaustive consideration of all potential stakeholders, especially as many of their expectations may be conflicting. The influence of the stakeholders

[27] In economics, a stakeholder is an actor internal or external to a company concerned by its functioning in terms of social responsibility. The concept of stakeholder is born out of a new ethical demand of the civil society, which requires that the companies account for the social and environmental consequences of their activity. It is in this sense that civil society stakeholders have an interest in the smooth running of the business. The concept of stakeholder thus covers ethical issues, which cover the fields of the environment, finance, and social. In its conceptual approach, it was born in the United States of the conjunction of the encouragement by religion of the need to exert philanthropic works and mistrust against the State. The name of stakeholders will be popularized by Ed. Freeman, philosopher and American academic born in 1051, in book *Strategic Management: A Stakeholder Approach*, 1984. The identification of stakeholders and the dialogue with them make this as part of the fifth part of the ISO 26000 Corporate Social Responsibility Standard, published in 2010. The Open Group Architecture Framework (TOGAF) standard also contains good practices on how to conduct this stakeholder analysis.

[28] Great Benchmarks: Manual Collection. La Découverte edition, Paris, January 2015.

therefore depends on the perception of the managers and the hierarchy that they establish between the different expectations. In terms of governance, faced with the contradictory expectations of the stakeholders, the leaders see their managerial latitude increase in application of the old adage, 'divide and conquer'."

After the solidarity, the SRI of which we did not already know what this last term covered precisely, this movement of the responsible finance has known, for about 15 years, a new extension of its domain under the influence of the new technologies. This is the impact investment[29] whose difference must be emphasized with its precursor qualified as manager. The Principles for Responsible Investment (PRI) were launched by the United Nations on April 27, 2006 in New York by Koffi Annan, then Secretary-General of the United Nations. It is a voluntary commitment to the financial system that encourages member companies to consider environmental, social, and good governance criteria when investing. This is in the context of CSR, rather than in the social impact as such. Impact investments include investments in companies, organizations and funds to produce social and environmental impact in addition to financial performance (from neutral to positive). Often confused or even interchangeable with SRI, impact investing can be defined as *"an investment that explicitly combines social return and financial return on investment. Social impact investing therefore implies the establishment of priority and specific social objectives whose impact is measurable through an ongoing evaluation process. These investments can be made in all legal types of organizations with a sustainable business model, and aim for compensation levels ranging from the absence of remuneration to returns close to the market."*[30] With the new technologies, investors tend to trust more resilient, innovative, and value-

---

[29]The term "impact investing," translated into French as "investment with social impact," was defined in 2007 at the Rockefeller Foundation meeting (Bugg-Levine and Emerson, 2011). The term is then adopted by the Global Impact Investing Network (GIIN), created in 2008, which brings together the various players in the sector—investment funds, banks, or foundations. In 2010, the Rockefeller Foundation, GIIN and JP Morgan joined forces for the first social impact investment publications, notably for the *Impact Investing: An Emerging Asset Class* report, which will contribute to the structuring of the sector. According to Wikipedia.org, social impact investing can sometimes be referred to as "impact investment," "double-bottom line" or "triple-bottom line investing" (investment for a financial, social and environmental return in the second case the "Triple Result"), "social investment" (or "social investment") or "blended value investing."

[30]Definition taken from the Report of the French Committee on Investment with Social Impact: "How and Why to Promote Investments with Social Impact," 2014.

oriented organizations that aim to achieve better long-term returns, contribute to the sustainability of businesses and financial markets, and to promote a more stable and inclusive global economy.

Impact investing is therefore distinct from SRI in that its primary motivation is a measurable impact over the life of a project. A portfolio that applies SRI principles generally excludes certain sectors, companies, or strategies or selects only the best firms (Best in Class ranking). The origins of the SRI movement date back to the 70s, when religious communities decided to limit their investments in certain sectors or societies, according to their values. Many in the investment industry believe that this approach to SRI can have a negative financial impact on investment performance because it limits the choice of potential investments. As a result, these SRI-focused strategies do not always reach to savers, as professional investment managers are usually required to seek the best possible returns for their clients. Investment decisions that take into account the restrictions imposed by the SRI principles, which exclude certain sectors or companies, could come into conflict with this obligation. A partially proven hypothesis, to which we must add the difficulty, to present this type of investment because of its diversity and its complexity for an uninitiated.

The impact investment strategy may apply: to all asset classes (private equity, debt, etc.); to various activities (environment, employment, housing, energy, etc.); to any country (emerging country as well as developed countries); to various organizations (supranational, public, associative, private, etc.); to micro finance and fair trade. According to the authors[31] of the book *High-Yielding Societal Investment, The Revolution of Impact Investing*, another qualifier for impact investing which is also defined by the JP Morgan bank is "an investment in socially innovative and commercially competitive unlisted companies intended to produce a return on investment."

We therefore see that several strategies are focused on this responsible finance, such as SRI, solidarity investment, ethical investment, sustainable investment, green investment, community investment, social investment, and more recently, the impact investment. The titles are multiple by integrating to varying degrees the environmental, social, and governance

[31] Cyrille (Antignac) & Bernard (Attali) *Essentials of Banking and Finance Collection*, Bank Revue Editions, Paris, 2016.

(ESG) criteria and shareholder engagement (or shareholder activism). The first imperative is that of clarifying the definition of this responsible finance.

The long march of solidarity to responsible finance: some benchmarks and definitions

Responsible finance is mainly embodied in responsible investment. The latter is not a revolution but an evolution in how to analyze, select, and manage investments, incorporating environmental, social, and governance criteria. Since antiquity, and over the centuries, the antagonism (we have also used the term oxymoron which combines two words of opposite meaning) between the concepts of ethics and finance (in the sense of wealth or profit) has constantly existed and has finally been invited today in the economic and social spheres, reinforced by recurring financial crises.

What are we talking about? Ethics, deontology, morals, sustainable development, ecological economy, solidarity savings, SRI, …, ethical finance? Responsible finance, similar to its predecessors, is developing into financing and prefinancing components consisting of the savings phase. This change is partially due to the rise of investment funds where the investor wants to increase his powers and sometimes it is necessary to reason in order to obtain some consistency with new values, shared or not. It is also developing because a certain number of financiers have become convinced that taking into account social and environmental criteria is likely to better identify the most successful firms over time. Responsible finance covers different practices, all of which aim for financial profitability as well as environmental, social, or societal impacts. It has evolved in particular to cope with emerging issues: inequalities, migration, resource use, climate, etc., but also by relying on available technologies such as digital and social networks. From now on, the term encompasses the previous concepts that remain: sustainable development, solidarity finance; social responsibility; SRI. This section will attempt to present the main definitions of the aforementioned concepts while preserving the momentum of how we moved from solidarity to SRI and solidarity savings of ethical finance to this finance called "responsible." Since several appellations overlap and designate neighboring concepts, a first clarification is necessary in order to better understand the whole phenomenon. Without pretending to draw up an exhaustive list of definitions, we will begin by specifying the main terms, sustainable development, CSR, SRI, that lead to responsible finance commonly used in recent years to qualify all areas. For more details on this, we refer the reader to "Responsible Finance Week,"[32] an annual event that took place from September 28, 2017 to October 5, 2017.

Indeed, since 2016, the Week has a new name and has become one of the responsible finance events. Launched in 2010, the SRI Week is evolving to allow all responsible financial actors who wish to organize such events. These events must promote the savings aimed at developing a sustainable economy, resolutely integrating environmental and social issues. For the last 5 years, the Week has been under the patronage of the Ministry of Ecological and Solidarity Transition, and since 2015, the Ministry of Economy and Finance joined the event.

Another sign of an attachment to this new globalizing name of responsible finance: the quarterly digital publication of Novethic under the title "The essentials of responsible finance" presents the progress and areas for improvement in this sector. For ESG, social, and impact bonds criteria, ESS fund (SSE), Novethic[33] asks questions—How to combine financial performance and social and societal responsibilities? What is the meaning of changes? Chance of success or failure?—directly related to the evolutions observed. These queries are powered by proprietary data from the research center on SRI and thematic funds presented in the Novethic Indicator.

If all these terms—socially responsible, solidarity finance, SRI, ethical finance—are now classified under the new general title of responsible finance, they certainly have common fundamental attributes of thinking about the meaning of money and the use of a currency, though each of

[32]The Responsible Finance Week is an opportunity to discover all forms of responsible investment: crowdfunding for societal impact, Solidarity Finance, SRI, and so on. During the week of the events are held everywhere in France, their organizers are financial institutions, platforms, associations, schools and universities ...

[33]Novethic, a subsidiary of Caisse des Dépôts, created in 2001, aims to make pedagogy on responsible finance. Media expert of the responsible economy fed, by professional journalists, who decrypt the economic and financial impacts of major environmental and social issues. Novethic is also a research center dedicated to Responsible Investment, which analyzes practices for integrating ESG criteria into financial management. It offers studies that allow investors to compare themselves and labels for financial products (SRI and green funds). Novethic has recently launched a web application, "Carbon Risk," which explains the links between fossil fuels, the maintenance of global warming at 2° and the commitments of governments, investors, and companies. The application is accessible at carbon-risk.fr. Each year, Novethic organizes an international symposium for institutional investors on mainstream ESG issues into financial management.

them retains its own specificity. This is what we will try to clarify. Previously, a word is recurrent and transverse to all these terminologies: "manage." So let us start by defining it. This adjective, according to "the little Larousse illustrated" means "to act as guarantor, who must answer, to be guarantor of his own actions or those of the persons in his charge, who weighs on the consequences of his actions." Being responsible is not just an act of power but it is also an act of humanity, it is also about taking risks.

A moderating behavior would advocate two facets: the moment when one does not know the consequences and the moment when one continues to do despite knowing them. One qualifies as the responsible, the other does not because it is a fault. Jean-Paul Sartre said today we are afraid of responsibility. It is necessary to situate the responsible term at the level of happiness and to "build happiness rather than look at misfortune." There is an ethics of responsibility. When the main state of the planet (the United States) refuses to sign the Kyoto Treaty on the environment or the COP 21 in Paris, can we talk about taking into account obligations and duties? This poses the problem of humanity and human dignity.

At the risk of being somewhat reductive, we will focus on the definition of five structuring pillars which, in our opinion, have somehow contributed to the evolution of the financial sphere toward responsible finance. It is about solidary finance, sustainable development, CSR, SRI, and ethical finance. As the boundaries of these concepts continue to widen, we do not claim to establish an absolute chronology of their genesis (that is, to answer the question: who appeared first?). Signs of their existence appearing in the historical review of the preceding section, it is also necessary to take into account the fact that they involve many interferences and similarities, even if their purpose is different.

Solidary finance, according to the association Finansol,[34] "connects savers who seek to make sense of their money to companies and associations with strong social and environmental benefits, they will finance

[34] Based on the website of Finansol created in 1995 (www.finansol.org). This association aims to promote solidarity in savings and finance. Through campaigns and various communication tools, Finansol makes everyone aware that they can play a role in establishing useful, fair, and reasoned finance. Its actions contribute, notably, through the promotion of the Finansol label, to publicize various solidarity savings products available. These investments make it possible to grow money while supporting access to employment and housing for those who are excluded, the development of ecological activities with organic farming and renewable energies, entrepreneurship in rural areas. developing countries … .

through the subscription of solidary savings products."[35] Solidary finance aims to finance operations that do not find an answer in traditional financial circuits, and may concern: integration, social innovations, social housing, and North-South Development.[36]

The mechanisms of the solidary finance distinguish the following products: *The products of partition* (they consist, for the saver, to donate all or part of the income of his investment to a work of general interest to a philanthropic, educational, scientific, social purpose. According to the criterion of the Finansol label, a sharing investment is a savings product, the subscriber of which, in the form of a donation to a charity, donates at least 25% of the income generated each year in order to benefit from tax cuts).

Solidary investment products: To obtain the qualification and benefit from special tax provisions, the law requires that at least 10% of the investment be devoted to the financing of solidary projects such as integration and creation of companies, social housing, and North-South development. Among these solidary investment products, there are 90/10 solidary funds of which from 5% to 10% outstanding amounts are invested in securities issued by approved integration companies and 90%–95% in conventional securities (equities, bonds, etc.), eventually managed by an SRI process. The funds collected are oriented toward the social and environment: 28% of investments go to integration through employment; 31% are injected into very social housing; the environment receives 36%; and 5% goes to international solidarity.

Solidary savings products: Represent savings whose outstanding income is intended, completely or partially, to finance solidary activities. The solidary saver chooses to put his money, not only according to what it will bring back to him, but also according to what he will bring back to

[35] From November 6–13, 2017, Finansol organized its annual communication campaign by launching the 10th edition of Solidarity Finance Week with the slogan: "Give your savings a face." A real awareness-raising operation, it aims to make everyone aware that it is possible to give meaning to their savings by supporting projects that meet the challenges of our society.

[36] According to the barometer of the newspaper *La Croix* in association with Finansol, in its latest edition published on May 22, 2017, 196,000 new subscriptions were made in 2016 for all of these different forms of solidarity finance representing €1.31 billion subscriptions and an outstanding amount of €9,36 billion as of December 31, 2016. Solidarity finance, mainly represented by employee and bank savings, results in, according to Finansol "confirm the French's appetite for solidarity savings," a financing method that has created or consolidated 49,000 jobs, relocated 5,500 people, and supported a hundred economic development actors in 2016.

society, in terms of social added value. Solidary savings can be broken down into multiple types of investments. The Finansol label is the only one distinguishing solidary savings products, essentially in the form of booklets, Undertakings for Collective Investment in Transferable Securities (UCITS) that life insurance contracts and some banks develop as an action on a daily basis. For example, "Crédit Coopératif" developed a service, which for any withdrawal made with the specific blue card transfers a fraction of the withdrawal to an association chosen by the cardholder or BNP Paribas who suggests paying the breakages of card purchases, that is to say, the cents of Euros to associations on a preestablished list.

Sustainable development

The emergence of the idea of sustainable development is concomitant with that of the industrial society. From the second half of the 19th century, Western societies began to find that their economic activities, and industrial ones, in particular, had a significant impact on the environment and social equilibrium. Then, the crises of the 20th century of economic (1907: American banking crisis, 1929, 1973, and the first oil shock) and ecological (1957: oil spill caused by the Torrey Canyon, 1976: Seveso and chemistry, 1986: Chernobyl and nuclear power ...) nature took place in the world and raised awareness of the need to establish a model of sustainable society.

The term "sustainable development," translated from English, appeared for the first time in 1980 in the "World Conservation Strategy," a publication of the International Union for the Conservation of Nature (IUCN). A formulation specified by Mrs. Gro Harlem Brundtland, Norwegian Prime Minister, who, in the framework of the United Nations World Commission for Environment and Development (WCED)—known as the "Brundtland Commission"—in 1987, set the definition as follows: "development that meets the needs of the present without compromising the ability of future generations to meet their needs." In 1992, the Rio Earth Summit, held under the auspices of the United Nations, formalized the concept of sustainable development and the three pillars (economy, ecology, and social): an economically efficient, socially equitable, and ecologically sustainable development.

A concept supposed to be able to combine several requirements going from the satisfaction of the essential needs of present and future generations, in relation with the demographic constraints (water, food, education, health, employment); improving the quality of life (social services, housing, culture); respect for human rights and freedoms; and the reinforcement of new forms of renewable energy (wind, solar, geothermal).

The Larousse encyclopedia speaks of a "*mode of development that ensures the satisfaction of the essential needs of current generations, especially the most deprived, while safeguarding the ability of future generations to meet their own needs.*"

Novethic's lexicon states,

> *It is a matter of successfully reconciling social and economic progress with the safeguarding of the planet's natural equilibrium; it is the major challenge of the beginning of the twenty-first century. Applied to the corporate world, the notion of sustainable development has led the latter to be more attentive to the concerns of all stakeholders ("stakeholders"). It is then for companies to engage in social responsibility (CSR) approaches, having an influence on the practices and processes implemented in areas such as, human resources, business practices, local impact, etc. For some, sustainable development is an ecological concept. This means that the processes of evolution of our societies must be long-term without altering the capacities of the ecosystems that support their needs, to leave future generations intact capital. Sustainable development therefore involves the exploitation of biological resources at a rate that does not lead to their depletion or even exhaustion but makes possible the indefinite maintenance of the biological productivity of the biosphere. This form of economic development respects the environment through a rational and moderate exploitation of nature and its many resources. It is with this in mind that the concept of energy transition has been put in place. It is a question of gradually abandoning the greenhouse gas emitting energies for the benefit of renewable energies.*

In 2005, in our book on ethical finance, we emphasized that the time when the financial sphere was not concerned with sustainable development seemed to be over. Financial industry has to play a considerably important role in terms of economic, social, and environmental responsibilities, because it is a sector that has the biggest structuring impact on the organization and functioning of the entire production system. For our part, we think that a first awareness is engaged, but it is not enough to clarify the concept in the hypothesis where several appellations are found under the same term such as sustainable development, social responsibility, or environmental and social responsibility. Why not talk about "PSP" without addressing a semantic reflection societal progress,[37] shared progress?[38] This last formulation avoids the harmful juxtaposition of the two terms, development and sustainability, leading sometimes to think the opposite of what they wanted to express.[39] On a separate note, the two components of the term sustainable development have the following definition. The World Report on Human Development (UNEP, 1994) describes development as a process that extends the decision-making potential of the human being both quantitatively and qualitatively. This distinguishes "development" from "growth," a quantitative increase measured by physical magnitudes.

The word sustainable, which is positively connoted, is often combined with different substantives in the most diverse contexts, which have little to do with the notion of sustainability. The term "sustainable development," which must therefore be used in its composite form, refers to the possibility of ensuring a necessary evolution, which is not limited in time or, in other words, the maintenance of a dynamic and increasing potential. On the other hand, it does not mean the maintenance of a status quo, as might be suggested by the word "durable" which refers to what is constant, permanent, persistent, long-lasting, and stable. However, since the status quo has no intrinsic value, it does not deserve to be maintained for the sole purpose of doing so. It is important to have a scale of values to decide what is worth keeping, and how it should be done. Despite the range of interpretations inherent in this term and the diversity of definitions, sometimes contradictory, that ensued, certain trends emerge from this confused set. According to the most common meaning, sustainable

[37] It should be noted that the word "social" does not have the same meaning in the French and English languages, which has led Francophone to distinguish between "social" and "societal" in order to bring out the responsibility vis-à-vis internal stakeholders ("social" in the sense of industrial relations) and external stakeholders ("societal" in the sense of the community in which the company is located, the pool of employment and life).

[38] Used by Michel Le Net in the editorial of the *Ethical Business Magazine*, no. 16, April 2002.

[39] Still according to Michel Le Net and in the context of the same previous reference: "Who says development, says growth. Who says sustainable, says permanence." So sustainable development = permanent growth, that is to say literally persistent over-exploitation of our planet. The second chapter of this first part of the book will give us the opportunity to discuss theories about growth and its limitations.

development results from the harmonious evolution of three interdependent dimensions

1. The economic component is linked to the creation of wealth and improvement of material living conditions.
2. The social component encompasses health, education, housing, employment, intra and intergenerational equity,[40] and the prevention of social exclusion.
3. The ecological component is concerned with the preservation of the environment. Sustainable development is not a separate field, but an integrative approach, a conceptual framework for an overall strategic assessment.

Corporate social responsibility

If we consider the CSR as of today, as a variation of sustainable development transposed to the company, it is clear that it may have been so earlier and leading to the fact two definitions of CSR that coexist in France. The first would come from the reflections on sustainable development applied to a player, that is, companies. The second definition would be a responsible attitude that stakeholders (stakeholders, but also governors and international organizations) would like companies to adopt with regard to the economic, social, and societal consequences of the financialization of the economy. The two streams of CSR that stem from the concepts of sustainable development (World Business Council for Sustainable Development) and the corollary of the bankruptcy of the welfare state, illustrated by the movements of "Corporate Social Responsibility and Business for Social Responsibility," come together under the auspices of the UN and European Union. The latter, in order to provide a framework for companies wishing to invest in sustainable development, published a Green Paper on CSR on July 18, 2001. It defines CSR as follows: *"the voluntary integration of companies' social and ecological concerns into their business activities and their relations with their stakeholders.*

[40]Complying with "intergenerational equity," as Cyril Demaria puts it, in his book, *Sustainable Development and Finance*, Maxima, Paris, 2004, p. 9, "means taking into account the future needs of future generations," "that is to say, to give them a path (even theoretical) in a current affairs debate such as that of energy choices or the financing of research."

Being socially responsible means not only fully meeting the applicable legal obligations, but also going beyond and investing "more" in human capital, the environment and stakeholder relations."

Citizenship or corporate responsibility is a commitment to respect, a set of principles that goes beyond the mere application of legal provisions. These principles are often based on universally recognized international instruments such as the International Labor Organization (ILO) conventions, human rights declaration, and Rio Declaration on Sustainable Development. The areas on which corporate responsibility is exercised are the environment, conditions, and standards of work; human rights; business ethics (or the fight against corruption) and corporate governance. Social responsibility is about taking the social, environmental, and economic consequences of one's actions and choices. Thus, this concept leads a certain number of companies to observe and act better on the impacts on their environment and on the community in which they operate (the respect of "stakeholders"). After inducing this policy of being "socially responsible," companies now seem to be able to claim some legitimacy because of its institutionalization and recent regulation, and it now seems to correspond to a certain corporate ethic: ethics being considered here as a science regulatory principles of action and moral conduct. It has now become an economic and societal norm (societal to express the social and environmental responsibility). The International Organization for Standardization (ISO), organization in charge of defining the international standards that govern business trade, also addressed the challenge of CSR in a document published by the working group on the ISO 26000 Standard on Corporate Social Responsibility. In these guidelines, the ISO defines the CSR as follows: "*the responsibility of an organization for the impacts of its decisions and activities on society and the environment, resulting in ethical behavior and transparent that*:

- *Contributes to sustainable development, including the health and well-being of society takes into account stakeholder expectations;*
- *Complies with applicable laws and is in line with international standards of behavior;*
- *And that is integrated throughout the organization and implemented in its relationships."*

To illustrate the evolution of the concept, we will illustrate this point by quoting a recent survey (2016) conducted by Global Compact France,

Havas Paris, CSA Research, and L'Express. The result of the study is entitled[41] "The new frontiers of corporate social responsibility: a model for performance?" Conducted on the basis of a survey of 192 companies, the study questions the role of social responsibility in business: What are its benefits? What are the brakes and levers? How does the social responsibility approach transform the business model? What actors do they rely on? On which major societal issues do businesses feel they have a role to play? According to this study, corporate social responsibility is now an unavoidable challenge for the future. Today, it seems to be well integrated into the overall strategy of companies, first and foremost by the businesses that come under the basic contract: Environment, energy saving, and human resources management. Beyond the benefits, in terms of image and even though it is not yet source of tangible profits, companies have clearly understood that their sustainability is at stake. Thus, is societal responsibility the meaning of history? For the majority of them, social responsibility is likely to transform their business model when, for the most pioneering, CSR has already become a factor of transformation, even giving rise to new products and services. Having become highly strategic, CSR has become a dedicated service under the responsibility of the general management, when it does not fall more directly to its missions. Customers and consumers as well as employees and suppliers embody key partners in a successful approach. However, many obstacles to the implementation of a CSR policy remain such as the lack of visibility on the creation of value, lack of time, mentalities, and costs. Asked about their power to act, companies believe they have a role to play in the first place on the place of women in society, youth employment, unemployment, and climate change.

It seems that the importance of CSR issues is not much debated. It is no longer a question of whether or not to treat this question, but rather how and with whom. For this, it remains to overcome the tensions between short-term constraints and long-term societal responsibility issues.

---

[41]The study, conducted online between May 10 and May 24, 2016, surveyed 192 respondents (CEO, DG, Director of Communication, Director of CSR) including 156 companies signed the United Nations Global Compact, or 46 companies fewer than 50 people, 111 more than 250 and 45 more than 10,000 people, interviewed on a corpus of 18 questions.

Socially responsible investment[42]

There is no common definition of SRI today for all investors. However, we can distinguish some major approaches: ESG selection, exclusions (sectoral or normative), thematic approaches, shareholder engagement, or impact investing. Each approach offers advantages and disadvantages, but all of them are not exclusive of one from another: management companies or institutional investors may choose to combine several of them to increase the ESG quality and the social or environmental impact of the funds. It was in the 18th century that the notion of SRI seemed to emerge in the Anglo-Saxon community of the religious philanthropic movement of the Quakers. The Larousse encyclopedia tells us that *"The Quaker term is a nickname given to members of the religious group who call themselves the "Society of Friends" because of the word of its founder, George Fox, who urged Judge Bennet to honor God and to tremble before his Word. Quoted as early as 1654, this sobriquet has been widely used since the end of the 17th century. Fox began preaching his doctrine in 1647."*

Born out of a revolt against the abuses of the ritualism, dogmatism, and conformism of the Anglican Church, this movement will have a great moment in its history under the aegis of William Penn who obtained the concession from the Crown for a vast territory in the American Northwest (present-day Pennsylvania), he undertook to install a religious democracy. Historically, the SRI originated in this Anglo-Saxon society of the 18th century, especially with Quakers who convey ideas of moral rigor related to a rigorous practice of solidarity and who are actively engaged against slavery (abolition of slavery as early as 1758), corsair activity, or any act of violence. In particular, they will become directors of the most important companies of the 19th century such as Barclays, Cadbury, Lloyds, and Price Waterhouse Coopers, which will allow them to increase their influence and take part in social struggles.

Also known as SRI for "socially responsible investing," the Anglo-Saxon tradition of SRI finds its roots in these Quakers, actively engaged against slavery, corsair activity, or any other act of violence. As early as the 1920s, American religious communities instituted a selective investment by forbidding their members to invest in "vice societies," that is, the sale of arms,

[42] 2015 key figures (source Novethic): French SRI outstanding reached nearly €746 billion at the end of 2015. The market grew by 29% between 2014 and 2015. Institutional investors held 90% of out standings. SRI employee savings accounted for 10% of outstanding.

alcohol, and tobacco. In 1928, in the United States, the first SRI fund was created—the Pioneer Fund, set up by Philip L. Carret. This is the first fund to systematically resort to a "sin screen," which prohibits any investment related to the tobacco and alcohol industries. In 1971, two pastors of the Methodist Church, Luther Tyson and Jack Corbett, launched Pax World Fund, whose various missions are to promote peace (making sure not to invest in companies related to the war industry, these founders did not endorse the Vietnam War, but committed to reduce social inequalities, protect the environment, and work for sustainable development (we will have the opportunity to re-discuss the activities of this investment fund later).

In France in 1983, the Catholic Committee against Hunger and for Development (CCFD) launched, along with Crédit Coopératif, launched the first shared investment fund "Hunger and Development." Part of the income of this UCITS is earmarked for business creation in the Third World. At the same time, the Meeschaert Asset Management Company created the first Ethical Mutual Fund New Strategy 50, at the instigation of Sister Nicole Reille,[43] steward of her religious community, the Congregation Notre-Dame. In April 2006, SRI was recognized internationally as these principles were part of an extension of the global pact initiated by the United Nations.

The main goal of this Global Compact is to strengthen the sense of societal responsibility and corporate citizenship in order to find solutions to the challenges posed by globalization.

In July 2013, the French Association of Financial Management (AFG) and the Forum for Responsible Investment (FIR) published a definition to clarify the role of SRI: "*SRI (Socially Responsible Investment) is an investment that aims to reconcile economic performance and social and environmental impact by financing companies and public entities that contribute to sustainable development regardless of their sector of activity. By influencing governance and stakeholder behavior, SRI promotes a responsible economy.*"

SRI is the systematic and traceable integration of ESG criteria into financial management. Very often, these criteria complement the traditional financial analysis and allow the creation of specific investment funds for individuals or institutional clients. All of these criteria are based

[43]Sister Nicole Reille, nicknamed "mother" of ethical savings in France, she was the first to realize that saving was not only a financial project, but, that it was also an social act. Visionary and pragmatic, the founder of France's first SRI fund, she died on Monday, May 7, 2012 at the age of 82.

on the previously defined concepts of "sustainable development" and "CSR," according to which any model of long-term economic growth must be based on respect for people and the environment, in order to protect the future generations. It is commonly accepted that SRI covers, mainly, the following components:

1. ESG selection: Investors select companies for their good ESG practices. In France, it is the so-called Best-in-Class approach that is the most widespread. It favors companies with the best ratings from an extra-financial point of view.
2. Exclusion: This is the first method used in SRI which results in an exclusion of portfolios of companies that do not comply with international conventions (normative exclusions). There are other forms of exclusions such as sectoral exclusions that exclude companies from certain areas of activity (tobacco, alcohol, weapons, pornography) from the portfolio.
3. The thematic approach: It favors investments in companies in the field of sustainable development and excludes companies from certain other fields (often the same as within the framework of sectoral exclusions).

Ethical finance

We have already discussed the functions, strengths, and weaknesses of finance in the first section of this chapter. The marriage between ethics and finance no longer holds utopia and gradually extends to all the economic actors, that is, from citizens' savings to sovereign wealth funds of the states. The dynamic "so that money connects men," according to the formula of the Finansol association, is well engaged. However, let us try to get to the bottom of the subject, at the risk of being somehow provocative. According to journalist Catherine Bernard,[44] in an article entitled: "*Ethical finance, it does not exist.* And why not?," wonders about its limits. Her article is devoted to the presentation of Gaëtan Mortier's book: *Ethical Finance: The Great Misunderstanding*[45] (an indictment trying to

[44] Former head of investigations at "Enjeux les Echos," in an article published on May 13, 2013 listed on the website www.slate.fr

[45] Mortier Gaëtan takes an uncompromising critical eye on this world of responsible finance. Considering that it has been misguided, it proposes, among other things, regulation, the independence of rating agencies and a revival of shareholder activism to put an end to the excesses of modern finance. Paris, April 2013, Fyp editions, stymulo collection.

show that this ethical finance would have lost its meaning!). The journalist considers that

> *to solve the big problems of our societies, there are two ways. First, the merciless way: tackling it frontally. Combat precariousness, unemployment, discrimination, fight against pollution, limit greenhouse gas emissions, reduce public debt, etc. at the cost of daily efforts, a general commitment from all actors in society. It's long, difficult, politically risky, in short, absolutely not sexy. Difficult, however, to cut. But in some cases, there is a second, much more attractive way: to change behavior, not by making citizens feel guilty or constraining them, but by rewarding them for their efforts, the reward being financial or purely social. The interest of this second method, which, moreover, generally fits in quite well with the market economy, is that it encourages innovation—how to invent more responsible products, services and behaviors—and therefore growth, and that it is relatively painless in the short term.*

The reality is probably between these two methods. As for ethics, we have had the opportunity to talk about it as a doctrine of the happiness of men and the means of access to the end, rules of conduct. It already has a history. Presented as a rising value of business life in the 90s (ethics committees, ethics officers, philosophers were the new sages of large companies) ethics has found, today, a powerful competitor in the modern managerial strategy, sustainable development. They have many points in common and the attempts to formalize the previously mentioned concepts present them well as guides of actions that integrate the impacts of the decisions of the firm well beyond its only immediate interests. As rightly pointed out by Guillaume Eliet in an article of the newspaper *Les Echos* dated Friday, July 16, and Saturday, July 17, 2004,[46] "*Ethics is not soluble in sustainable development or even in corporate social responsibility. On the contrary, in essence, ethics transcends each of these subjects, which constitute, in a way, only* concrete versions."

In the face of the value conflicts that shake capitalism—progress and employment, money and labor, the long-term market and investment, and profit and sharing—ethics must be wary of any dogmatic attitude, but adopt an approach of openness to lead minds to respect confrontations

---

[46]The point of view of Guillaume Eliet, attorney at law, cabinet Coudert Frères, director of the Business Ethics Circle: "The New Business Ethics," p. 13.

and challenges. With humility, and without behaving as judge, ethics, which transcends sustainable development and CSR, must take a stand. This is what sets it apart from the deontology, which it does not intend to judge on the purpose of the activity deployed, since the latter is part of a legal framework. While ethics focuses on the meaning of acting, financial ethics refuses to intervene in the choice of investments, including in the area of ethical funds, which may have to discard values contrary to the moral order or not to invest in "sin stocks" ("sin values") of arms manufacturers and dealers, tobacco or alcohol companies, or those involved in gambling or producing pornographic movies.

For ethical finance to resume its original meaning, what role should ethics play in the financial sphere? Can the individual exercise of virtue suffice to bring about the general functioning of finance? Does not its systemic logic of functioning tend to impose a loss of ethical sense of individual behavior? This is money and moralists of all persuasions, as the philosopher Paul Ricœur (1913–2005) pointed out, "the hunger for gold is insatiable; a kind of "bad infinity" inhabits this ever more that is never enough." Our ancestors treated the problem by the laws of religious morality. Today, it is mainly in the realm of politics and public regulation that we can act.

The words "moral" and "ethical" refer to the sphere of values and moral principles. Are they synonymous? Do they have different meanings? Different schools of thought exist on this question. For some thinkers, "morality" and "ethics" have the same meaning: the first comes from a Latin word ("mores") and the second from a Greek word ("ethos"), which both mean "manners." For others, these terms take different meanings and are not equivalent. Through time and culture, individuals and groups have defended different conceptions of these principles and values. For our part, we will not make any distinction between ethics and ethics considering Jean Moussé[47] or Paul Ricœur,[48] already quoted, that nothing in the etymology or in the history of the use of words imposes a distinction, the two terms referring to this idea of morals. It is for all these reasons that we deliberately chose to speak, more willingly, of ethical finance, because of the more general scope of the term and new issues that the news makes it,

[47] Moussé (Jean), *Business Ethics: Freedom, Responsibility, the Decision-Maker Facing the Ethical Question*, Dunod, 2001.

[48] Paul (Ricœur), "Ethics and Morals," Rev.; Catholic Institute of Paris, no. 34, April–June 1990, p. 131.

at the risk of not succumbing in the vocabulary, a laughingstock or fashion. Ethical finance is a broad notion that covers several definitions, but can be summarized as follows: all practices aiming to reconcile performance with social, environmental, or societal impact.

For us it encompasses the concepts previously explained and defined above: solidary finance, sustainable development, CSR, and concepts like SRI along with microcredit[49] and extra-financial rating[50] will be specified in the second part.

After these various and divergent definitions of the main concepts, we will consider that responsible finance is, for us, an even more generic term, encompassing many new players and their new financing tools. It can range from finance that fights against climate change and promotes the green economy, to participatory financing under the aegis of FinTech (micro savings, crowdfunding, etc.), through "impact investing," changes in the traditional shareholder engagement, the ethical indices, the labeling of the funds. This list is not exhaustive, it is necessary to decipher this nebula that represents the responsible finance, and to realize a typology of its main actors and products. Prior to this analysis phase, let us understand the principles and the new regulatory and tax framework in which this responsible finance evolves.

Principles, regulatory, and fiscal frameworks of responsible finance in the world

This subsection, for CSR and SRI, essentially distinguishes between general principles and taxation. The approach will focus on presenting the different elements for France and other countries in chronological order.

---

[49] Microcredit is a tool for fighting poverty. It consists of the granting of small loans to entrepreneurs or artisans who cannot access conventional bank loans. It also offers non-financial services such as training, advice, professionalization, and awareness activities on various topics.

[50] Extra-financial rating was born out of the need for SRI assessments which is not based solely on the economic performance of the company, but also on its behavior toward the environment, on the respect of social values, societal commitment, and corporate governance. The extra-financial rating mainly comes from the specialized rating agencies. Unlike financial rating, they are paid by investors to establish these ratings and not by companies. According to Novethic, we speak of declarative notation as opposed to the rating requested by certain agencies and which consists in carrying out extra financial audits at the request of the companies.

Principles and law

In France

In France, there are no parameters to define the CSR performance standards. For example, there is no law requiring companies to reduce their greenhouse gas emissions, or to put a waste reduction strategy in place. On the other hand, there are public information obligations. Companies subject to the Grenelle laws must carry out extra-financial reporting containing, among other things, their CO_2 emissions and other indicators of economic, environmental, and social performance. As a result, this is an incentive for companies to undertake strategies to reduce their impacts.

While in France, CSR is largely governed by regulations, standards, and good practices (some experts are happy to talk about institutionalized CSR), in the United States a more philanthropic and individual approach prevails. In France, Article 116 of the New Economic Regulations (NRE) Act passed in 2001 introduced a social and environmental reporting obligation for the first time intended solely for listed companies, without imposing any sanctions. This legislation was amended by Article 225 of the Grenelle 2 law, adopted in July 2010, which gradually extends the obligation to make this type of reporting to companies with more than 500 employees. It adds the need to certify these extra-financial data by a third party and introduces the idea of the relevance of indicators left to the free choice of companies. In certain sectors, such as real estate, companies have worked together to develop practical guides for the application of Section 225. More specifically, it should be noted that it was a long process that led to the introduction of this concept of CSR. For the record, the table below traces some of the most significant stages of the birth of the "social economy."

In *"The critical dictionary of CSR,"* a collective work published under the direction of Nicolas Postel and Richard Sobel, a chapter[51] devoted to the NRE[52] law (NRE) and Grenelle I and II laws,[53] written by Sylvaine

[51]Septentrion University Press, 2013, pp. 294–298.

[52]Law No. 2001-420, May 15, 2001, relative to the NRE.

[53]Respectively, Law No. 2009-967 of August 3, 2009 on the implementation of the Grenelle Environment Program and Law No. 2010-788 of July 12, 2010 on the national commitment to the environment.

SOCIAL ECONOMY is born out of workers' movements and is progressively differentiated by its legal forms: association, cooperative, foundation.	**From the mid-19th century to the beginning of the 20th century**
Affirmation of the SOLIDARITY ECONOMY which is defined by its solidarity purpose rather than by a particular status.	**Year 1980**
IMPACT INVESTING, use of the term for the first time at a conference of the Rockefeller Foundation.	**Year 2007**
ECONOMIC MODERNIZATION ACT with the growth of solidarity employee savings and the funds 90/10.	**Year 2008**
LOI DE L'ÉCONOMIE SOCIALE ET SOLIDAIRE qui précise le concept et créée le statut d'Entreprise Solidaire d'Utilité Sociale (ESUS) leur permettant de bénéficier d'aides et de financements spécifiques (accession à l'épargne salariale et réductions fiscales).	**Year 2014**

Laulom, retraces the slow maturity of the reporting obligation for companies. Laulom is careful to specify the impact of this legal framework with regard to CSR. "*While CSR is most often defined as a voluntary process, the fact remains that it is part of a legal framework that will not be without influencing business practices. Three types of legislative rules may interfere, directly or indirectly, with corporate actions. On the one hand, some rules, a priori indifferent to the problem of CSR, can indirectly encourage companies to engage in practices that can be considered as CSR. This is the case in France for health and safety rules and the risk prevention policy that the employer must implement in the company, obligations to inform and consult employee representatives. On the other hand, CSR can generate self-regulation that the law can't seize. So it's not just here only simple incentive rules, not fundamentally calling into question the voluntary nature of CSR, but rules that may come to frame a renewed expression of the employer's regulatory power (Rules of Procedure, Charter ...). Finally, the third type of legislative intervention, which interests us here, has a different nature. It is for the legislator to directly encourage companies to adopt CSR practices.*"

This NRE law, through a management report ("reporting"), provides a guide to transparent and virtuous behavior to listed companies, but without any real sanction and limited to the national territory. It will be necessary to await the decree of February 20, 2002 to define more precisely the content of the social and environmental information that must be given. According to Article R 225-104 of the French Commercial Code, social information is based on a range of factors, from workforce management (types of contracts, reduction and safeguarding plans, parity of remuneration for men and women), training, hygiene and safety in the company, disabled people, etc. This management report must specify how the company takes into account the territorial impact of its activities (Article R. 225-105 of the French Commercial Code). The idea of subjecting companies to an extra-financial reporting obligation is growing in many countries. It makes it possible to measure the environmental and social impacts of their activities through the indicators they choose and the objectives they set themselves.

Companies must include, for example, in their extra-financial reporting, their CO_2 emissions, energy consumption, or the gender distribution of senior executives, not to mention the investments in training or the number of accidents at work.

The Grenelle I and II laws are directly in line with the NRE law, of which scope of application they intend to broaden and bring CSR into the governance of major firms. Thus, article 53 of the Grenelle I law states that: "the quality of the information on the way in which companies take into account the social and environmental consequences of their activity and the access to this information constitute conditions essential elements of good corporate governance." While the NRE law was previously only concerned with the companies listed on the stock market, it is now the companies whose total assets or turnover are €100 million and 500 employees.

A new paragraph of Article L. 225-102-1 of the French Commercial Code provides that *"social and environmental information appearing or to be included in the light of legal and regulatory requirements shall be verified by an independent third party in accordance with the terms and conditions laid down by decree of the 'Conseil d'État' (Supreme Administrative Court that also has a role to give opinion to the government on important Decrees). This audit gives rise to a notice that is sent to the shareholders 'or partners' meeting at the same time as the report of the board of directors or the executive board."*

From now on, with the Grenelle Laws, the information provided is consolidated and "relates to the company itself as well as to all of its subsidiaries."

We cannot, here, ignore the work of France Strategy[54] in the context of its CSR platform[55] and in particular its January 2016 report entitled "Studies, Corporate Social Responsibility and Competitiveness, Evaluation and Strategic Approach" by Salima Benhamou and Marc-Arthur Diaye in collaboration with Patricia Crifo. This document recalls the will of the Prime Minister to amplify the implementation of CSR by installing in April 2013, a consultation platform on this theme under the aegis of France Strategy composed of representatives of civil society, companies, unions, associations, NGOs and experts, and so on. This CSR platform includes, in particular, a working group on the theme "CSR and competitiveness" which testifies to the place taken by this topic in the social debates. In their introduction, the authors of the study questioned such important questions as: *"Can we consider that the concern for social responsibility is compatible with the concern for competitiveness? In other words, can CSR be apprehended not as an additional constraint but as a tangible economic contribution for companies? And in this case, how to encourage companies to include CSR approaches in their development strategy?"*

After an inventory, this study seeks to identify the main factors that can encourage the adoption of "responsible approaches and the link that these approaches have with economic performance." To assess this possible link, the study is backed by a survey of 8,500 French companies with at least 10 employees on several dimensions of CSR (environment, human resources, stakeholders, etc.). The main results revealed that the structural factors of companies (size, sector, etc.) influence the implementation of responsible practices, but sometimes differently prioritized depending on the dimensions of CSR. CSR is significantly correlated with the economic performance of companies and it must become an integral component of their organizational capital, which argues for a new form of governance and more partnership-based management. The study also seeks to formulate some recommendations where financial incentive would not be the most appropriate method. A voluntary approach should be favored in a regional framework of proximity with specific indicators and a facilitation of access to certification for small and medium enterprises (SMEs).

[54] France Strategy ("France Stratégie") is defined as a public think tank, a singular institution at the heart of public policy. Heir to the Commissariat du Plan founded in 1946, created by decree on April 22, 2013, modified by decree on March 24, 2017, France Strategy participates and testifies to the evolutions and transformations of French society.

[55] www.strategie.gouv.fr/travaux/instances/plateforme-rse

In addition, for information, it should be noted that the referenced European Directive 2014/95/EU, devoted to the publication of nonfinancial information by certain large companies, has not been the subject of a French Council of Ministers' treatment (July 19, 2017).

The Minister of Economy and Finance has issued an order for the publication of nonfinancial information by certain large companies and groups of companies.

According to the extract from this report of the Council of Ministers,

> *This order, made pursuant to Article 216 of Law No. 2017-86 of 27 January 2017 on equality and citizenship, makes it possible to take provisions in the field of law necessary for the transposition of Directive 2014/95/EU as well as the adaptation measures related to this transposition. The transposition of this directive leads to a substantial modernization of the nonfinancial information publication system. The latter was introduced by Law No. 2001-420 of 15 May 2001 on new economic regulations and supplemented by Law No. 2010-788 of 12 July 2010 on the National Commitment to the Environment, accompanied by Decree No. 2012-557 of April 24, 2012 relating to the transparency obligations of companies in social and environmental matters. The number of topics covered by the scheme has steadily increased since then.*
>
> *At the end of this transposition, the extra-financial performance declaration, which replaces the Corporate Social Responsibility (CSR) report, becomes a tool for strategic management of the company, concise and accessible, focused on significant information interesting its stakeholders.*
>
> *The scope of the companies required to produce such a statement is evolving in order to orient the device towards large companies. Thus, small and medium-sized listed companies are no longer subject to this system, which is an important simplification measure. In addition, the new system exempts subsidiaries from filing such a declaration, since the information concerning them is presented by the group head company in a consolidated way, which gives a complete picture of the extra-financial impacts of the group's activities, while limiting the reporting burden on subsidiaries.*
>
> *The format of the extra-financial performance declaration is also clarified. The content of this statement includes a reference to its business model, a*

presentation of the extra-financial risks it faces, a description of the policies implemented to limit these risks and the results of these policies.

Resulting from an in-depth analysis of the extra-financial issues facing the company, the extra-financial performance declaration is intended to become an essential information document for all stakeholders.

Consequently, the system for verifying published information is also simplified: it now only concerns companies with more than 500 employees and more than 100 M € in total balance sheet or turnover, whereas the former regime applies to all companies required to file a CSR report.

The ambition of transparency in the publication of extra-financial information resulting from the legislation currently in force has, moreover, been confirmed. In fact, the extra-financial performance declaration will now have to be published on the website of the targeted companies and maintained online for a period of five years. As a result of preparatory work involving all interested parties, the new extra-financial reporting regime provides companies with a renewed framework that is distinguished by its flexibility and contributes positively to their corporate social responsibility commitments. The provisions of the Ordinance apply to reports relating to fiscal years beginning on or after 1 August 2017.

Compared to the existing obligations (NRE law of 2001 supplemented by the Grenelle laws), this new regime is distinguished by its flexibility and is more oriented toward large companies. SMEs are no longer subject to it, neither are subsidiaries. The information verification regime is simplified. While the previous regime applies to all companies subject to the extra-financial reporting obligation, it only concerns companies with more than 500 employees or €100 million of total balance sheet (total liabilities or assets) turnover. These obligations will apply to reports relating to financial years beginning on or after August 1, 2017. It should be recalled that, according to European regulations, this transposition should have been made before December 6, 2016, thus putting France in breach of Community law. CSR leads companies to make commitments that go beyond law enforcement in the countries in which they operate. They rely on international standards. The framework that companies must respect is laid down by international conventions such as those of the ILO

(International Labor Organization), the OECD Guidelines or the Universal Declaration of Human Rights.

On the other hand, ADEME[56] (the French Environment and Energy Management Agency) and the French Association for Standardization (AFNOR)[57] are two public instances responsible for supporting companies in their CSR/Sustainable Development approach. They provide advice and means to companies that are moving in this direction, and are the relay of international CSR standards. In addition to the quality management supported by the ISO[58] 9001 standard, which is closer to our problems, let us specify the definition and objectives of the 14001 standards for environmental management and 26000 for CSR as follows.

- In force since 1996, the international standard ISO 14001 is recognized worldwide as a benchmark for environmental management. It is an international standard defined by the World Organization for Standardization (ISO, the term ISO stands for International Standard Organization), which is a worldwide federation of national standard bodies comprising about 140 countries. It defines the requirements to be met by an Environmental Management System (EMS) to be recognized through a certification. It is based on a voluntary approach putting a policy with regard to the environment in place. According to ADEME, the organization thus has a framework enabling it to identify and control the environmental impact of its activities, products, or services; continuously improve its environmental performance and fight against all types of pollution; comply with the regulations in force; define environmental goals and targets.

[56]The French Environment and Energy Management Agency (ADEME) is a French public industrial and commercial establishment (EPIC) created in 1991. It is placed under the supervision of the ministers in charge of research, ecology, and energy, and its mission is to generate, animate, coordinate, facilitate, or carry out operations aimed at protecting the environment and controlling energy.

[57]The French Association for Standardization (abbreviated as AFNOR) was created in 1926. It is the French organization that represents France at the International Organization for Standardization (ISO) and the European Committee for Standardization (CEN). Since January 1, 2014, following the merger of AFNOR and Technical Union of Electricity (UTE), it is also a member of the European Committee for Standardization in Electronics and Electrical Engineering (CENELEC) at European level, and the International Electrotechnical Commission (IEC) at the international level.

[58]ISO, the International Organization for Standardization is composed of 163 members who are the national standards institutes of industrialized, developing, and transition countries of all sizes and in all regions of the world. ISO's collection of more than 18,400 standards provides business, governments, and society as a whole with concrete tools for the three dimensions—economic, environmental, and societal—of sustainable development.

- ISO 26000 is the international reference framework on CSR. It is the first definition of CSR on a global scale and should apply to all types of organizations, companies, local authorities, or NGOs. Seven areas have been identified: organizational governance (transparency, accountability, and stakeholder engagement); human rights; conditions and working relationships; environment; good business practices; consumer issues; societal commitment. The ISO 26000 standard, published in November 2010, represents the first true international standard of Social Responsibility that has been the subject of an international consensus; clearly defining "Sustainable Development" and "Social Responsibility"; being recognized and taken into account the State Strategies; prefiguring the future architecture of all SD/CSR approaches; enabling companies to deploy comprehensive and ambitious CSR policies.

International

The ISO 26000 standard does not only apply to CSR, but to the social responsibility of any type of organization. ISO 26000 incorporates the many texts issued by international organizations (UN, ILO, UNEP, Global Compact, European Union, OECD ...) dealing with CSR issues.

In parallel with the aforementioned standards, let us recall some international principles, among them: the "Global Compact" and *the OECD Guidelines for Multinational Enterprises.*

- The "Global Compact" tries to promote, in a way, the "10 commandments" of CSR that companies must respect. Born out of an international initiative launched in 1999 by the United Nations Secretary General, the Global Compact offers member companies the opportunity to adhere to 10 key principles in the areas of human rights, labor, the environment, and human rights corruption. The 10th principle was added in 2004. The 10 principles of the Global Compact according to the website www.lobalcompact-france.org:
  1. Businesses are invited to promote and respect the protection of international human rights law.
  2. Businesses are urged to ensure that they are not complicit in human rights abuses.
  3. Businesses are invited to respect freedom of association and to recognize the right to bargain collectively.

4. Businesses are invited to contribute to the elimination of forced or compulsory labor.
5. Businesses are invited to contribute to the effective abolition of child labor.
6. Businesses are invited to contribute to the elimination of all forms of discrimination in employment and occupation.
7. Businesses are invited to apply the precautionary approach to environmental issues.
8. Companies are invited to take initiatives to promote greater environmental responsibility.
9. Companies are encouraged to promote the development and diffusion of environmentally friendly technologies.
10. Companies are encouraged to take action against corruption in all its forms, including extortion and bribery.

Since 2003, the signatory companies must publish good practices in at least one of the 10 principles of the Covenant, failing to be excluded from the list of signatories. As of January 1, 2014, more than 8,000 companies had signed the Global Compact in 145 countries.

Then, on August 2, 2015, 193 countries approved and increased to 17 the objectives of the UN. They are gathered in the 2030 Agenda. This agenda was adopted by the UN in September 2015 after 2 years of negotiation including both governments and civil societies. It defines targets to be reached by 2030, defined objective by objective. Thus, hunger, poverty, climate change, health, inequalities are the main themes of the United Nations Sustainable Development Goals (SDGs). Entered into force in early 2016, it clearly illustrates the ecological and societal challenges facing our world. Targets aim to encourage global economic growth and promote sustainable development for the planet and humanity. We report these SDGs with short and precise titles as follows:

1. Eradication of poverty
2. Fight against hunger
3. Access to health
4. Access to quality education
5. Equality between the sexes
6. Access to safe water and sanitation
7. Use of renewable energies
8. Access to decent jobs
9. Build resilient infrastructure, promote sustainable industrialization that benefits all and encourages innovation

10. Reduction of inequalities
11. Sustainable Cities and Communities
12. Responsible consumption and production
13. Fight against climate change
14. Aquatic life
15. Terrestrial life
16. Justice and peace
17. Partnerships to achieve the objectives
    - The OECD Guidelines for Multinational Enterprises, less known than the United Nations Global Compact (2000) and the ILO Tripartite Declaration of Principles (1977), are precursors to the global instruments of CSR, adopted in 1976 and revised five times between 1976 and 2011. They constitute recommendations that governments send to multinational businesses operating in or from the acceding countries. They constitute the most in-depth frame of reference at the international level. The 34 member states of the OECD and 12 nonmember states, or 46 countries accounting for 85% of foreign direct investment, have joined. They set out principles to promote reasonable business conduct in a globalized environment, in accordance with applicable laws and internationally recognized standards. Thus, according to the official website "*France Diplomatie*" (www.diplomatie.gouv.fr) on May 25, 2011, the governments of 42 member and nonmember countries (Argentina, Brazil, Egypt, Latvia, Lithuania, Morocco, Peru, and Romania) of the OECD, which adhered to the OECD Declaration on International Investment and Multinational Enterprises and the related Decision, has completed a revision of the most important Principles ever after one year of work. The updating work was carried out by the acceding governments in close consultation with the Economic and Industrial Advisory Committee to the OECD (BIAC), the Trade Union Advisory Committee to the OECD (TUAC), and NGO OECD Watch.

The highlights of this update are

- A new chapter on human rights inspired by the Guiding Principles for Business and Human Rights: Implementing the Protect, Respect and Remedy Framework established by the United Nations Human Rights Council.

- A new approach to responsible supply chain management based on the concepts of due diligence and influence Clearer and stricter procedural guidelines that strengthen the role of National Contact Points (NCPs).
- A proactive implementation agenda to help companies apply the Principles, including through sectoral guides. To ensure that these principles are respected, each of the acceding countries has set up NCPs often addressed by NGOs wishing to challenge multinationals who have committed acts in violation of these Principles.
  - At the European level, mentioned for the first time in the Lisbon Strategy in March 2000, CSR has since gained prominence in the discourse of the European institutions with a first step: the Green Paper "Promoting a European framework for CSR," published in 2001 by the European Commission. It launches the debate between the partisans of the voluntary approaches, leaving as much latitude as possible to the companies and the proponents of the regulation wishing to establish a framework setting obligations in term of CSR.

In 2002, the second step taken was the "Commission Communication on CSR," a policy paper advocating a new social and environmental role for business in the global economy and launching the "*European plurilateral Forum*" with representatives of the parties stakeholders, trade unions, businesses, investors, NGOs, researchers, and national governments on six themes: responsible consumption, responsible investment, the links between CSR and competitiveness, transparency and reporting, human rights, as well as the global dimension of CSR. In 2006, the Commission published a new communication, confirming the voluntary dimension it wished to give to CSR and excluding any regulation, including on corporate reporting.

In 2011, the Commission adopts a new strategy on CSR and a new definition. For it, CSR is "the responsibility of companies towards the effects they have on society." The Commission states that "*it is appropriate that companies, in close collaboration with their stakeholders, have embarked on a process to integrate social, environmental, ethical, human rights and consumer concerns into their business activities and their basic strategy, this process aimed at: 1/ creating a community of values for their owners / shareholders, as well as for other stakeholders and society as a whole; 2/ to identify, prevent and mitigate the potential negative effects that companies may have.*"

In April 2014, an accounting directive introduced an extra-financial reporting requirement for all listed companies with more than 500 employees in the European Union and marks a new construction stage for European CSR. Note that the transposition of this directive (2014/95/EU), for France, was presented in the Council of Ministers only on July19, 2017. Published in the Official Journal, it will then have to be ratified by the Parliament and followed by an application decree.

- Finally, still on the international scene, are we moving toward a standardization of extra-financial information, although little used by France, the case of integrated "reporting"? Integrated reporting consists of a synthetic presentation of the company's strategy based on financial and extra-financial data. The concept is promoted by the International Integrated Reporting Council (IIRC), an international association created in 2010 that brings together leading companies, investors, promoters of reporting standards, and large audit firms. For ICRI, integrated reporting is based on six different types of capital that define the value of a business: financial and manufacturing capital, natural and social capital, and human and intellectual capital. This reporting seeks to achieve several objectives: improve the quality of information provided to investors and stakeholders; promote the inclusion of extra-financial criteria in reporting and propose a repository for companies; encourage the introduction of integrated management in companies so that their actions are focused on the creation of values (other than financial ones). The aim is to bring out a new international standard for synthetic reporting that combines financial and extra-financial data to provide transparency and, above all, to restore investor confidence. An article published in Novethic's professional letter "Essence of CSR," no. 110, July 2015 sought to explain the reasons for the French delay in the implementation of this tool. According to this text and a Europlace survey (March 2015) with some 50 large companies, only three of them were experimenting with integrated reporting in 2014. This lack of interest would result from: its complexity, time-consuming aspect, and implicitly its cost of development, because this new reporting is not content to collect data, it is necessary to draw a global prospective vision of the firm.

For SRI, let us focus on "PRI": on April 27, 2006 in New York, and May 4 in Paris, the launch of the PRI took place. These are the products of a working group of international experts and financial directors, under the auspices of UNEP-Fi, a unit of the United Nations Environment Program, to encourage the adaptation of environmental best practices by finance professionals, and the Global Compact. For Kofi Annan, *"this initiative stems from the growing recognition that, while finance is driving the global economy, investment decisions and shareholder practices do not sufficiently reflect policy social and environmental considerations."*

PRIs define a framework that goes beyond the field of SRI. It is a voluntary commitment aimed at the financial sector and encourages investors to integrate ESG issues into the management of their portfolios. The PRI addressed three types of potential signatories: asset holders (pension funds, insurance companies, etc.); portfolio managers (investment management companies, etc.); and professional services offering products in the two preceding categories. The PRI includes 6 principles in more than 30 possible actions:

1. Take ESG issues into account in their investment decision-making processes.
2. Take ESG issues into account in their shareholder policies and practices.
3. Ask the companies in which they invest to publish reports on their ESG practices.
4. Promote the acceptance and application of PRIs among asset managers.
5. Work in partnership with those in the financial sector who have committed to respect the PRI to improve their effectiveness Financial Professions Center/Bank Review, Chapter.
6. Report on their activities and progress in implementing the PRI.

Implicitly linked to environmental law, for some of its assets, SRI raises a multitude of questions. Thus, for Maître Romain Lemaire, based on an interview published on September 5, 2016, in the "Footprint Earth" section of the Novethic professional magazine, *"Environmental law is two-tiered ... one mature in the industrialized countries ... the other sentence to the other pain to develop in nations where the rule of law is stammering ... this state of affairs raises the question of the responsibility of the parent companies in the event of an ecological disaster"*

A right of a rich person who questions the duty of vigilance in the chain of the supplies. In France, if our environmental law is institutional (Environmental Charter is an integral part of our constitution), it is still true that the negative image and the lack of notoriety for a multinational can weigh more than the right, especially in unstable countries for the compensation of victims.

About 40 years after the 1976 law on the protection of nature, the National Assembly has definitively adopted Wednesday, July 20, 2016 the Law for the Reconquest of Biodiversity, Nature, and Landscapes. With this, the French law was innovated and became more restrictive. In addition to the creation of a French Agency for Biodiversity (FAB), the law gives a precise definition of biodiversity: a complex and dynamic system, set of genes, species, and ecosystems that interact, and of which humanity is a part (Article 1). New principles are laid down: ecological solidarity, which requires taking into account the possible environmental effects of a decision on neighboring territories; the nonregression of environmental law, which means that the level of environment protection cannot be lowered (Article 2). It integrates nocturnal landscapes into the nation's common heritage and recognizes the place of soils and their diversity. Some will consider that the result, as often in France, is half-hearted because of the pressure lobbies: hunters, farmers, and industrial agrochemicals, palm oil or deep-sea fishing. Nevertheless, this text contains measures offering a new harmony between man and nature. The stakes were all the more crucial as France, since its overseas territories and the importance of its maritime space, is home to ecosystems that are just as rich as they are endangered.

At the international level, there are a number of conventions (dealing with nuclear pollution, oil pollution, regulation of greenhouse gas emissions, pollution of ships, treatment of hazardous waste, etc.) which aim to better compensate the victims. Are they sufficient to regulate everything and make SRI more attractive to investors? The increasing consideration of the societal dimension makes it possible to affirm the principle of reciprocity which opens up the universe of sensitivity of all stakeholders.

From Some Complements to the Regulatory Framework with Text References

The law of February19, 2001 on the generalization of employee savings schemes has introduced in the Monetary and Financial Code an incentive for managers of employee savings funds to take environmental and social criteria into account in their asset management policy, and opens the possibility of creating solidarity savings funds.

The law of July 17, 2001 on various social, educational, and cultural provisions, including the creation of the pension reserve fund, stipulates that its executive board, which implements the guidelines of the establishment's investment policy, reports to the supervisory board on "the way in which the general investment policy of the fund has taken into account social, environmental or ethical considerations."

As early as 2005, the Board of Directors of the Public Service Supplementary Pension Institution, whose scheme was created by the Pension Reform Act of August 21, 2003, decided to adopt an investment policy that takes into account in a resolute and permanent way, the search for the general interest. In 2006, this resulted in the adoption of a charter that sets out the guidelines, resources and resources needed to implement this 100% SRI policy.

The law of July 12, 2010 on the national commitment for the environment stipulates that *"SICAVs and management companies shall mention in their annual report and in the documents intended for the information of their subscribers the terms and conditions for taking into account in their investment policy Investment of criteria relating to the respect of social, environmental and quality objectives of governance. [...] They indicate how they exercise the voting rights attached to the financial instruments resulting from these choices."*

The law of August 17, 2015 on the energy transition for green growth extends these obligations to institutional investors and broadens the scope to climate risk management and the means implemented to benefit the energy and ecological transition.

Equivalent obligations are made to companies with the law of May 15, 2001 on NRE, amended by the law of July 12, 2010 on the national commitment for the environment, supplemented by the law of August 17, 2015 on the energy transition for green growth and the law of August 8, 2016 on work, the modernization of social dialogue and securing career paths. For memory and sources: www.legifrance.gouv.fr)

- Finally, on December 15, 2016, between principle and right, a new "process or protocol" has been published to integrate climate change into finance. This is the report of the "Task force on climate-related financial disclosures" (TCFD) sponsored by the G20, Finance Ministers and Regulatory Authorities of the Financial Stability Forum. Its purpose is to strengthen the transparency of finance to make it a lever for greater mobilization of the financial sector in effectively taking into account the objectives of mitigation and adaptation to the effects of global warming. This report provides climate reporting guidelines for both regulators and investors. It raises, in particular, the following questions: How to enable regulators to better understand the potential climatic component of systemic risk? How, then, can investors be provided with data enabling them to better assess the financial impact of climate on the strategy and situation of the issuers—financial and nonfinancial—in which they have invested? The responses of the TCFD consist in suggesting a reference system articulated around a categorization of risks upstream (physical, judicial, and transition) and a typology of downstream solutions which declines a chain of current value in the methodologies of evaluation of the extra-financial performance, from governance and covering strategy and risk management to consistency analysis of indicators.

EVALUATING FINANCIAL IMPACT Climate-related risks and opportunities can impact organizations financial performance.

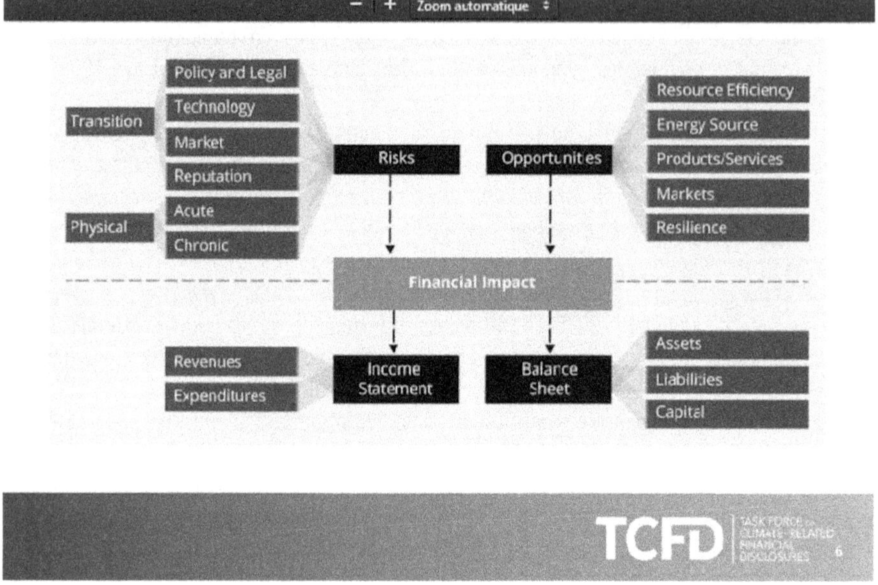

Source: TCFD Report (2016, p. 6).

This TCFD report is based on the idea that climate change is a systemic risk for the economy and finance. As a result, companies and the various financial players must evaluate and quantify their exposure to this risk in order to put in place the necessary strategies to limit their impact. The diagram below, extracted from the report, summarizes its main recommendations:

This "process or protocol" for materializing the risks associated with climate change reflects the research efforts undertaken over the last decade by SRI investors who have sought to reconcile managers and analysts in order to bring the two phases together: value creation and a sense of purpose values n fiduciary responsibility.

In terms of governance for the case of France and its large companies, we cannot ignore an obligation now imposed in the composition of the Board of Directors. Indeed, from January 1, 2017, companies with more than 500 employees will have 40% women on their boards. The law on the balanced representation of women and men on the boards of directors, known as Cope-Zimmermann, was passed in 2011, 6 years ago. The companies had therefore 6 years to make their turnover joint. After this date, the bad students who will summon a nonjoint CA will be exposed to sanctions: blocking of the remuneration, cancellation of the new nominations, if they are men, and so on.

Taxation

As for the previous subsection and according to the information held for the main countries, we will study successively the case of France then the international one.

In France

Savings products relating to solidary finance and SRI are the main ones affected by the tax provisions. Although distinct, they can be found in investments under UCITS allowing investors to entrust the management of their capital to a professional who undertakes to invest them in one or more specific financial markets. Essentially, for tax reasons, we will distinguish solidary finance or solidary investment from shared savings.

Solidary finance

According to the portal of the French Minister of Economy, of Finance, and of Action and Public Accounts (economie.gouv.fr), we speak of "solidary investment" or solidary saves" when the savings are invested for fully or partially (5%, 10% ...) in so-called social utility projects: microcredit, integration, and other solidarity projects. The "90/10" funds are invested for 90% in SRI (funds belonging to ethical finance) and for 10% in unlisted companies with strong social utility (actors of solidarity finance). For example, mutual funds of solidarity enterprises (PEE for Company Savings Plan, PERCO for Group Retirement Savings Plan) are all "90/10" funds. They are also found in solidary investment savings products offered by banking institutions.

As part of shared ownership, since February 17, 2001, the Fabius law requires all companies that have set up a PERCO (Collective Retirement Savings Plan) to offer a solidarity fund among all funds selected. This is called FCPES for Joint Venture Fund of Solidarity Enterprises and operates as a traditional fund to which we add a solidarity added value distributed to solidarity companies. In 2008, the law extends this obligation to the PEE (French: "Plan Epargne Entreprise" for Business Savings Plan).

The solidarity shareholder allows the investor to invest directly in social or environmental projects via specialized solidarity funders. Two types of investments can be subscribed; unlisted shares and term accounts. The first type of investment offers investors the opportunity to acquire shares in the capital of a charity. He becomes a partner (shareholder or member according to the legal structure of the organization) and can participate directly in the management and orientation of the funds. Here, the risk can be quite significant and the capital is generally invested minimum for 5 years, because these investments provide a tax benefit. For their part, term savings accounts allow solidarity organizations to have resources for a limited period of time. Indeed, the money can be immobilized for a minimum of 12–25 months, with a rate of remuneration that depends on this period of immobilization.

Share savings, also known as a "sharing product" consists of an investor to donate all or part of the income from his or her investment to a work of general interest that is philanthropic, educational, scientific, social, humanitarian, cultural, or environmental.

Share-based savings appeared in France in 1983 with the creation by "Crédit Coopératif" of a "Hunger and Development" mutual fund. The principle of this investment, still existing, is to pay part (50% or 75%) of the profits made in this fund to the Catholic Committee against Hunger and for Development. The funds are then used to finance the development of the countries of the South and to fight against hunger in the world. Unlike "90/10" funds, sharing funds are not necessarily invested in solidarity-based businesses, but they offer to redistribute part of the fund's income to social or humanitarian institutions in the form of donations. The share of distributed income comes either from management fees that the bank transfers directly to the social, or humanitarian organization, or from the saver himself who decides to donate a percentage of his income from the sharing fund in which he has invested. We distinguish different products of sharing:

1. Savings books and mutual funds: The principle of sharing is based on the sharing of interests between the investor and one or more associations proposed by the bank and chosen by the client. In addition, some financial institutions participate in donations from their clients in the form of an employer contribution.

2. Life insurance: the principle of sharing is based on the payment of a portion of the entry fees at the time of the subscription of the contract or on an annual payment of a portion of the profits made by the contract.
3. Bank cards: as a sharing product, they bear the double logo of the bank and the association designated as the recipient of donations. The principle is either to round the amount paid by the customer with his credit card to the higher euro, or to repay a percentage of the amount of the purchase made, or to repay a portion of the membership fee.

Presentation of specific French products (without translation) of solidarity investments and sharing savings

On the left side of the table: the solidary investment for the social enterprise; to the company and financial institutions (banks, insurance, and asset managers).

On the right side of the table, mainly, savings sharing (philosophy of donation) of individuals made in the form of savings booklet; investment companies with variable capital; cash vouchers; life insurance; by credit cards.

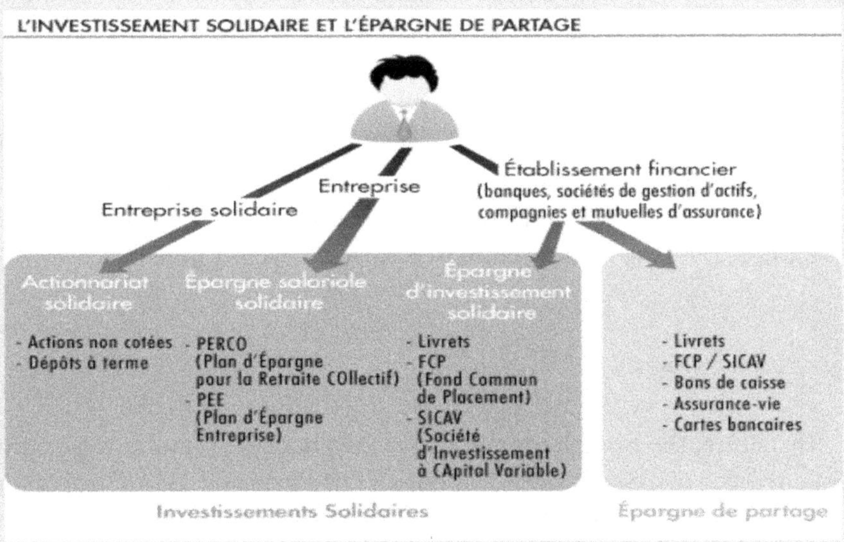

Source: www.economie.gouv.fr

In a market where rates remain potentially low, the investor must accept controlled diversification of his investments. Responsible finance is able to support this strategy. The year 2017 ended with an upheaval in the taxation applicable to the individual with the adoption of a Single Flat Levy (PFU) which modifies the taxation of income from the heritage and implementation of the Real estate tax (IFI = Impôt sur la Fortune Immobilière), which replaces the Solidarity Tax on Fortune (ISF = Impôt de solidarité sur la fortune) by focusing on real estate. According to the latest survey carried out by KPMG, the crowdfunding recorded a 44% increase in its amounts raised with €336 million in 2017. This evolution was made possible thanks to opening the sector to different types of financial tools (bond issues, mini vouchers, equity securities) accessible to individuals. Although to be considered with caution, the financing of real estate projects remains the sector which concentrates the biggest part of collection (42% according to the barometer) with an average annual yield of 10%, for Duration of immobilization of approximately 18 months for average bets of €4,900. The future Action Plan for Growth and Transformation of Enterprises (PACTE) concocted by the Ministry of Economy and Finance should include "virtuous" mechanisms to better skew the savings of the French and make them invest in companies.

The deputies finally adopted, on December 22, 2017, the draft budget law for 2018 in the National Assembly. The "Conseil Constitutionnel" (French Supreme Court) also validated most of the projects on 29/12. This budget law includes a set of measures that affect the taxation of wealth, including the increase of the generalized social contribution (CSG) by 1.7 points and the flat tax of 30% on income from capital (or PFU, Single Lump Sum). How do these measures affect the taxation and taxation of income from wealth and investments (real estate, booklets, PEL, life insurance, PEA, dividends, employee savings, capital gains)?

Taxation in general

By nature, the French tax system is very changeable and involves multiple derogations. Some savings methods, whether real estate investment or financial investment allow to escape or reduce taxes on income and on capital gains, most often with long-term conditions savings. This is particularly the case for the Stock Savings Plan, life insurance contracts, employee savings plans, or retirement savings plans.

The taxation of savings products (shares, bonds, passbooks, etc.), starting in 2018, is undergoing profound changes. Thus, the new finance law for 2018 introduces a proportional rate (flat tax) that calls into question the evolution made by the Finance Act for 2013. The latter had submitted the capital gains (incomes, capital gains) to the progressive scale of the tax. All financial and wealth products are not subject to the same tax regime. Article 28 of the new Finance Act for 2018 introduced a Single Flat Levy (UTP) for income and capital gains received by natural persons as of January 1, 2018 at a rate of 30%. This overall rate includes the tax itself (12.8%) and social security contributions which rose to 17.2% (compared to 15.5%) in 2017. In return, the various abatements in force are removed. This Single Lump Sum Withdrawal relates to: share income (dividends); income from collective investment schemes; fixed income investment income (bonds, bank savings books); revenues from housing savings plans and accounts subscribed from January 1, 2018 (from the first year); capital gains realized.

This One-off Lump Sum Payment does not apply to certain areas: share savings plans; life insurance contracts (for premiums paid before September 27, 2017 and when the capital paid is less than €150,000); employee savings; housing savings plans (under 12) and home savings accounts purchased before 2018.

In general, all savings incomes, regardless of the type of investment, are subject to the annual rate currently set at 17.2% since January 1, 2018. However, there are notable exceptions such as a savings account, blue savings account, Booklet of Sustainable Development, young booklet, the Savings Booklet Popular, which is exempt. These are the only products that cannot bear social or other taxes.

If the flat tax rate is not attractive to the taxpayer, it is always possible to opt for progressive taxation on the tax scale. But beware! This is a global option integrating all financial income, as well as realized gains (gain). In this situation, it is then possible to benefit from the dividend deduction (40%) and the deductibility of part of the CSG (6.8%).

We will endeavor to present in a simplified way the general framework of the main fiscal measures concerning solidarity economy, participative financing, initial coin offering, donations, and philanthropy.

Special and complex case of the taxation of companies and structures of the social and solidary economy

Companies and structures of the ESS are distinguished by their social utilities (support to vulnerable publics, territorial cohesion or sustainable development) and the orientation of their surpluses toward the continuation of their activities often not lucrative. Approval of a social enterprise of social utility (ESUS) allows them to benefit from aids and specific financing, in particular, accession to employee solidarity savings and the companies and organizations of the ESS are eligible to Approval of Social Solidarity Enterprise (In French ESUS = "Entreprise Solidaire d'Utilité Sociale"), if they fulfill the following conditions: The main objective of the business must be the search for social utility; the expense generated by the social utility objective must have a significant impact on the income statement (at least 66% of all operating expenses over the last 3 years ended; senior management is limited (7 times the insertion minimum wage and the amounts paid must not exceed 10 times the insertion minimum wage); the company's equity securities must not be traded on a financial market.

Some structures in the SSE benefit from legal approval because of their activity (integration, social assistance, etc.). They are therefore not obliged to comply with the conditions for obtaining approval, except that which concerns the absence of listing on a financial market. Accreditation is issued for a period of 5 years or 2 years, for companies less than 3 years old at the time of application. The Prefecture of Department must publish the decision of approval to the collection of administrative acts. The holding of shares does not give rise to the payment of dividends. However, the ESUS authorization allows investors to benefit from the tax advantages associated with the Share Savings Plan.

Crowdfunding is a new method of responsible financing. Crowdfunding literally means "crowdfunding." It is generally translated into French as "participatory funding"! We can distinguish crowdfunding for real estate from individuals, for example, crowdInvesting for businesses.

The real estate crowdfunding allows individuals to invest in real estate construction programs, whether housing or offices. When a real estate developer starts a project, he or she creates a dedicated legal structure whose purpose is to manage the construction and commercialization of the real estate program. The company, thus created, borrows, generally, in the form of bonds. When all the properties of the program have been sold, savers recover their investment plus borrowing interest. Property income, already heavily taxed (property income and real estate gains are subject to income tax and social security), will suffer the increase of the CSG. With the real estate crowdfunding, the bonds will be able to benefit from January 1, 2018 of the flat tax. Today, income from bonds is subject to income tax and social security contributions. The tax rate can range from

15.5% (for households that do not pay income tax) to 60.5%. With the flat tax, the tax rate will be 30% and those who have interest can stay in the current tax system.

Concerning the identification of ethical and social links between the three actors in the practice of CrowdInvesting—the platform, the entrepreneur, and the crowd of investors—confirms the existence of the ethical dimension of CSR in the context of CrowdInvesting. Here the motivations of investors are aligned with those of responsible finance, including SRI. The "Crowd" is identified as a stakeholder of the company. Overall, CrowdInvesting appears as a flexible and connected solution, closely linked to the evolution of digital technologies, promoting the commitment of companies in responsible projects. The challenge today is to skillfully manage the integration of this funding practice which not only gives greater visibility to responsible projects, but also encourages the engagement and participation of employees and individuals.

The Finance Act for 2018 provides for several measures in favor of companies in order to increase their attractiveness and competitiveness. The most emblematic measure lies in the gradual reduction of the IS rate, until it reaches 25% in 2022 (In 2018, IS 28% for all companies in the limit of €500,000 profit and 33.3 rate beyond). Crowdfunding also provides access to tax benefits. This is the case when it comes to certain donations or investments in SMEs.

Crowdfunding covers several different mechanisms. Public funding of projects, or crowdfunding, raises funds from the public to finance a project. The project leader can be a company, an individual, an association, or since 2016, a community. There are several large families in crowdfunding: crowdgiving, loans (or "crowdlending," which also includes bond and minibond issues), and equity crowdfunding (equity financing).

The latter category is favored by start-ups who prefer to give securities of their company to investors, giving them financial rights and more specifically rights on profits rather than repaying them a loan with interest. Equity crowdfunding players, and in particular Investment Service Providers (ISPs) and Participatory Investment Advisors (CIPs), are currently facing significant changes in their regulatory and economic environment that could lead them to rapidly evolve their practice, or even their model business.

The new fiscal order introduced by the Finance Act for 2018 should, moreover, speed up the movement, as this investment does not enter into the real estate tax base. Revive growth by reducing some of the tax; this is the objective that the government sets with the creation of the IFI (Tax on Real Estate). As its name suggests, it will only concern the entire household property portfolio. The entry threshold (set at €1.3 billion), the rates, and the 30% abatement on the main residence do not change. The government also clarified that real estate for the operation of a taxpayer's business was not affected by the IFI. Ultimately, most of the reform comes from the withdrawal of securities in the calculation of this tax (this includes securities in shares or bonds, income from certain booklets, and other savings solutions). The new property wealth tax (IFI) concerns real estate assets with a net worth of debts of more than €1.3 million. The IFI base includes all real estate assets that are not assigned to a professional activity by their owners. Capital gains from real estate crowdfunding are financial products and therefore do not enter into the calculation of the Fortune real estate tax (in French = "Impôt sur la Fortune Immobilière," IFI).

In addition, concerned by the "flat tax," all gains from investment (interest, dividends and similar income, capital gains ...), unless otherwise specified by the legislator (Booklet A, Stock Saving Plan). By definition, capital gains from real estate crowdfunding are therefore part of the flat tax regime. These gains will be taxed at 30% (a fixed income tax rate of 12.8% and an overall social tax rate of 17.2%), and it will be left to taxpayers who have an interest, the opportunity to opt for progressive taxation of the income tax.

Recall that crowdfunding real estate offers to finance the construction real estate, offering short-term investments (6–36 months) with annual returns of 8%–12%. "For the investor, it is a loan to a promoter and therefore a financial product on offers of equity securities or debt securities. In no case is it an investment in real estate or in stone-paper.

If the project holder is an individual, and therefore a natural person whose tax domicile is in France, he is liable to French income tax due to the entirety of his income from any source. It is therefore an "unlimited" tax liability, regardless of its nationality (French or foreign), the taxpayer must, in principle, be subject to tax in France on all of his income from French sources or foreign. It would therefore be logical to declare the contributions collected in the BIC income category (industrial or commercial profits).

If the contributor is an individual, donations to a project carried by a natural or legal person who is not an association or a nonprofit organization do not qualify for any tax reduction. They are considered a purchase of goods or services.

Crowdfunding before and after the decree of October 28, 2016 on securities and loans offered as part of crowdfunding

	Before the decree	***After the decree***
Maximum amount that an individual is willing to lend	***€1,000***	***€2,000***
Ceiling of the loan that the company can realize	***€1 million per year***	€2.5 million per year
Types of financing	Donations Loans Simple shares	Donations Loans Shares Convertibles bonds ***Equity shares***

According to "To Inform Itself on the New Framework Applicable to the Participative Financing (Crowdfunding)," published by the Authority of the Financial Markets on September 30, 2014—Update Guides on August 26, 2016 and the May 9, 2017.

What is the taxation of funds invested via crowdfunding? It varies according to the type of crowdfunding.

Donations: If the promoter of the project is a foundation, an organization of general interest or an association recognized as being in the public interest, the donor benefits from a tax reduction equal to 66% of the sums paid within the limit of 20% of the taxable income. If the gift is made with counterparty (in kind, for example), the value of the gift must not exceed one quarter (25%) of the donation amount. The taxpayer must keep the CERFA (administrative form) form for 3 years in case of request from the tax services.

Loans with interest: Interest is subject to a mandatory deposit at the source of 24% plus 15.5% of social security contributions (CSG and CRDS) (through the crowdfunding platform) and then a progressive tax rate Income; the deposit of 24% giving right to a tax credit chargeable on the IR. The investor receives each year a single Tax Print (IFU) which allows declaring his income to the tax administration.

Private equity: The sums invested are eligible for either tax benefits on entry or exit. At the entrance: there are tax cuts in the framework of schemes for the financing of SMEs via crowdfunding. This is a tax reduction of 18% of the amount invested within the limit of €50,000 (therefore, a maximum reduction of €9,000), taken into account in the cap of tax loopholes to €10,000. The saver can choose a reduction of wealth tax. It is 50% of the payments taken into account in the limit of €90,000 (a maximum reduction of €45,000). At the exit: if subscriptions for unlisted shares are lodged in a Plan in Savings in Actions, they benefit from the advantageous taxation of this envelope (no tax on capital gains).

The direct catch of the equity crowdfunding with the savings of French led the public authorities to control the activity of the CIP strictly, with the aim of protection the investors. The CIP are in particular subjected to the obligation to subscribe a contract of professional third-party insurance. They are also constrained to respect a significant number of rules of good behavior (management of the conflicts of interests, level of the resources allocated with their activity, etc.) whose contents will be reinforced and modified in-depth by the transposition in French right of European directive 2014/65/EU (known as MIFID II). These modifications relate in particular to the character independent of their advices and their remuneration. In spite of the hardening of certain rules, the legislator increased ceiling of the naps which can be raised by a company. The ceiling of the funds raised by the same transmitter over a 12 running month period thus passed from a million to 2.5 million in October 2016. Let us specify, however, that when the lifting of funds exceeds a million Euros, this one should not exceed 50% of the capital of the transmitting company.

In order to set up a homogeneous device, reliable and transparent, the French State deposited at the National institute of industrial property (INPI in French) the collective brand "Platform of participative financing controlled by the French authorities." By using this brand, the Advisor in Participative Investment, registered with the ORIAS[59] (In French ORIAS stands for Organisme pour le registre unique des intermédiaires en assurance, banque et finance, the organization of recording of the platforms of participative financing) informs the public which platform is subjected to the respect of the requirements fixed by the French regulation.

The new competition of the Initial Corner Offering

For a few months, the Initial Corner Offering (ICO) has come to hustle the world of the financing of start-ups. This mode of fundraising through the emission of exchangeable digital credits is the "token" against crypto currencies during the launching phase of a project. The carriers of project

[59]Organization for the single register of the intermediaries in insurance, banks, and finances.

offer either titles of their company or the subscription of tokens conferring of the very diversified rights: right on dividends related on the future profits, the handing-over of a product of a service, and so on. The investors speculators being primarily justified by the profit generated in the possibility where the value of the tokens exceeds that of the price of ICOs. According to the Authority of Financial Markets (MFA) at least four emissions of tokens were carried out in France in 2017. The amounts raised via these four ICOs would add up in the order of magnitude €80 million. The level of market capitalization of the corresponding tokens would have reached approximately €350 million.

Thus, to the regulated character of the participative financing comes to be opposed a quasi-absence of regulation of ICOs. This situation could, however, develop with more or less short-term because a consultation of the MFA is currently in hand. In this state, if the lifting of funds in crypto currencies makes it possible to be freed from the constraints related more to the traditional lifting of funds or the crowdfunding. The innovative ICOs market still provides poor protection for investors and savers. Very a greatest caution thus remains of setting for these operations.

2018 income tax return: Donations to organizations of general interest made in 2017

The donation can take one of the following forms:

- Payment of sums of money
- Gift in kind (a work of art for example)
- Payment of contributions
- Abandonment of income or products (e.g., waiver of copyrights)
- Costs incurred as part of a volunteer activity

To benefit from the tax reduction, the payment, in whatever form, must be made without any direct or indirect consideration. In the context of contributions, the institutional and symbolic advantages obtained are not considered as real counterparts; for small goods (greeting cards, badges, etc.), the value of these counterparties must not exceed one quarter of the donation amount, with a maximum of €69 per year. Beneficiary organizations must meet three conditions: be nonprofit; have a social purpose; and selfless management. Do not work for the benefit of a small circle of people.

Type of organization	Amount giving right to the tax reduction	Maximum reduction
Organization of general interest or recognized by public utility	66% of the versed sums	20% of taxable income
Organization of free assistance to the people in difficulty	75% of the sums paid up to €531 66% of donations greater than €531	€399 20% of taxable income

The sums paid at approved organizations located in a Member State del' European Union, in Iceland, Norway, or in Liechtenstein also entitle to the tax cut. Taxation, the gifts profit from a tax cut of 66% (Article 200 of the CGI), should not exceed 20% of the assessed income. The surplus can, however, be deferred. While giving to organizations of assistance to the people who provide free a meal, a housing, or care (the Red Cross, the "Resto du coeur," the Little brothers of the poor, Apprentices of Auteuil ...), the tax cut of 75% of the amount of the gift within the limit of €531 is a maximum saving in tax of €399.

Philanthropy: The tax applicable reduction is identical to that to the old wealth tax. Since the Tepa law (August 21, 2007), the donations of sums of money, but donations of listed securities in freehold, allow reduction of wealth tax. Are excluded donations in kind and donations of securities whose tiles are dismembered? The lists of eligible organizations are smaller than the list of income taxes. Unlike recognized utility foundations, associations recognized of public utility do not use most of this device. While giving before the real declaration of wealth tax 2018 (next May), the Wealth tax Real will be decreased to a total value of 75% of the value of the gift within the limit of €50,000 (or of €45,000 in the event of office plurality with an investment SME realized before December 31, 2017), which corresponds to a maximum gift of €66,667.

In addition, according to the Ministry of Ecological and Solidarity Transition, in addition to regulatory and tax regulations, three types of system have been developed to make savers aware of SRI:

- *The transparency Code* for socially responsible funds open to the public. The Transparency Code of the AFG and the FIR is the French version of the European Code of Transparency for socially responsible funds open to the public initially developed by Eurosif in 2005 and revised in 2013 to bring it into conformity with the aforementioned Article 224. Its objective is twofold: to improve the readability and transparency of the socially responsible funds approach for investors and savers, and to set up a framework of best practices for the transparent management of financial investments. It is mandatory for all socially responsible funds open to the public managed by a member of the AFG or the FIR.

- Sponsored by the Ministry since its first edition, the continuation of the organization of the "Responsible Finance Week" (already mentioned, took place in 2017 from September 28 to October 5), which brings together the actors of the alternative finance and provides a forum for exchange and reflection.
- *Two Labels*, worn by this ministry, were created in late 2015 and early 2016:
  1. The energy and ecological transition label for the climate, Decree No. 2015-1615 of December 10, 2015, guarantees the orientation of investments toward the financing of the ecological and energy transition. From the investors' point of view, it guarantees the transparency and quality of the environmental characteristics of these financial products, confirmed by the audit of Novethic, a third-party expert and independent, selected to be an auditor by the Ministry.
  2. The SRI: a public label promulgated by Decree No. 2016-10 of January 8, 2016, which sets the criteria to be met by SICAVs and mutual funds in order to benefit from this label. The decree defines SRI as a management method that consists of selecting corporate securities by incorporating extra-financial criteria. In their selection, the funds must take into account the impact of companies on their environment, society and integrated governance issues. Companies' management wishing to obtain this label for any of their financial products will have to appeal, at their own expense, to an external certifying body approved by the French Accreditation Committee (Cofrac). The label will be awarded for a period of three years following an audit of the fund's investment policy. To be labeled "SRI," the funds must meet one or other of these requirements:
     - i. Exclude from their initial investment universe 20% of securities on the basis of these famous ESG criteria.
     - ii. Or build a portfolio whose average rating in terms of ESG will be significantly higher than that of the benchmark index they use to compare their financial performance. These labels require a measure of the actual societal impact of the labeled

funds and, for the energy and ecological transition label for the climate, a minimum level of investment in companies and green projects, as defined by a precise and internationally recognized nomenclature.

Work on these two labels has led the AFG and the FIR to change the definition of SRI to focus on its objectives, its link with the issues of sustainable development, and its impacts on society: *"socially responsible investment is an investment that aims to reconcile economic performance and social and environmental impact by financing companies and public entities that contribute to sustainable development regardless of their sector of activity. By influencing governance and stakeholder behavior, socially responsible investment promotes a responsible economy."*

The lack of harmonization in this area may not favor the "jungle" of SRI tools and benchmarks for the uninitiated saver. In an article in the newspaper *Le Monde*, dated January 19, 2016, Anne-Catherine Husson-Traore, Novethic's general manager said about the public label SRI: *"It is not sure that this label will be a guarantee of clarity for the General public. But it has the merit of existing. It is the first time that the public authorities have labeled a financial product. It's more about promoting the financial center of Paris than providing a tool for individuals."*

Of some examples of the taxation of the SRI and solidary funds in the world

For Europe, the report 2018 heading "Financing a Sustainable European Economy," published at the end of January 2018 by the High-Level Expert Group on Sustainable Finance, presents the challenges. This report, which extends the work initiated by the Cop 21 of December 2015 in Paris, is interesting for its general recommendations concerning finance, the bank, the insurance, agriculture, the sea. However, the budgetary priority and the necessary fiscal harmonization between the states are not evoked. It is noteworthy that "problem of sustainability is a 'double compression': a compression of time and a compression of risk, now, it is necessary to pass to the action, but, which tools should be used?"

To illustrate the complexity of this tax issue, consider a few situations:

Some examples on the specific taxation of solidarity savings or investment products according *to the Dutch Ministry of Finance*:

a. The MIA (environmental investment rebate) and Vamil (arbitrary depreciation of environmental investments) are two different schemes. Using the MIA/Vamil schemes, you can:
   - Invest in environmentally friendly products or company resources with a tax advantage.
   - Get innovative environmentally friendly products onto the market more quickly.

Investing with a fiscal advantage

Through the MIA, you can deduct up to 36% of the investment costs for an environmentally friendly investment on top of your regular tax deductions for investments, and with the Vamil you yourself may decide when to write off these investment costs. This provides you with an advantage in liquidity and interest.

For all entrepreneurs

All entrepreneurs in the Netherlands who pay income or company tax can make use of the MIA/Vamil. The arrangement is interesting, for example, to entrepreneurs in agriculture, shipping, and industry, and also for those who invest in sustainable transport, sustainable recreation, and sustainable buildings.

The environment list

Do you want to know which investments you can use the MIA and/or the Vamil for? Then look at the current Environment list (in Dutch). This includes about 270 investments that are eligible for the MIA and/or the Vamil. These investments, called company resources on the Environment list, are minimally damaging to the environment. They often have a wider scope than the obligations in the law.

b. Energy-saving investment credit
   You may opt for the energy-saving investment credit if, in 2017, you invested more than €2,500 in new business assets that are recognized by the Ministry of Finance and the Ministry of Economic

Affairs as energy-saving investments. The energy-saving investment credit is 58% of a maximum of €120,000,000.

The minimum investment amount is €2,500 per business asset. Do you opt for the energy-saving investment credit? In that case, you are not entitled to the environmental investment credit for the same business assets.

A reporting procedure applies to the energy-saving investment credit. You must file a digital report through the e-desk of the Netherlands Enterprise Agency (Rijksdienst voor Ondernemend Nederland, RVO.nl). Visit rvo.nl for more information.

c. Environmental investment credit

You may opt for the environmental investment credit if, in 2017, you invested more than €2,500 in new business assets that are recognized by the Ministry of Infrastructure and the Environment and the Ministry of Finance as environmental investments. There are three categories to which different percentages apply. Do you opt for the energy-saving investment credit? In that case, you are not entitled to the environmental investment credit for the same business assets.

If you want to make use of the environmental investment credit, you must report your investments to the Netherlands Enterprise Agency (Rijksdienst voor Ondernemend Nederland, RVO.nl).

d. The Green Funds Scheme

The Green Funds Scheme is a tax incIn Switzerland, the tax on financialentive scheme enabling individual investors to put money into green projects that benefit nature and environment. Individuals who invest in a green fund or save money with financial institutions practicing "green banking" receive a lower rate than the market interest rate, however, this is compensated by a tax incentive. In return, the banks charge green projects a lower interest rate. The Green Funds Scheme is a tax incentive scheme launched in 1995 by the Dutch government to encourage green initiatives. In a nutshell, it comprises the Green Projects Scheme (which establishes the conditions governing the projects), the Green Institutions Scheme (which regulates the role played by the financial institutions), and finally the tax incentive for individual investors (which gets the flow of funds moving).

Green projects

The Green Projects Scheme designates projects that are eligible for green project status. There are a few technical and financial conditions, but the main requirement is that these are new projects providing a significant and immediate environmental benefit. Projects are divided into categories covering a broad range of activities from high-tech environmental innovation to low-tech improvements in the area of nature and the landscape.

Green institutions

The majority of Dutch banks have a "green fund" or a "green bank" which meets the strict requirements imposed by the Green Institutions Scheme. The banks issue bonds with a fixed value, term and interest rate, or shares in a green investment fund. Usually, the interest rate or dividend paid out by the bank is lower than the market rate, which means that the bank can in turn invest the funds in green projects for a lower interest rate.

Tax incentive

In the Netherlands an individual investor would normally pay a presumptive capital income tax (see explanation below) on the amount invested, but green capital is exempt up to about €57,845 per person (€115,690 fiscal partners). Green investors also pay less income tax on their green capital. Their reduction is 0.7% of the amount exempted. This means they can accept a lower interest rate or dividend on their investment.

e. Donations

Did you donate money to charities or church or social organizations in 2017? Or did you incur expenses for such an organization? In that case, you may deduct these expenses under certain conditions. This also applies to donations in kind.There are two types of donations:

1. Ordinary donations (You made these donations to a Public Benefit Organization [Algemeen Nut Beogende Instelling or ANBI] or to certain supporting foundations for a Social

Benefit Organization [Sociaal Belang Behartigende Instelling or SBBI]).

2. Regular donations (You made these donations to an ANBI or an association that meets the conditions).

Public benefit organization

A donation to an organization is deductible if this organization has been recognized and registered by us as a public benefit organization (ANBI). An ANBI is an organization that focuses on public benefit for at least 90%. There are more than 43,000 ANBI's.

Organizations may request us to register them as ANBIs. If they meet certain conditions, we recognize and register them as ANBIs. One of the conditions is that they publish every year on the Internet some facts about their financial situation.

Foreign organizations

An ANBI could be established in the Kingdom, in another Member State of the European Union or in a state designated by ministerial regulation. Other organizations could also be designated, if they meet the conditions.

Donations to a cultural ANBI

Did you donate money to a cultural ANBI? In that case, you may, in order to calculate the deductible item, increase the amount of the donation to this cultural ANBI by 25%. The total increase of the ordinary donations and regular donations to a cultural ANBI may be no more than €1,250. This increase is calculated on the ordinary and regular donations jointly.

Another example with Switzerland: Low pressure and complexity characterize double taxation.

The results of the 2018 Swiss Sustainable Finance survey on sustainable investment speak for themselves and bear witness to the growth of sustainable investment in Switzerland:

1. Sustainable investment up 82% to CHF 390.6 billion.

2. 92% increase in SRI funds held by institutional clients and 38% for private clients.

In 2017, capital invested in a sustainable manner rose by 82% year-on-year to 390.6 billion francs (215 billion in 2016), according to the latest report on Sustainable Investment in Switzerland 2018, published by 66 financial institutions. Excluding the so-called "sensitive" sectors (tobacco, nuclear, weapons, etc.) is currently the most popular strategy. The increased role played by institutional investors in sustainable investments is the main factor explaining the spectacular increase in investments observed last year. Sustainable assets managed directly by pension funds, insurers, and other institutional investors more than doubled (+128%) to CHF 238.2 billion, representing four tenths of the Swiss sustainable investment market. Last year, sustainable investment funds reached 94.4 billion (+47%), representing a quarter of the total market in this category in Switzerland, followed by sustainable management mandates with 57.9 billion (+25%), representing 15% of this market.

In Switzerland, the tax on financial investments differs according to the type of return, the product in question, and the investor's domicile. Coupon, dividends, and interest are included in income tax and subject to the marginal tax rate that applies to the last CHF 1,000 of taxable income. The Swiss tax system reflects the federal structure of the country, which is composed of 26 autonomous cantons with about 2,294 independent municipalities. The Swiss constitution confers full tax powers on the cantons, with the exception of taxes which are reserved exclusively for the federal government. There are therefore two levels of taxation in Switzerland: the federal level and the cantonal/communal level. Generally speaking, the taxation of legal persons on profits—at federal level: The Swiss Confederation levies a fixed rate tax on the after-tax profits of companies and cooperatives. Associations, foundations, and other legal entities, as well as collective capital investments, are taxed at a fixed rate that is generally half the federal rate. No capital tax is levied at the federal level.

Tax advantages are granted at cantonal and municipal level and also, in certain specifically defined regions, at federal level, for approved investments (economically disadvantaged regions). At cantonal and municipal level, most cantons offer partial or total tax relief on cantonal or municipal taxes for a maximum of 10 years, depending on the case. In particular, relief is granted in the event of the establishment of a new company or an expansion project of economic importance to the canton.

Income tax Persons subject to federal and cantonal/communal income tax are all natural persons who have their domicile or stay in Switzerland (at least 30 days with an activity). Tax rates for individuals are progressive, with a maximum rate at the federal level. The cantons may freely set their tax rates. The tax burden can therefore vary greatly from one canton to another.

Conclusion: What to remember

Responsible finance is necessary for the capitalistic system; will it be sufficient to change the conceptual framework and content? We no longer judge the financial operation itself as belonging to the realm of good or bad, we begin to recognize the soundness for development, insofar as it is treated in a legal framework with the concern of the general interest. The way is still long. Concerning the interest of this responsible finance, awareness now seems firmly rooted in people's minds; a real pathway to action is another matter. Many questions remain and it is the sense of the necessary decryption carried by our second part which will contribute, perhaps to enlighten the debate. Questions remain about the lack of transparency, the heterogeneity of evaluation methods, the validity of value selection processes, and the explanation of the rapid expansion of the number of funds. A certain doubt is maintained by the critics of ethical finance on the real "ethical" motivation of the actors. Between solidarity and the effect of communication, the small amounts mobilized by ethical finance lead, again, to relativize their scope. Often presented as an alternative mode of management, is ethical finance able to reconcile modern finance with solidarity and to influence its methods? SRI assets in France represent around €746 billion in 2015, an increase of nearly 30% compared to 2014, according to a survey conducted by Novethic in partnership with the FIR. This growth is supported by employee savings and the shy awakening of individual savers. However, the latter would hold only 10% of total outstanding. However, it is difficult to have precise figures, since SRI is not regulated strictly speaking and remains only a "label" of voluntary commitment by investment actors. On the other hand, while institutional investors have been turning to SRI for 15 years, individuals have not yet taken the lead, despite an offer of more than 300 funds already available. And that is the whole current debate around SRI. Is there a real benefit to investing in these types of assets rather than "traditional" funds?

Many managers, who are particularly committed to sustainable development, say that in the long term, SRI positions earn more than global assets with better risk management. This is conceivable and easy to understand, especially on thematic SRI funds, such as water or renewable energies, which are indisputable planetary subjects. However, the figures, for all that, do not yet clearly show a real advantage in terms of purely financial management (return, volatility, liquidity, etc.). This is still a choice of financial strategy but also convictions for investors.

One of the limits which thus appear in this SRI approach can be in the standardization of the concept itself. Limiting a responsible approach to common sense by excessive standardization could be a hindrance to a positive momentum and reduce the areas of application of the concept. Take the example of EHPAD (Accommodation Facilities for Dependent Old People, nursing homes), a major national cause for necessary investments that do not meet the SRI criteria and are focused on nonfinancial assets. However, they are part of the steps to improve the latter years of life of our elders. There is a contradiction and there will be others! Who owns the choice to integrate a notion of utility with investments or a notion of morals and ethics? Could not all asset classes one day be responsible finance? SRI is still largely unknown to French people. For Grégoire Cousté, General Delegate of the FIR, this is to expand this type of investment to the general public. All the big banks have SRI products, brochures, but the account managers do not market them enough yet. This is not yet a priority for the individual. Yet, the demand for SRI investment is increasing among savers. The weak link lies in the marketing, distribution, and training of counselors still marked by transactional marketing more than relational and explanatory. Stimulate supply by demand as we demand organic products. It requires interaction: create a dialogue between account managers and savers to make the products known, but, it remains, still, time-consuming.

The systematic search for the accumulation of profits and growth, long considered sufficient to give meaning to production and the capitalist system, clearly shows its limits and no longer appears to be able to bring perpetuation of the model. The French market for responsible finance is still an emerging market in search of its structure. But, with what levers, what products and what actors? All these elements coexist in certain vagueness and a rapprochement of facade; it is appropriate to analyze the essence and purposes to understand their necessarily differentiated methodologies and their perspectives of evolution. It is these legitimate questions and this deciphering that the second part of the book tries to treat.

Actors and principal products of responsible finance in the world

"A pessimist sees the difficulty in every opportunity; an optimist sees the opportunity in each difficulty."
Winston Churchill, English Politician (1874–1965)

Introduction

Pascal Bruckner, in his book *La sagesse de l'argent*,[1] reminds us that "Money is a promise that seeks wisdom. The expression must be understood in two meanings: it is wise to have money; it is wise to wonder about it. It makes every man a philosopher in spite of himself: to think well is also to learn to spend well, for oneself and for others. With money, no one is comfortable: those who think they hate it secretly idolize it. Those who idolize it overestimate it. Those who pretend to despise it lie to themselves. Problem craze, impossible disapproval. This is the difficulty. But if wisdom does not consist in attacking that very thing which seems to all the symbol of madness, what is the point of philosophy?" Similar to Victor Hugo, who sees a source of opportunities in all difficulties, and Pascal Bruckner, who is in search of wisdom, after questioning about responsible finance, its origins, and its prejudices, we will try to analyze the reality and the modes of intervention of responsible finance.

[1] Essai Grasset, Paris, 2016.

This part presents and puts the new tools and players in responsible finance into perspective, along with a panorama of current events that seeks to understand and enrich the debate. We are still not completely aware of what responsible finance is, and even less, *a priori*, what it can be sometimes used for. Concepts such as socially responsible investment, sustainable finance, solidarity savings, shared finance, micro credit, green bonds, crowdfunding, most of which are recent, are now, in one way or another, a part of responsible finance. However, many questions still remain, for example, is the "nebula" of socially responsible investment (SRI) a reflection of sustainable awareness or just a marketing trick? How to promote a management style that remains difficult for the general public to understand? Social relations seem to be increasingly turning toward a set of transactions, and therefore, would social functioning be increasingly based on a vast commercial network marked by a tendency to put a price on everything? Moreover, the flagship indicator for measuring economic performance only includes paid activities, while countless activities that are essential to the proper functioning of society (free Internet services, child and/or elderly home-care services, private garden crops, etc.) are excluded. If the paying transaction facilitates the choices of disposing of the sum, would this intrusion of the payment not constitute a form of attack on morality? Is it morally acceptable that everything can gradually be bought, starting from human organs to elections? The national and international financial sphere is also confronted with a growing complexity of questions ranging from the financing of the economy by nonbank actors to the growing role of technologies, behavioral and societal changes, and evolving and costly regulatory pressure.

"Disruption" is the trendy barbarism that all those who want to describe the changes we are experiencing are characterized by four key words: creativity, flexibility, reactivity, and proximity. Disruption is a mode of organization of work that corresponds to the industrial age, period when the time of presence in a production line was assimilable to the total production time. However, it becomes unsuitable in a world where robots do fragmented work. Thus, as Patrick Artus and Marie-Paule Virard pointed out in their book, "*Et si les ouvriers se révoltaient, Pour un nouvel âge du capitalisme*,"[2] the current dynamics of capitalism are producing not only a worrying increase in economic inequalities, but also a bipolarization of the labor market, with a very sharp increase in the gaps between

[2]Fayard Documents, March 2018.

highly skilled (high-tech industry, technological services to enterprises, finance, etc.) and low-skilled workers, the latter being increasingly confined to low-value-added services. However, one should not be overly optimistic about the virtues of the mechanism of "creative destruction," once described by Joseph Schumpeter. Indeed, far from promoting productivity gains and creation of better quality, more productive, and better paid jobs, this expected evolution is not corroborated by the observation of facts in developed countries. Rather, the latter shows a distortion toward unsophisticated and unproductive jobs in services, accompanied by a scarcity of jobs with intermediate qualifications. Patrick Artus and Marie-Paule Virard readily spoke of the bipolarization of labor markets, to describe this situation as "an imponderable," which Schumpeter had not envisaged. Similarly, the observations made by Alfred Sauvy, according to whom, since the beginning of the industrial revolution, the migration of agricultural workers toward industry, relayed by the "spill" of industrial jobs toward services since the 1970s, no longer operates today. These two remarks imply a necessary modification of the reasoning on this subject. In this phase of growing technological change, while increasing flexibility and reducing job protection still represent the dominant trends in order to face the exacerbated competition on the labor and goods markets, and to adapt to our economic model, it is necessary to revisit our way of thinking. All the more so, since sharing the wealth created is hardly favorable to employees in most of the advanced economies that do not have a powerful income redistribution system. Our economic system is increasingly evolving toward a model where shareholders strive to secure their dividends and return on capital at all costs, while employees bear an increasing share of economic risks on their shoulders. Patrick Artus and Marie-Paule Virard do not hesitate to use the expression "asymmetry of sharing" for OECD countries and note that over the last 20 years, real per capita wages have barely increased by 20% when the productivity increased by 37%, with a fall in the share of wages in GDP.

Disruption is management hit by an announced end of the hierarchy, where the diploma based on a transmitted knowledge is erased to the detriment of competence in a perpetually moving and increasingly politically unpredictable (Brexit, rise of populism, and protectionism ... weakening of the European institutions ...) international society. Without anticipating the recommendations of the third part, more than an upheaval of the firm's management, promotion of a better sharing of the wealth created by all stakeholders could constitute the solution to avoid the downward spiral of social regression and tensions. A management disruption has to be integrated in an economic context affected by automation and artificial intelligence (AI) destroying jobs. Many are concerned that the expected productivity gains may be reallocated to the rest of the economy.

Disruption in Europe and in Euro! In a recent column in *Les Echos*, Joseph Stiglitz, 2001 Nobel Prize winner for economics,[3] expressed concerns about a new crisis in Europe and the Euro and stressed, "The promoters of the single currency promised prosperity, but they refused to give the member countries the tools that would enable them to get through the crises. The impatience of the populations grows in the face of the intransigence of a Germany which continues to impose austerity on all. What if Italy breaks everything?" Considering that the Member States have lost the main adjustment mechanisms at their disposal (the interest rate and the exchange rate), according to Stiglitz, "Political leaders across the euro zone are increasingly paralyzed: voters want to stay in the EU, but they also want an end to austerity and a return to prosperity." Is that compatible?

It is within this economic and political framework of multiple constraints, of which the preceding list is not exhaustive, that responsible finance is trying to develop. The financial sector is still unstable. European banks, in particular, enjoyed sustained activity and growth in their earnings in 2017 despite low interest rates. However, there are still some gray areas with the rise in provisions for litigation, the limits of cost hunting, and the mapping of market risks and opportunities in the face of FinTech.

Sustainable finance, responsible investment (RI), (environment, social, and governance [ESG]) integration, impact investing, shareholder commitment, and so on are all practices that designate the economy's instruments and savings mechanisms. Would responsible finance be a way to invest without mortgaging our future? However, in the absence of legislation, investors must still make their choices and remain prudent if they want to invest their money in the right place based on their social and environmental values. It is not about reinventing finance, it is about making it more accessible. Finance has become the master of the world rather than its servant, though the loss of confidence generated by successive crises is not yet overcome. Under these conditions, what next phase should be expected for finance? In 2018, the trade resistance sought by the United States and China is not likely to restore the confidence that the 2015[4]

---

[3] *Les Echos*, newspaper website, *Chronicle*, June 28, 2018.

[4] Including: the Third International Conference on Financing for Development in Addis Ababa; the United Nations Summit on Sustainable Development in New York and COP 21 in Paris.

conferences had generated through a desire to regulate and harmonize financing flows.

In a world where financial innovation is stubbornly focused on creating differentiation to generate increased margins, the first imperative is therefore to try to present a more precise mapping by focusing, essentially, on new concepts. The four tables below (extracted and completed on the basis of our book *Ethical finance, Structures, Actors and Perspectives*), although simplistic, summarize the major developments recorded by the concepts and practices of more responsible finance:

1. Awareness

	1850	1936	1945	1970	1990	2010
Events	Industrial Révolution	Socialist Theses	Recon-struction	Crisis of the Welfare State	Globalization	Transitions: Energetic and Digital
Innovations	Discovering oil at sea, the electric train	Nylon, the tape recorder	The H Bomb	The Moon (69)	Internet	FinTech and new actors
Socio-economic facts	Paternalism	The rise of trade union-ism	National-izations	The cor-porate citizen	Deontology	Collaborative economy

2. Evolution of concepts

	1987	1992	2002	2010
Events	Brundtland Commission	Earth Summit, Rio: UNCED	World Summit on Sustainable Development, Johannesburg	Digital Transition
Concepts	Slowdown in economic growth	Sustainable development and CSR	Triple performance: economic, environmental, social	Impact
Actors	Scientists NGO	Nations, Governments	The company	Social networks, collaborative economy FinTech

3. Products and practices

Categories	Selection mode	Practices	Criteria	Expected Performance
Ethical Funds, Socially Respon-sible Funds, Impact invest-ments	• Negative criteria • Positive criteria	• Exclusion or selection based on those that best meet the ESG criteria • Participatory activism	• Benchmark • Introduction of extra-financial data • boycott	• Financial capital gains • Citizens or ethical values
Solidarity Funds	Positive criteria-oriented citizenship and /or solidarity	Partial or total distribution of the result solidarity-based	Citizenship Sharing Solidarity Excluded from conventional institutions	Yield • Social value

4. Outstanding amount of solidarity savings in millions of euros at December 31, 2016

	2010	2011	2012	2013	2014	2015	2016	2017
Savings collected by solidarity companies	293	348	395	429	474	444	502	550
• Unlisted shares	220	259	295	324	367	428	484	
• Other investments	73	89	100	105	107	16	18	
Solidarity banking savings	1,329	1,479	1,718	1,894	2,225	2,819	3,059	3,600
• Accounts on booklet	491	714	823	895	1,105	1,522	1,668	
• Term deposits	1	1	1	1	113	195	198	
• Collective investment • scheme	781		832	902	864	937	1012	

(continued)

(Continued)

	2010	2011	2012	2013	2014	2015	2016	2017
• Life insurance contracts	56	65	62	96	143	165	181	
Solidary salary savings	1,460	1,721	2,577	3,695	4,137	5,195	6,204	7,400
Total	3,082	3,548	4,690	6,018	6,836	8,458	9,705	11,550

The resources collected come from various solidarity investments. Savers can subscribe to these savings products via their banks or mutual insurance companies (solidarity bank savings), via their employers (solidarity employee savings), or directly by opting for one of the investments offered by solidarity companies (savings collected by solidarity companies).

As on December 31, 2016, more than 2 million solidarity savings products had been subscribed, mainly by individuals, of which €9.76 billion had been invested. About 63.5% of this stock comes from solidarity employee savings, 31.3% from solidarity bank savings, and 5.2% from investments offered by solidarity companies.
Source: FINANSOL's 2018 Zoom report on solidarity finance.

Concerning solidary savings, a French specificity born in the 1980s with the social shares and the CIGALES network,[5] we will limit ourselves to recalling only a few characteristics linked to France because of employee savings not widespread in other European countries. In the South of Europe, ethical finance and microcredit is discussed in more details. In Anglo-Saxon countries, proximity can be found in Social Impact Investing. For this solidary finance and/or solidary savings, which meet the expectations of a growing fraction of the French population wishing to give meaning to their investments, there is no standard definition in Europe. In the case of France, we could not ignore this form of savings.

In this second part, it is advisable to continue the process and analyze, only, the new products and actors joining the concept of responsible finance. However, our desire to broaden the field of international comparisons has run up against many problems, for example, the collection of statistical data because the concepts do not have standardized definitions recognized by different countries; the multiplicity of actors of different sizes (the association of a few members is confronted with large mutual

[5]The CIGALES movement, which emerged from the social and solidarity economy (ESS) in the 1980s, was built on the observation that it is possible for ordinary citizens to support those who embark on the great adventure of creating or developing a company.

This support takes the form of a financial contribution to the capital, but also of human support and appropriate advice. An outside glance allows the company to spend more serenely its first year of existence.

Today, all CIGALES clubs have their raison d'être in territories often marked by crisis; the link between the entrepreneur and the members of a club increases the viability of each project accompanied.

companies in banking or insurance); and various approaches (the militant discourse can move away from the scientific objectivity that we have tried to preserve to deal with our subject). Real subjects will appear during the presentation of the products and the modes of governance of the actors—militant representation and expertise of the latter risk management. How far can we go in the social economy while facing regulatory requirements of the financial profession measurement, creation of value, and performance of the partnership? We reassure the reader, the third part will advocate elements of answers to these multiple questions.

After Brexit, compared to other continental European cities, Paris is a major financial center, in terms of size and economic weight, likely to welcome new players in responsible finance.

Similarly, France's exponential growth in the FinTech industry represents a decisive attraction for international investors in financial technology innovations, digital and new products of responsible finance. New paradigms are needed: social and solidary economy, circular economy, governance rating, green financing. The integration of green and sustainable financing is a major issue addressed by international finance. Investors are withdrawing from coal and fossil fuels. At the same time, the green bond market is growing both in France and other countries. It is necessary to understand and decipher these new products and players. Are they able to influence future investment strategies?

This second part, after presenting the main players and their products of what we believe to be the current area of responsible finance, attempts to address innovations under the influence of digital change both for "traditional" financing and solidary finance.

If we are saying that the internationalization of the economy has shifted the world from a State/Nation model to a model seeking proximity, we are therefore looking for a responsible finance that would be more relevant for the economy as a whole. Local banking systems industrialized their production by adapting other banking companies. The so-called "solidary" finance branches of responsible finance then increasingly took over the financing of very small and emerging companies as in the middle of the 19th century and early 20th century. They now meet financial needs that the financial system rejected and for which they had neither the organizational model nor the appropriate know-how. Thus, in addition to the traditional profession of lender, the professions of guarantor (guarantee) on loan, venture capital, investment fund manager, or life insurance contracts have been added. Responsible finance professionals use all existing financial products except the speculative products responsible for the latest crises. The marriage between ethics and finance is no longer a naive utopia and is gradually gaining ground at all levels of the economy—from citizens' savings to sovereign wealth funds. It is possible to affirm that responsible finance, which has become universalist in terms of territories and professions, represents a relevant financial system even though it is not free from questioning and that is what we will try to analyze. We will try to present succinctly, without absolute exhaustiveness (please forgive in advance possible omissions) and on the basis of examples, these actors of responsible finance starting from research and promotion to give us an analysis of an evolving offer of products and services (section "Actors and product offerings in responsible finance: From research to promotion and distribution"). Then we will discuss the innovations of responsible finance under the influence of the new digital economy (section "Responsible finance and the digital economy").

Actors and product offerings in responsible finance: From research to promotion and distribution

Our goal here is to offer a critical analysis of the concept of responsible finance through its current inclusion in mainstream international finance. The challenge is therefore to understand whether the latter must be more structured to avoid the risk of dilution in the financial mass, to the detriment of its ethical identity, since finance itself systematically implies a search for performance. The development of responsible finance is at the origin of new businesses, new forms of cooperation between shareholders, and new tools. The "Doing good after doing well" model is increasingly being discussed today because of the growing weight of social investors (individuals, social economy enterprises, universities, foundations, institutions, etc.) who are often nonprofit-making and concerned with promoting a fairer and more sustainable economy that reconciles efficiency and well-being. This approach integrates social and environmental concerns in the choice of investments. Responsible finance brings together the players and their products impacted by this dynamic. The SRI approach, "a polymorphic and evolving concept that is sometimes difficult to grasp,"[6]

[6]Formulation by the AMF in a report mentioned above: "on SRI in collective management," November 2015.

continues its development and is gradually affecting all financial management. Today, criteria related to environmental, social, and corporate governance risks are commonly used by the financial community through socially responsible or sustainable development funds that select the best performing firms; exclusion funds (no investment in arms, nuclear, gaming or tobacco, etc.); or shareholder commitment, which consists, for investors, in demanding a stronger social responsibility policy from companies. In addition to these different approaches, other types of financial products are also developing under the names of mutual funds and solidarity financial products. The first consists in transferring part of the profits generated by the fund to charitable associations or NGOs, the second are savings products intended to finance solidary economy projects. Similar to other types of UCITS, SRI funds (SICAVs or mutual funds) are created by management companies and custodians (the latter having the task of monitoring the regularity of the UCITS' management decisions and the responsibility for safekeeping its assets). They are managed by management companies licensed by the "Autorité des marchés financiers" (AMF = Financial Markets Authority, in English). Management companies that offer SRI funds set up special mechanisms for these products, often creating an extra-financial analysis unit or sometimes entirely dedicated to SRI. SRI products are available through multiple banking and financial distribution networks. The offer to retail investors is increasingly expanding and SRI products are now offered by insurance companies, and even by new players (retail banking) and new banks (banking via mobile phones).

SRI fund management generally involves answering the following two questions regarding the identification of values and firms. The identification of companies eligible for a SRI fund is based on a combination of two complementary analyses.

1. Extra-financial analysis consisting of identifying and promoting companies' ESG best practices
2. Financial analysis consisting in identifying and evaluating the most attractive companies from a financial point of view.

Based on this dual reading, the fund manager buys or sells shares, bonds, or corporate debt securities to form the SRI fund. As with any investment, it must also take into account the macroeconomic context (changes in currencies, sectors of activity, etc.) in compliance with the constraints and management rules specified in the fund's prospectus (document describing the borrowing company's strategy and the characteristics of the proposed security).

For example, the Établissement de Retraite Additionnelle de la Fonction Publique (ERAFP), which manages €28.4 billion in assets in market value as of September 30, 2017, in accordance with the provisions of Article 76 of Act 2003-775 of August 21, 2003 reforming additional civil service pensions, has taken an original investment approach. This institution acts as a responsible investor (61.5% in bonds; 32.1% in diversification assets; 6.4% in SRI-oriented real estate).

Although SRI, mutual funds, and solidarity-based financial products are developing, they still remain niche markets (recall €746 billion of SRI outstanding in 2015, including €54 billion of "conviction," according to Novethic[7]; nearly €10 billion of solidarity savings outstanding in 2016 and €11.5 billion in 2017, according to Finansol. These data can be reported to the 4,400 billion assets under management in France).

If responsible finance has to increase its role, before presenting its current and future main broadcasters, let us ask ourselves: how does academic or private research contribute to this momentum? Which organizations contribute to its promotion? While there is often a consensus in the discourse to recognize the virtues of responsible finance, it is more difficult to put it into practice in order to ensure its sustainability. Our rapidly changing ecosystem must preserve the robustness and resilience of the financial industry while valuing a nonfinancial economy that combines long-term risk-taking with investor protection. This first section of the second part is divided into two subsections: the first is devoted to the presentation of the actors involved in promoting responsible finance. The second addresses the particular role of SRI.

Promoting responsible finance

Responsible finance is rapidly gaining interest among French people, but, as in case of economics, they have little knowledge on the subject.

[7]Fund category created by Novethic in 2016 to qualify the portfolios most impacted by the ESG assessment of issuers and their activities.

This finding was established at the beginning of 2018 by a survey conducted by Infopro Digital Etudes[8] among 1,000 people representing all categories of the French population (millennials = 18–34 years; xennials = 35–41 years; generation X = 45–52 years; baby-boomers = 53–72 years; and silent generation = 73 years and over). The main focus of this survey was to identify the knowledge of the topic. For the French, the concept is, mainly, assimilated to an action of public utility (13%) participating in economic development and business support. Almost 4 out of 5 French people would be interested in "useful" savings products (another way of describing responsible finance). According to the survey, 26% of them declare that they have directed their savings toward the "Plan d'Epargne en Action," the "Livret de Développement Durable et Solidaire," or life insurance, but only 5% have invested directly in "responsible" companies. For the French, the environmental impact of investment is the priority for 73% of them. Finally, one in three French people wait for a RI to give them a return of 3%–6%. The survey also reveals that the general public is still unfamiliar with this concept of responsible, sustainable, and useful finance.

We will address, successively, the following themes: clubs; some training, chairs, and academic research; committees, forums, poles; non-financial rating agencies; labels; ethical stock market indices; "ZinZins" or institutional investors; some promoters, and so on. Let us try to find our way with some examples!

Clubs

- The "Mines-Energy and Mines-Environment and Sustainable Development Clubs" of **Paris Mines Tech and Inter mines Paris, Saint-Étienne, Nancy**, an association set up in June 1983 within the framework of the law of July 1901 by the three alumni associations of the Mining Schools of Paris, Saint-Etienne, and Nancy, runs the classic alumni association activities (solidarity, school promotion, employment aid, magazines…) and specific activities such as organization of training sessions, conferences, and seminars dedicated to Sustainable Development and CSR (examples of topics covered, in 2009, "CO_2 emission rights: can financial sophistication serve

[8] Survey results reported by *Funds Magazine*, No. 112, April 2018, p. 12.

the protection of the planet?" "New businesses/New challenges," in 2010; more recently, on September 26, 2017, "How Sustainable Development is transforming finance."

- Sustainable Development Club of the **Association Française des Investisseurs en Capital (AFIC)**. AFIC is an association aiming at the promotion of private equity. It includes all the Private Equity structures set up in France. In December 2010, its sustainable development club published a document introducing Sustainable Development and implementing an ESG policy for private equity professionals.

Some training, chairs, and academic research

In France, it can be estimated that between universities and grandes écoles d'ingénieurs et de commerce, more than 50 courses at the "Bac + 5" level are oriented toward the Social Environment (ESG) and the ESS. Forum Responsible Investment (FIR)[9] has published a directory of initial and continuing training courses on RI in France. About 20 courses are listed in this directory ranging from a period of 3 hours to more than 300 hours as part of its Masters or MBA courses at universities or Grandes Ecoles. These figures should be compared to the Masters of Science, MBA, and all of the third cycles given by Universities and Grandes Ecoles exceeding 4,000 in number in France (more than 400 of which include the term finance). In the absence of homogeneous statistical data, research in social and solidary economies remains marginal in France. It represents less than 1% of the budgets. As for consulting firms, more than 200 one- to three-day ESG-oriented training seminars are offered to companies.

Associations

- "ADERSE" (Association pour le Développement et l'Enseignement de la Responsabilité Sociale de l'Entreprise) is an academic association founded in 2002 by François Lépineux (INSEAD), Arnaud Pellissier-Tanon (Paris I), and Yvon Pesqueux (CNAM), with the aim of promoting the theme of corporate social responsibility in

[9] www.frenchsif.org

higher management training courses and in the field of management research. Its president is Madame Véronique Zardet. Recognized by FNEGE as a French academic association for management sciences, ADERSE already has more than 150 members, most of whom are teacher-researchers from universities and "grandes écoles" interested in the subject.

- "Association Française de la Gestion Financière" (AFG) brings together all the players in the asset management industry, whether individualized under a mandate or collectively. Its members are entrepreneurial management companies or subsidiaries of banks or insurance companies. AFG's involvement in SRI is part of its broader action to promote long-term savings (employee and retirement) and the quality of assets (determined action in terms of corporate governance, etc.), levers for sound financing of the economy, and effective protection of savers' interests.
- "Les Amis de la terre" is an association for the protection of man and the environment, which notably campaigns on the responsibility of financial actors. It has a critical point of view on SRI and has developed an "eco-citizen" guide "Environment: how to choose my savings?"
- "Observatoire sur la Responsabilité Sociétale des Entreprises" (ORSE) is an association of large companies, portfolio management companies, professional, and social organizations that informs and reflects on corporate social and environmental responsibility, sustainable development, and SRI in France, Europe, and internationally.
- "International Network for Research on Organizations and Sustainable Development" (RIODD), created in 2006 and currently chaired by Mrs. Frédérique DEJEAN (University Paris Dauphine) is an association which:
  1. brings together researchers and people interested in research and determined to give it their support;
  2. is international, because the problems tackled are global in scope, even if they are at regional and local levels;
  3. is multidisciplinary in the social sciences (philosophy, law, economics, sociology, management, political science, communication, etc.), because the scope of the issues to be dealt with cannot be satisfied with a single approach or with the perspective of a discipline alone.

The association is a member of the National Platform of Global Actions for CSR which was set up by the Prime Minister in June 2013 and is placed under the responsibility of the Commissariat France Strategize. Within this platform, the RIODD is part of the "researchers and developers" cluster.

Committees, forums, poles

- Created in 2002 "Comité Intersyndical de l'Epargne Salariale," CIES comprises the CGT, CFTC, CFE-CGC, and CFDT Confederations (worker unions), and has set itself a goal, among others, of promoting SRI. It awards its SRI label to a certain number of employee savings funds. Among its objectives are the following: Facilitate all employees' access to employee savings, by offering "tools" for controlled and monitored employee savings products; promote socially responsible corporate behavior; obtain the most favorable legislation possible for employee savings, in strict compliance with the primacy of wages.
- "European Sustainable Investment Forum" (ESIF) is a European network dedicated to promoting the integration of ESG criteria in financial management, mainly through lobbying European institutions, publishing research reports, and organizing events to raise investor awareness of ESG issues. Based in Brussels, Eurosif is a nonprofit organization founded in 2001 to promote SRI throughout the Europe. It is the European reference organization for the development of RI practices. Every 2 years, Eurosif publishes a report on the SRI market in Europe. There are also Social Investment Forum (SIF) in the United States, Canada, Australia or Asia, Hong Kong. It organizes SRI Week every year.
- "FIR" was established in 2001 at the initiative of fund managers, social and environmental analysts, consultants, trade unionists, academics, and citizens. Since then, they have been joined by investors. It brings together fund management professionals, specialists in social and environmental analysis, consultants, trade unionists, academics, religious leaders, and citizens. Its objective is to lobby the various financial institutions to adopt RI practices, that is, to integrate nonfinancial criteria into various management methods. Their common concern: promoting SRI, ensuring that more investments integrate social cohesion, and sustainable development issues. FIR

is a founding member and stakeholder of the European network of RI forums, such as Eurosif.

- "Finance Innovation" (finance-innovation.org) is one of the seven world competitiveness clusters, out of the 71 approved by the CIACT (Comité Interministériel d'Aménagement et de Compétitivité des Territoires).[10] In France, the Finance Innovation division, specializing in innovation in finance, has FBF, the FFSA, the French Management Association, the CCIP, NYSE Euronext, the Paris City Hall, and the Île-de-France Region as its founding members. The Finance Innovation Global Competitiveness Cluster has been carrying out concrete actions to encourage and facilitate the development of innovative projects and research with high added value in the financial sector since its certification by Mrs. Christine Lagarde, Minister of the Economy, in July 2007.

About 350 projects led by startups, small and medium- sized enterprises (SMEs), large companies, and academics have already received the Finance Innovation Label of Excellence, and more than 1,000 companies have been supported. Finance Innovation is a true financial innovation cluster, with a network of 340 members from finance, technology, and the new economy, facilitating exchanges between all stakeholders in the financial ecosystem.

Very small businesses (SMEs) are still 90% dependent on bank credit and will be more affected by the prudential rules in force. The diversification of resources therefore remains a major challenge for them, and new financing solutions specific to them are emerging: participatory financing, new financing of trade receivables, dedicated products to optimize, and secure working capital needs…are gradually taking their place. These solutions contribute to the digitization of finance, strengthening of savings investment in companies, and extension of financing methods generally reserved for large companies to SMEs, modestly because they are still embryonic and little known, but usefully because they explore new

[10]Created in 1963, the Délégation à l'aménagement du territoire et à l'action régionale (DATAR) had a role of réflexion, impulse, and animation of the policies of the French State with regard to territorial planning. It has been replaced by the Délégation interministérielle à l'aménagement et à la compétitivité des territoires (DIACT), created by a decree of December 31, 2005. The latter has a wider field of action than the DATAR. Indeed, this development reflects the government's desire to promote the attractiveness and competitiveness of the national territory while pursuing a policy of solidarity toward fragile or outlying areas.

avenues. Finance innovation contributes to the dissemination and accessibility of these new financing methods through collective actions aimed at raising awareness, informing and supporting local companies in their search for innovative financing, whether complementary or alternative to traditional bank or private equity financing.

Nonfinancial rating agencies

Created in the late 1990s and early 2000s, nonfinancial rating agencies assess and rate the social and environmental responsibility and governance policies of large listed companies. Their ratings are mostly sold to SRI fund managers. Today, this sector has around 30 players located in Europe, North America, and Asia. These agencies work through the analyses of public documents, specific questionnaires, and meetings with company managers. Each has its own methodology, which does not simplify the response work of companies and the comparison between their different ratings.

In France, the main agency is Vigeo, taking over from ARESE in 2002, which had long been managed by Geneviève Ferone, a pioneer in social and environmental rating, specializing in corporate social responsibility, SRI, and development. In January 1997, Ferone founded ARESE, France's leading social and environmental rating agency for listed companies, which she chaired until June 2002.

On October 13, 2015 Vigeo, the French agency for the analysis of companies on ESG criteria, headed by Nicole Notat, merged with its British counterpart Eiris and is now called Vigeo Eiris.

- "Vigeo Eiris" (www.vigeo-eiris.com/fr)

  "We need to be a global player in an ultra-competitive market" explains Nicole Notat, Vigeo's President, before adding that "the very thorough analysis of this market very quickly showed that EIRIS was the best possible choice for us. We were compatible in terms of ESG rating methodology and culture, EIRIS also had an international influence and finally our synergies were strong since there was very little overlap between our two companies."

  Vigeo, the French company with 120 employees, with offices in Paris, Casablanca, Brussels, Milan, London, Tokyo, and Santiago de Chile, married the British company EIRIS, which has around 60 partners and operates in Australasia and the United States, in addition to its country of origin, through a dozen exclusive partnerships.

  The first was born in 2002, the second in the late 1980s. At a time when SRI took off 10 years ago, they each embodied two different

trends. Vigeo is associated with the Best-in-Class approach, that is,. a rating and management system that seeks to identify and select the best performing companies based on environmental and social criteria in each sector without exclusion.
EIRIS, which counts among its clients numerous religious foundations and congregations, has rather an image linked to the exclusion of sectors or activities for ethical reasons. "This is partly true," confirms Nicole Notat. "But our merger, which only took a few months, showed that we actually had common approaches since Vigeo responds to all of its clients' requests, including exclusion, and that EIRIS also does global rating. That is why we will very quickly be able to build a unique organization with a shared methodology." This could be done as early as 2016. Extra-financial rating is more than ever becoming financial and American: it is an intense symbol of the competition that is taking place in responsible finance with the takeover, in April 2019, by Vigeo Eiris' MOODY's agency.

- "Ethi Finance" (www.ethifinance.com)
  This is an independent extra-financial analysis agency specialized in the evaluation of corporate social responsibility (CSR). Founded in 2004, EthiFinance has become a European leader in the rating of small and medium-sized listed and unlisted companies. EthiFinance is an extra-financial analysis and advisory agency that assists its clients in managing risks and opportunities related to sustainable development. Since its creation, EthiFinance has developed tailor-made offers to meet the specific expectations of its clients, be they investors, companies, or organizations.
- "BMJ ratings," created by Pascal Bello in 1993, and a European market leader in sustainable development ratings (i.e., the agency is generally paid by investors and not by issuers) has been part of the Singer group since 2009.

Labels

From SRI to responsible finance, is the long march of investors to contribute to a better visibility of the SRI fund offer among investors, particularly individuals who show a growing interest in SRI, more committed? We have come a long way in the past 20 years. Between SRI, a confidential niche created in the 2000s, and the global responsible finance movement that mobilizes eminent insurers and pension funds, the scale has obviously changed. However, there was much dithering between rating agencies and investors. This was the case between the management company Amundi, a subsidiary of Crédit Agricole, and Novethic. Amundi preferred to boycott Novethic by turning to Afnor, another association, for certification. The dispute mainly concerned the methods of evaluation and awarding labels. In May 2012, the television program "cash investigation" castigated Novethic's SRI label in a report entitled "Green marketing: the big make-up," which revealed the presence of oil companies within funds labeled "SRI." In a report published in November 2015,[11] the AMF threw fuel in the fire. Great similarities between SRI and non-SRI portfolios left the financial regulator perplexed. This result is due to the Best-in-Class selection of capitalizations, which consists of selecting the firms with the highest social and environmental ratings in each industrial sector, including the most polluting. There is also a serious controversy over the evaluation of environmental and societal criteria. Although companies have no interest in lying under the Grenelle II law, their performance is nonetheless self-declarative. They can be assessed internally or by nonfinancial rating agencies, whose independence and reliability have often been criticized. Moreover, it must be recognized that SRI has often been suspected of "green washing," the Volkswagen affair and the control of CO_2 emissions from its vehicles continued investment in natural resource extraction. Despite repeated requests from the financial professions, there are still many steps to be taken to make SRI labels a quality signal identified by investors on all sides. The market had 366 funds managed by 71 management companies in September 2017. It is very difficult to know how many of them will experience labeling and for which funds! Nevertheless, we present you the main labels as follows:

www.novethic.fr The SRI Novethic label (•):

It is awarded to SRI funds whose management systematically takes into account ESG criteria. It attests to the impact that ESG analysis has on the composition of the portfolio. This Label does not address the financial characteristics of the funds; it is neither a guarantee of financial performance nor an incentive to purchase.

[11] AMF report (www.amf-france.org) published on November 26, 2015 on SRI in collective investment schemes. In addition to the stages in the development of SRI and attempts to define the concept, this report highlights the need for consistency, accessibility, and reliability of the information made available to investors.

- Novethic Green Funds label (www.novethic.fr)
  Launched in 2013 by Novethic, it allocates the funds to the finance companies which provide solutions to environmental problems. It guarantees investors the quality and transparency of the environmental characteristics of these funds and their contribution to sustainable development.
- Finansol label (www.finansol.org)
  It distinguishes solidary savings investments on the basis of criteria of solidarity and transparency. It guarantees investors that the fund contributes to the financing of activities with a strong social and/or environmental impact. The label also certifies the financial intermediary's commitment to provide its subscribers with reliable, regular, and clear information on the labeled savings product.
- CIES label (Comité Intersyndical de l'Epargne Salariale) labels SRI funds and employee savings funds (www.ci-es.oeg). The Comité Intersyndical de l'Epargne Salariale (CIES) was created by four trade union confederations (CFDT, CFTC, CGT, and CGC). Considering that it was not the responsibility of trade unions to manage funds directly, but was necessary to control and secure the use of employees' money managed by specialized and socially responsible bodies, CIES created a label for the product ranges offered by different management companies (banks, insurance companies, social protection groups, etc.). This label is an incentive for employees to choose these products and for union negotiators to retain these organizations.
- State labelsIn 2015, the Ministry of Ecology launched the Energy and Ecological Transition for the Climate (TEEC) label. Bercy (Designation of the place of the Ministry of Finance and Economy) followed in 2016 with its own 3-year SRI certification (www.lelabelisr.fr).
  a. State SRI labels
     1. AFG is an organization promoting the SRI label alongside the FIR. The first labels were issued in September 2016. At the end of September 2017, the amount of labeled funds outstanding exceeded €23 billion for 114 funds managed by 23 management companies. They are distributed by many banking and insurance networks in France and Europe, and many financial advisors. Decree 2016-10 of January 8, 2016 concerns the creation of this label requested by the profession. The accessory

decree completing the decree notes the creation of the specifications of this label by recalling the eligibility criteria and the labeling criteria divided into six pillars (considering ESG criteria; issuer analysis and rating methodology; integration of ESG criteria into the life of the portfolio; ESG engagement policy (dialogue and voting) with issuers; enhanced transparency; highlighting positive impacts on the development of a sustainable economy).

2. AFNOR's SRI label (www.certification.afnor.org) was also selected by the public authorities. This label meets the aforementioned specifications which integrate ESG practices in asset management and impact measurement indicators of the approach. In a press release dated August, 2016, Amundi declared that it was the first beneficiary of this AFNOR SRI label supported by the State for four requests made (concerning four funds: Amundi Crédit Euro ISR; Amundi Actions Euro ISR; Amundi Actions Europe ISR; and Amundi Actions USA ISR) representing 633 million assets under management.
3. Energy and Ecological Transition for Climate Label (TEEC) ensures that investments are directed toward financing the ecological and energy transitions. For savers, it is supposed to ensure the transparency and quality of the environmental characteristics of these financial products through the audit by a third independent expert entrusted by this Ministry to Novethic.

Though the transition is underway, responsible finance remains a minority movement. Let us hope that these recent tools promote its development and diffusion, but difficulties persist in terms of methodology, the labeling of moral principles and behavior, the holding of a monopoly on ethics, and the universality of concepts.

This list is not exhaustive and we refer the reader to the following two sites www.financefortomorrow.com and www.paris-europlace.com which published a brochure entitled "The sustainable future begins in Paris" for more details.

With the help of the official site www.economie.gouv, portal of the Economy, Finance, Action and Public Accounts and the dossier produced by FACILECO, financeforall.com (educational site on money and finance), let us look deeper at some actors and promoters of this responsible finance.

"Ethical" stock market indices

The major international nonfinancial rating agencies have formed partnerships with companies that produce stock market indices (Financial Times, Dow Jones) to create indices that bring together the companies with the best social, environmental, and governance ratings. Today, these indices are used more by these companies as a communication tool than by the financial community to build products or as a performance comparison tool. Companies that appear in one or more of these indices mention this in their "sustainable development reports."

- One of the main indices is, the *Dow Jones Sustainability Indices* (DJSI), built in collaboration with STOXX Ltd from scores provided by a Swiss evaluator, SAM. Worldwide, more than 2,500 companies are members of the various indices. For Europe, it is the Dow Jones Europe Sustainability Index (DJSEUR). The Dow Jones Sustainability Index (DSJI), the NYSE's global 30 stock index, was created in 1999. It classifies these values according to their CSR practices around three main directions: economic, environmental, and social.
- The *FTSE Group Indices* (Financial Time Stock Exchange, a joint group of the London Stock Exchange and the Financial Times) launched in 2001 are a range of socially responsible stock market indices (for Europe, for example, the FTSE4Good 50 Index appears alongside an index reserved for UK stocks, US stocks, and derivatives indices, etc.). The selection is based on the ratings of the English agency EIRIS (Ethical Investment Research Service) and includes exclusion criteria. The FTSE4Good index distinguishes the best performing companies worldwide in terms of their Sustainable Development policy (French companies include: BNP Paribas, Danone, Société Générale, SEB).
- The *ASPI Eurozone Index* (Advanced Sustainable Performance Indices), developed by Vigeo, is made up of 120 Dow Jones Euro Stoxx stocks with the best Sustainable Development performance. It also proposes US; UK; and Japan indices.
- *Ethibel Sustainability Index* (ESI) was launched in 2002 in partnership between the Belgian ethics consultancy ETHIBEL and Standard & Poor's. This index is concerned with the financial and societal performance of 198 stocks. It consists of a global index and three regional indices (ESI American; ESI Europe; and ESI Asia Pacifica).

- The *ECPI Range of Ethical Indices* (made up of three indices each grouping 150 firms: The ECPI Ethical Index Euro; the ECPI Ethical Index EMU; and the ECPI Ethical Index Global) managed by the European rating agency, E. Capital Partners, which studies a panel of 4,000 companies listed worldwide, mainly on social and environmental criteria.

  More generally, in France and throughout the world, it should be noted that nonfinancial rating agencies, such as the extension of the areas of responsible finance, have considerably extended their scope under the pressure of the development of SRI funds, whether or not based on conviction but, above all, because of the gradual integration of ESG criteria into asset management. In addition to the main indices mentioned above and the new environmental assessment indices, such as Trucost, South Pole Group, Carbone 4, several nonfinancial rating agencies have chosen to approach financial rating agencies or to offer additional assessments in order to meet the growing demands of issuers. Vigeo, known as Vigeo Eiris, has acquired Ethibel, Avanzi, and Eiris in addition to its operations in Morocco, Chile, and Canada. In addition to this, EthiFinance did not hesitate to approach the traditional Spread Research agency, leaving the classical rating oligopoly insensitive to this business expansion. Standard & Poor's entered into agreements with the British carbon and water footprint agency Trucost at the end of 2016. While Moody's has long used ESG criteria in its risk analyses, the agency did not hesitate to adhere to the UN-supported Principles for Responsible Investment (PRI) in 2016. In its credit risk analysis, the Banque de France, after experimentation, integrated this CSR theme. Another example is the creation of the new Euronext index in association with Vigeo Eiris: the "CAC 40 Governance." This thematic index, launched in March 2017, evaluates good governance practices based on three criteria: (1) the effectiveness of the Board of Directors, its composition, and its ability to deal with CSR; (2) internal audit and control, which is independent of the Board of Directors; and (3) the Board of Directors' independence.

"ZinZins" or Institutional Investors

Institutional investors (nicknamed "zinzins" or "large investors") are organizations that collect savings and place them on the financial markets.

These are mainly investment companies, pension funds (pension funds to finance funded pensions), banks (383 credit institutions in France at the end of 2015, including 160 traditional banks, 90 cooperative banks, 96 specialized credit institutions, 20 branches of banks outside Europe, and 18 Municipal Credit Banks) and insurance companies (365 insurance companies manage over €2,300 billion in financial assets), and collective investment schemes (Sociétés d'Investissement à Capital Variable et Fonds Communs de Placement). They are mostly long-term investors who only hold minority stakes (less than 10%) in the listed companies. The portfolio of institutional investors is broken down into different asset classes (at the end of 2015, equities represented 12%; bonds 72%; loans 2%; real estate 5%; alternative management, private equity, and infrastructure sharing the balance). Many institutional investors delegate the management of their assets to management companies with a defined mandate. The share of delegates thus represented more than 65% in 2015. Institutional investors are increasingly concerned to respect environmental and social criteria that allow their investments to be more and more in line with this search for meaning expressed by savers. In France, institutional investors represent over 70% of the SRI market. At European level, they account for 92% of SRI outstanding.

Some promoters

In addition to already mentioned bodies such as Novethic, the FIR belonging to the European Eurosif network, there are also SIF in the United States, Canada, Asia, and Oceania. For the record:

- *Novethic (www.novethic.fr)*
  This SRI research and expertise center created in 2001 is a subsidiary of the Caisse des dépôts et consignations. Thanks to its regular studies, it is today the main source of data on SRI in France in terms of statistics and analysis of market trends. An almost exhaustive list of SRI funds available on the French market can be consulted on its website. Novethic evaluates their extra financial characteristics. Ratings allow investors to find their way around.
- *Eurosif* (European Sustainable Investment Forum, www.eurosif.org) is a nonprofit organization based in Brussels and founded in 2001. According to Novethic, this network aims to promote the integration of ESG criteria in financial management by lobbying the European

institutions, publishing research reports (including a biannual report on the European SRI market), and organizing events to raise investor awareness for these issues.

- *Paris Europlace (www.paris-europlace.com)*
  It was created by the main institutions representing the Paris financial center to promote French financial players. It brings together and represents the diversity of players in the financial industry: issuers, investors, banks, insurance companies, financial intermediaries, and auxiliary professions. It intends to position Paris on SRI. In 2008, the Paris financial center launched an initiative in the field of sustainable finance with the signing of a "Responsible Investment Charter" completed in 2012 with "10 SRI and CSR proposals for Europe." These issues have been taken up in strategic priorities and at European and international levels, notably in the G20 meetings. With the COP 21 in Paris in December 2015, Paris EUROPLACE has taken three initiatives: (1) Organization of the "Climate Finance Day," to close the "Climate Week Paris," organized by UNESCO in May 2015, the priority objective of which was to mobilize the financial sector in favor of the fight against global warming in preparation for COP 21; (2) signature of joint declarations by Paris financial center players on climate change, both in May 2015 and June 2016 during the "2nd Business Climate Summit" in London; (3) Publication of a guide on the Green Bonds to demonstrate the commitment and expertise of French players in the field of green bonds. A final point to which we will return very largely in the next section.
- *French Financial Management Association (AFG)*
  The Association Française de la Gestion Financière represents and defends the interests of portfolio management professionals on behalf of third parties. Founded in 1961, it brings together all the players in the asset management industry.
  Its involvement in SRI management is part of its more global action to promote long-term savings (savings invested in shares, employee savings, retirement savings, etc.) and the quality of assets (corporate governance action in particular), levers for the proper financing of our economy, and the protection of citizens against the risks of life. French management companies are fully committed to this approach and adapt their offer to the concerns of their institutional and individual investors, by offering products corresponding to different degrees and types of commitment—SRI funds, integration of ESG criteria,

shareholder commitment, thematic investment, and son on—that share the values of sustainable development. The management players have also organized themselves to meet their clients' expectations and comply with the new legislative provisions on financing the energy transition.

- *Shareholder activism*
  Shareholder activism refers to the actions that many responsible minority shareholders take as owners of firms in which they own a portion of the capital. These efforts consist, on the one hand, of dialogue with company executives on issues of concern to investors and, on the other hand, of proposing and submitting to a vote, by proxy, resolutions containing the concerns in question. Socially responsible voting resolutions generally aim to guide corporate behavior toward greater levels of corporate citizenship, lead management to implement actions that will enrich the well-being of all the company's stakeholders and increase its financial performance over the long term. In France, we are far from the dynamism of the American "shareholder activism," however, a growing demand for shareholder democracy and responsible[12] finance appears, and those in spite of the presence of mechanisms of double voting and anti-BPO devices are obliging the abandonment of the principle of neutrality by the directions in the event of hostile takeover bid. In France, for example, in 2016, 45 external resolutions were tabled at the General Meetings of CAC 40 companies, including 33 by shareholders and 12 by employee shareholders. About 8 of the 45 resolutions were adopted, that is, 18% against 8% 2 years ago. Through written and oral questions from NGOs and minority shareholders at general meetings, negative votes were cast on resolutions relating mainly to the "say on pay"[13] (SoP), the capital increase, not conferring double voting rights, and the contestation of corporate officers. Transparency and

[12]According to the 2015 European Voting Result Report, which analyzed 788 listed European companies in 17 countries, including the SBF 120 in France. In total, more than 12,000 general meeting resolutions were examined with the rise in participation (62% as opposed to 61% 5 years ago), minority resolutions (15% in 2015 against 12% in 2008), and rejected resolutions.

[13]English wording meaning that listed companies must allow their shareholders to decide on the remuneration levels of their executives. In France, although favoring self-regulation as recommended by the ethical code of governance jointly defined by the Association Française des Entreprises Privées (AFEP) and the Mouvement des Entreprises de France (Medef), in 2014 CAC 40 managers were subject to the "Say on Pay" system, which introduced the concept of consultation on their remuneration.

accountability of leaders are increasingly guiding both public and corporate governance. There is a need to organize and regulate relations between managers and shareholders, even minority shareholders, and this in the name of the growing weight of societal issues where ESG criteria may well go from minority to majority.
The investment programs and responsible actors we have just presented certainly provide capital to private or legal persons who have difficulties raising funds through conventional channels or who are poorly served by conventional credit institutions. These institutions mainly include credit institutions, but also venture capital to finance social housing programs and the development of small businesses both in France and abroad. Responsible, sometimes solidarity-based, investments enable the various economic players to raise their standards of living, develop their own businesses, and create jobs for themselves and their fellow citizens. But the boundaries of responsible finance do not stop at these areas alone. They must integrate new areas that we will analyze in this section, areas that fall within the financial sphere but are also impacted by the digital changes that are sources of multiple innovations affecting the traditional business models of the banking profession. Does the profusion of tools, standards, and indices help attempt to import ethical values into finance? Wouldn't technology be able to drive the changes we are looking for in financial practices even faster?

- At the European level, initiatives are multiplying and in the first part of the book devoted to regulation, we have already had the opportunity to highlight the role of promoter that the European Commission plays, notably through its work. For the record, in May 2018, the Commission presented a package of measures as a follow-up to its action plan on financing sustainable growth. The package includes three proposals aimed at
  - Establishing a unified EU classification system of sustainable economic activities ('taxonomy').
  - Improving disclosure requirements on how institutional investors integrate ESG factors in their risk processes.
  - Creating a new category of benchmarks which will help investors compare the carbon footprint of their investments.

In addition, from 24 May to 21 June, the Commission has been seeking feedback on amendments to delegated acts under the Markets in Financial Instruments Directive (MiFID II) and the Insurance Distribution

Directive to include ESG considerations into the advice that investment firms and insurance distributors offer to individual clients.

The role of SRI: National and international panorama

SRI covers investment practices that consist in integrating sustainable development criteria into the management of financial assets with the goal of encouraging companies to respect these criteria in their business models, as well as in their relations with their economic partners.

In principle, philosophy, and implementation, SRI can therefore be seen as both a financing mechanism for ecological transition and a factor accelerating changes in production and consumption patterns, by choosing to finance, for example, only the most virtuous companies in terms of sustainable development. It appears as one of the action levers to be activated to encourage companies to adapt to advanced social responsibility practices.

The international panorama of SRI that we propose below was conceived by the reconciliation of the data communicated on the sites of Novethic, the FIR, and Eurosif.[14] We will present, successively, first French, then European, and world data for the leading countries.

SRI is a polymorphic and highly evolving concept whose scope is difficult to define. It covers different realities depending on the countries, approaches, and objectives defined. SRI is also a relevant method for validating stock selection in portfolio management. It makes it possible to invest in quality companies positioned for growth, which brings the investor closer to the real economy. Cross-functional, it aims to help company's all businesses combine economic efficiency with a positive impact on society.

AFG and FIR attempted to define SRI in July 2013, saying SRI "is an investment that aims to reconcile economic performance and social and environmental impact by financing companies and public entities that contribute to sustainable development regardless of their sector of activity. By influencing governance and stakeholder behavior, SRI promotes a responsible economy."

For Novethic, "Responsible Investment is a generic term that refers to the different approaches that consist of integrating environmental, social,

[14] www.novethic.fr; www.frenchsif.org; www.eurosif.org/sri-study-2016

and governance issues into financial management. When it is used in a structured and systematic way to select the securities of a fund to identify and finance the players in an inclusive, low-carbon economy, we speak of SRI funds, or SRIs. Thus, the indicators determining investment decisions are no longer solely financial, but combine the financial and nonfinancial performance of issuers (companies, local authorities, governments, etc.)."

According to www.vernimmen.net, SRI represents "the practice of socially responsible investing (SRI), which involves taking into account social, ethical or environmental criteria in addition to traditional financial criteria in investment and asset management decisions. This practice can take several forms, including investment in funds that refuse to invest in certain areas (tobacco or armament for example) or that use social/environmental ratings in their choices or in funds that seek to influence the decisions of companies in which they are shareholders in the sense of ethics or sustainable development. It can also take the form of financial products that contribute part of its performance to social or sustainable development projects. Although SRI still represents a marginal share of the amounts invested on the financial markets, this practice has been growing rapidly for several years."

SRI seeks to combine performance and risk management. The PRI, launched by the United Nations in 2006 (see Part I), represent a voluntary commitment to integrate ESG issues into investment choices. The integration of ESG criteria is part of a dynamics aimed at limiting exposure to regulatory, operational, financial, and reputation risks.

SRI consists of investing in investment funds that take into account, in addition to traditional financial criteria, the company's social and environmental behavior.

SRI corresponds to three major approaches:

1. Socially responsible or sustainable development funds: They evaluate a listed company by integrating social and environmental criteria (environment, social, ethical issues, governance in investment decisions, etc.) which are crossed with financial criteria to select the best performing companies from a sustainable development point of view in a portfolio.
2. Exclusion funds (also called "ethical investments"): More widespread in Anglo-Saxon countries, they exclude, for moral or religious reasons, certain sectors such as arms, gambling, tobacco, or even activities considered by their holders as dangerous for the environment, for example, GMOs, nuclear.

3. Shareholder commitment or shareholder activism: It consists, for investors, of demanding from companies a stronger social responsibility policy, either by asking them directly, or by exercising voting rights at general meetings.

SRI should not be confused with solidary savings, which consist of saving in activities with high social and environmental utility but not necessarily immediately profitable.

Multiple other approaches are possible depending on the weight of history and the sociocultural issues specific to each country, thus, one finds the Best-in-Class which retains the best performing companies financially and socially responsible in their sector of activity. Some take care to distinguish between ESG rating, that is, analysis from an environmental, social, or governance point of view that leads to an evaluation of the firm, and SRI, which corresponds more closely to the principles of sustainable development applied to the financial sphere. Vocabulary is important and French people are sensitive to sustainable development. They will therefore favor an SRI in their choices that will incorporate ESG criteria in its selection. They will select firms with ESG best practice through thematic funds, for example.

SRI in France

SRI is strongly growing on the French market. Management companies have deployed innovative offers to meet the demand of institutional investors for whom ESG criteria have become indispensable. However, if multiple surveys show a growing interest on the part of individuals to give meaning to their savings, this does not trigger a demand for SRI products. The plurality of terms and approaches (SRI, ESG, sustainable finance, useful finance, responsible finance, etc.) are difficult to understand. This complexity is probably one of the major obstacles to the development of SRI.

According to data provided by Novethic and the FIR, SRI already covered nearly €750 billion of assets under management in 2015, that is, nearly 25% of French management assets. In addition to the relevance of the ESG analysis, the fight against global warming was also promoted by the climate conference in Paris in December 2015. In 2016, Novethic introduced a new classification of SRI funds. This new concept of SRI conviction offers investors' portfolios built with strong and assumed ESG bias: these are the so-called Best-in-Universe, environmental and social thematic funds. It is on this dynamic segment of the SRI fund market that Novethic has focused its "Indicator" analysis since 2016. Far from the logic of volume, the goal is to focus Novethic's expert analysis on an innovative and promising market dynamics. In 2017, Novethic's 123 SRI conviction funds posted significantly stronger growth (+42.5%) than all 404 SRI funds distributed on the French market (+14%), accounting for nearly a quarter of total assets under management. Thematic funds constitute a large half of the SRI conviction offer and are predominantly environmental, even if funds on social themes are developing to a lesser extent. For 2018, sustainable development objectives (SDOs) will become an investment benchmark. The year 2017 saw the emergence of the first impact funds based on the MDGs.

SRI in Europe

The 7th edition of the SRI Study 2016 highlights the scale of SRI practices and trends in Europe and across 13 European countries.

The 7th Eurosif study on the SRI market in Europe reveals strong growth in, among other things, thematic investments, impact investing, and green bonds. Normative and sectoral exclusions continue to predominate in a dynamic environment that encourages such development, particularly, thanks to a political context that supports this growth, such as article 173 of the "energy transition law for green growth" of August 17, 2015 in France.

According to Novethic, Europe is the most active and dynamic RI market in the world with many SRI funds and innovative investment approaches. Yet the European SRI market is not a homogeneous whole. Consequently, ESG practices differ from one country to the other. Novethic examines the key components of the European market, as well as develops a case by case study of the main European actors. In November 2016, Eurosif, the European network for promoting SRI, published its 7th edition of its market study.

The Eurosif Market Study reveals double-digit growth for SRI. The growth ranges from 30% for stewardship (engagement & voting) to 385% for impact investment. SRI is growing faster than the broad European investment market (25%) with retail investors returning to the market (up to 549% since 2013).

1. *Sustainability themed investments more than double their growth*
   Sustainability themed investments grew by 146%, with the most assets under management in France at €43 billion. An indicator that investors are increasingly looking at climate sensitive topics such as energy efficiency and renewable energy.
2. *Exclusions still dominate*
   Exclusions are still the most popular SRI approach with over €10 trillion of assets under management, showing a 48% increase. Leading countries are Switzerland, with €2.5 trillion and the UK and Germany with almost €1.8 trillion. This is in line with a wave of divestments that has been fueled by the climate change debate.
3. *Norm-based screening remains a popular strategy*
   Norm-based screening has now become the second most significant SRI approach with over €5 trillion assets under management and a growth rate of 40%. France dominates with €2.6 trillion.
4. *Impact investing and green bonds continue their rapid growth*
   Impact investing is the fastest growing SRI strategy up to 385% with €98 billion, from only €20 billion in 2013. The Netherlands leads with over €40 billion. This growth is supported by the significant raise in Green Bonds.
5. *Policy tailwinds*
   Across all the surveyed member states, there has been a positive response to the EU legislative agenda on enhanced transparency and corporate governance which aligns with long-term sustainable investment. Examples include Spain and Italy who had policy developments which have driven a greater awareness of SRI across those markets. The pension fund disclosure requirements in Spain and the industry engagement with government in Italy on SRI have been important developments which have contributed to the growth in those countries.

Although there is still no European consensus on a definition of what SRI is, there are local efforts to clarify and define it. The objective of this effort is to increase the visibility of SRI among investors (Figure 1 and Table 1).

SRI: characteristics of some European examples

1. *Germany*: from sectoral exclusions to shareholder commitment
   Outstanding subjects to sectoral exclusions (weapons, nuclear, tobacco, etc.), the most utilized by fund managers, totaled nearly

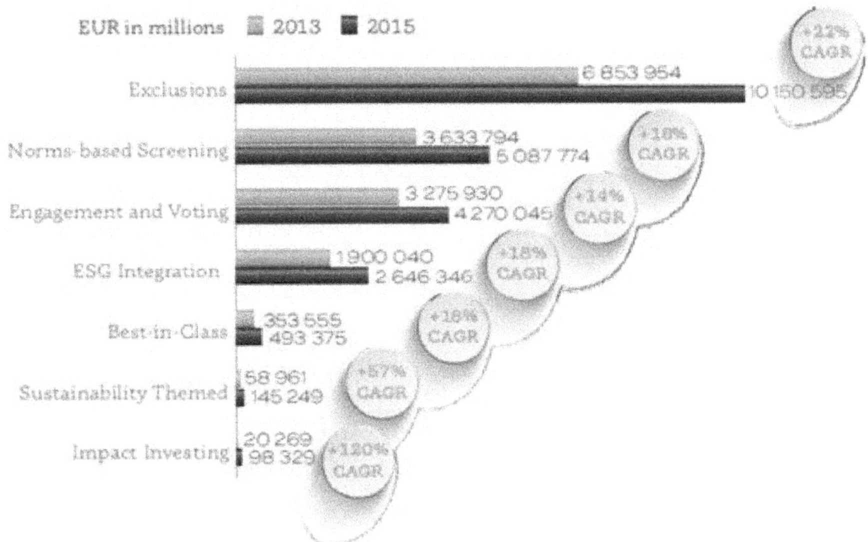

FIGURE 1. *Overview of SRI strategies in Europe*

€45 billion, compared with €25.6 billion in 2013 and only €17.1 billion in 2011. After exclusions, the most widespread SRI strategy in Germany is now voting and commitment, totaling nearly €32 billion at the end of 2015 (compared with €11.7 billion at the end of 2013. Institutional investors hold more than 85% of the SRI assets on the German market, which is marked by the importance of religious institutions and charitable organizations.

2. *The United Kingdom*
Shareholder engagement remains the dominant practice in the United Kingdom, followed by transparency on climate risk. Exclusions, mainly by religious congregations and foundations, are the third most common strategy. Best-in-Class, thematic approaches, and normative exclusions are only poorly developed in the UK SRI market.
3. *Switzerland*
The results of the 2018 Swiss Sustainable Finance Survey on Sustainable Investment speak for themselves and bear witness to the growth of sustainable investment in Switzerland:
   a. Sustainable investment up 82% to CHF 390.6 billion

TABLE 1: *A total sum of each individual strategy per country and the total of all strategies grouped together without overlap*

Countries	Best-in-class	Sustainability themed	Norms-based screening	ESG integration	Engagement and voting	Exclusions (all)	Impact investing	All strategies combined
Austria	8,153	271	7,920	1,363	3,791	42,736	323	52,184
Belgium	17,542	275	50,426	90,384	45,645	253,946	340	315,900
Denmark	15	5,232	261,776	63,149	227,651	305,109	31,500	118,376
Finland	439	656	111,868	44,210	46,711	138,422	444	67,978
France	321,984	43,065	2,650,582	338,170	38,500	666,215	1,138	3,121,081
Germany	21,088	8,157	15,379	27,733	31,880	1,803,473	4,763	1,786,398
Italy	4,058	2,064	565,607	45,008	43,303	569,728	2,927	616,155
Netherlands	56,645	37,114	936,399	440,695	726,314	1,123,133	40,791	991,427
Poland	2,717	3,762	2,769	–	–	2,769	34	5,998
Spain	2,535	300	24,003	8,283	10,455	123,516	267	95,334
Sweden	10,967	2,315	378,189	358,520	444,719	714,638	1,421	791,739
Switzerland	38,866	21,017	75,051	92,876	77,345	2,536,014	9,818	1,527,582
UK	8,368	21,022	7,806	1,135,955	2,573,731	1,870,896	4,564	1,555,328
Europe (13) in € million	493,375	145,249	5,087,774	2,646,346	4,270,045	10,150,595	98,329	11,045,479

Source: European SRI Study 2016 (Bi-annual report, next publication November 2018). *www.eurosif.org*.

b. 92% increase in SRI funds held by institutional clients and 38% for private clients

> *"We perceive a new interest on the part of institutional actors to participate and communicate on sustainable investment." From ESG integration to impact investment, sustainable finance comes in various approaches. Excluding so-called "sensitive" sectors (tobacco, nuclear, weapons, etc.) is currently the most popular strategy. There are also new efforts among institutional investors, such as the intensification of shareholder activism and the implementation of commitment policies to build best practices in the profession. Private Banks are beginning to offer a sustainable investment offer aimed particularly at Millenials for whom investment decisions are a way of expressing their social, political and environmental convictions. "75% of private clients are interested in sustainable development and this proportion rises to 88% among Millenials,"* says Claire Douchy, SRI and philanthropy manager at Société Générale. See previous section on taxation (end of Part I)

4. *The Netherlands*

The SRI market in the Netherlands has become increasingly mainstream. Levels of SRI implementation tend to vary according to market sectors—banks, pension funds, or insurance companies—but there are also interesting variations within each sector.

The SRI market in the Netherlands is rather fragmented. The 30 biggest insurance companies and 50 largest pension funds manage assets for over €1,370 trillion in total and therefore have a big impact on the financial services industry.

[See previous section on taxation (end of Part I)]

5. *Italy*

Institutional investors continue to lead the Italian SRI market, for the most part composed of a few large insurance companies. At the end of 2015, the total assets managed by institutional investors in Italy (insurance companies, pension funds, mutual funds, and wealth management) amounted to about € 1,400 billion. The market is mainly driven by a few big players, in particular insurance companies. Indeed, Italy represents one of the top four insurance markets by GWP at European level.

6. *Sweden*

   In 2015, a net total of €9 billion was invested in investment funds. During 2015, total fund assets under management in Sweden increased from €27 billion to €353 billion. Most of the Swedish financial institutions can be considered mature SRI players as a large number of asset owners and asset managers have been active in the Swedish SRI space for more than 10 years. Almost all of the large institutional investors in Sweden have some form of policy for sustainable, responsible, and/or ethical investing in place and they constitute the majority of the leaders in this industry.

   In summary, the most significant trend in the European SRI market is in thematic investments. In 2015, they recorded the highest growth rate (+146%). While they can focus on social themes, the international mobilization in favor of the climate at COP 21 has strongly contributed to the growth of green investments, in particular on the theme of renewable energies and energy efficiency. However, exclusion for controversial activities remains the most common strategy in Europe, ahead of ESG integration or shareholder engagement.

SRI around the world

Every 2 years, the Global Sustainable Investment Alliance (GSIA) publishes a report compiling global RI figures. The report is the result of collaboration between regional RI forums, including the European Eurosif, to which Novethic provided data on the French market. The latest report, published in 2017, shows that investments integrating environmental, social, and governance criteria reached $22,890 billion at the beginning of 2016, an increase of 25% since 2014. This subsection on the global SRI landscape focuses on the main features of North American and Asian markets.

1. *Northern America*

   The *American* SRI market has a certain history: the first American SRI fund, Pax World Fund, was created in 1971, some 10 years before the first French fund of the same type. Today, the definition of SRI is very broad and the outstanding amounts recorded include very diverse RI practices, hence the difficulties in comparing outstanding amounts. The SRI market in the United States is characterized by a strong involvement of institutional investors, primarily pension funds. According to US SIF, the US FIR, the volume of SRI outstandings more than doubled between early 2012 and early 2016. Over the 20142016 period, the market grew by +33%, from $6,570 billion at the beginning of 2014 to $8,720 billion at the beginning of 2016. Thus, SRI represents more than 20% of assets under management in the United States. This growth is strongly driven by institutional and private investors, who are increasingly demanding products that incorporate ESG criteria.

According to US SIF, until 2017, two main practices dominated: ESG incorporation and shareholder resolutions. The first includes the selection of issuers on ESG criteria, the exclusion of companies operating in particular sectors (alcohol, arms, tobacco), and/or having condemned commercial practices (presence in Sudan, etc.). The outstanding amounts concerned represented more than $8,100 billion in 2016 and covered not just open, dedicated, and indexed funds (Exchange Trade Funds [ETFs]) but also private equity funds, real estate, hedge funds, and so on. The second category, shareholder resolutions, corresponds to the shareholder commitment to change the ESG practices of companies. The year 2017 saw the election of a new Chairman change the orientations, by supporting fossil energies and renouncing the Paris agreement.

2. Canada

SRI is a concept that emerged in the 1980s and focused on the exclusion of certain sectors. Today, shareholder activism, the integration of ESG criteria, and the selection of portfolios of well-rated companies based on these criteria are the most widespread. Canada also has the particularity of having significantly developed community investments and sustainable development venture capital.

Shareholder activism is the most widespread strategy and concerns nearly 87% of SRI assets. The main issues of shareholder engagement were executive compensation, respect for human rights, and greenhouse gas emissions. The ESG integration concerns 77.5% of SRI stocks, while normative exclusions and sectoral exclusions (notably the exclusion of controversial weapons which is not subject to a legal obligation in Canada) are applied, respectively, to 56% and 51% of Canadian SRI Stocks.

In its latest report published in 2015, at the beginning of 2014, the Association pour l'Investissement Responsable (AIR)[15] estimated the amount of SRI assets under management at $1,000 billion, which represented a growth of 68% compared to 2012, and 30% of total assets under management. With 81% of the market, pension funds represent the largest share of the Canadian SRI. The size of the outstanding amounts should be put into perspective insofar as all the assets under management of these pension funds are recognized by RIA as soon as they adopt a RI approach (ESG integration, shareholder commitment, exclusions, etc.) for at least part of their portfolio.

3. Asia

There are many differences in a scope and actual development levels of the SRI market between Asian countries. SRI is a kind of approach that considers the environmental and social impacts of investments in financial socially responsible investments in Asia analysis. Consequence of SRI is two forms of returns for investors: financial return and added value, based on social, environmental benefits and nonfinancial management of risk.

Western patterns have been inspiration for many actions taken on the internal market in Asian countries. Globalization and its cultural, social, and financial impacts support global growth in the popularity of SRI. Therefore, the concept of corporate social responsibility quite freely settles among Asian companies and financial institutions which are signatories of the UN PRI Principles.

The climate change and environment protection will be one of the crucial challenges for adopting new solutions in the Asian market. SRI may help catalyst investor's activities in this problem, which is now mostly driven by religious attitude.

[15]The Responsible Investment Association (RIA) is Canada's membership association for RI. Members include mutual fund companies, financial institutions, asset management firms, advisors, consultants, investment research firms, asset owners, individual investors, and others interested in RI. Our members believe that the integration of ESG factors into the selection and management of investments can provide superior risk-adjusted returns and positive societal impact. The RIA's purpose is to support the RI activities of its members; promote and support an integrated reporting framework in which there is standardized disclosure of material ESG information; promote the integration of ESG factors into investment analysis and decision-making processes; promote the practice of responsible investing in Canada.

Unlike Northern America and Europe, SRI in Asia is largely driven by demand from individuals. Indeed, there are very few ESG mandates except for a few Japanese and Korean pension funds motivated by a long-term vision.

The growth of SRI in Asia is driven by an increase in the investment capacity of regional players and international investors. However, the lack of reliable ESG data has often been cited as a constraint to the development of SRI in Asia. Nevertheless, there has been an improvement in corporate transparency on ESG issues and exchanges in the region are mobilizing to provide companies with tools to improve their ESG reporting. Singapore was the first Asian stock exchange to decide in 2014 to introduce ESG reporting requirements for listed companies, followed by Taiwan in 2015.

The importance of environmental issues in Asia, such as climate change, water, and energy, as well as the weight of regulators, contribute to the development of thematic investments, and in particular green investments. Assets under thematic management grew by 56%, from $886 million at the end of 2011 to $2.1 billion at the end of 2013.

During 2015, AsRIA (members of the PRI) launched several initiatives, such as Private Equity ESG Initiative or AIGCC (Asian Investor Group on Climate Change), aimed at raising awareness among investors of all types (institutional investors, management companies, private equity companies, etc.) of the risks related to climate change, and more broadly on ESG issues, so that they are able to take them into account in their investment strategies.

The Green Bond market in Asia is beginning to emerge and expected to rapidly grow, driven by the growing appetite of investors and the support of regulators who must respond to a dual challenge: fight climate change and its impacts on the environment, and set up financing mechanisms for infrastructure development.

4. The Japanese SRI market

It started in the late 1990s with the launch of the Nikko Eco Fund in August 1999. The Japanese SRI market, which experienced a period of stagnation at the beginning of 2010, then a phase of decline until 2014, is now undergoing a second wind.

The amount of SRI outstanding at September 30, 2014 was $8 billion, compared to a $10.2 billion 2 years earlier. The majority of the SRI market in Japan is held by individuals. SRI in Japan is largely dominated by impact investing and microfinance funds (73.8% of outstandings), particularly in the fields of education, sustainable agriculture, health, and the environment (green bonds, energy efficiency, and the environment).

In early 2015, the Japanese stock exchange published a governance code for listed companies that came into effect in June 2015. This code provides for reporting on issues and improving the transparency of information for stakeholders.

Rest of the world: South America and Oceania

SRI in South America is beginning to emerge, thanks in particular to initiatives that LatinSIF, is multiplying to raise awareness of ESG issues not only among investors but also among companies and regulators. To restore investor confidence affected by issues such as deforestation, social inequality, and corruption. The most advanced country would be Brazil.

According to the latest survey by Responsible Investment Association Australasia (RIAA), an organization that brings together Australian and New Zealand SRI professionals, the Australian RI market experienced very strong growth in 2014. It now represents 47% of assets under management in Australia and stood at $633 billion at the end of 2015. The New Zealand market is more modest and recent.

Pension funds remain the main drivers of the market growth, but the concern of individuals for the management of their savings is growing, particularly since the campaigns of activist groups on the disinvestment of fossil fuels. The RIAA thus believes that the demand from individuals is real and that it will certainly be the driving force behind the growth of SRI funds in the years to come.

Responsible finance and the digital economy

Global finance has entered a new field, disrupted by emerging markets and technologies. The digital transition, that is the implementation of technologies based on applicative programming interface,[16] big data, artificial intelligence, the Internet of things, or the blockchain, has already

[16]In computing, API stands for Application Programming Interface, translated into French as interface de programation applicative ou interface de programation d'application. The

found multiple applications in the financial sphere. Responsible finance is not immune to this digital evolution, which the time being does not seem to have had all its effects on market finance, whereas retail banking is experiencing significant disintermediation and beginning of the disintegration of its economic model, to an extent where the question of bank profitability is becoming a concern. Despite a good resilience, the major French banks continue to destroy value with a ROE of 6.3% in 2017, which does not cover the cost of their capital while the average of their main competitors is higher. Under the observation of investors and regulators, French banks sort through activities with low profitability.

In this context, as you may have understood, for us the term responsible finance means not a limited field where investment is practiced, with goals of responsibility (what is often called SRI). Our perception is more global: responsible finance is a changing financial system that contributes to responsible growth by enabling efficient financing of the economy while reducing system instability and protecting the individual and collective interests of savers and investors, hence the need to expand and analyze these new scopes. A new economy where, often, the value of use supplants property, where sustainability prevails over property, and where cooperation would tend to surpass competition. The rules of the world economy are evolving and new paradigms are being established under the name of collaborative projects such as crowdfunding, car-sharing, contributory production of green energy, or 3D printing of various objects, often within the framework of self-managed organizations. In addition to the transformation of the organizational modes of our society, these collaborative local authorities contribute to democratizing the world economy, making action sustainable, and reduce income disparities. Are we moving toward a hybrid economy shared between the competitive market and the collaborative experience? Is this first observation likely to have an impact on finance? To progress in our approach marked by the search for meaning and weight of new technologies, we will be interested in the new actors and instruments of responsible finance (decarbonization, green bonds, etc.), then, we will try to understand how the digital transition (from Blockchain to FinTech) could amplify the emergence of this same responsible finance. Competitive intensity exacerbated on

---

API can be summarized as an IT solution that allows applications to communicate with each other and exchange services or data. It is actually a set of functions that facilitate, via a programming language, access to the services of an application.

the value chain by the Payment Services, Directive 2 and FinTech, the ultra-standard framework of financial regulation, not to say intrusive or sometimes counterproductive, the continued presence of low rates (but for how much longer!), not to mention cyber security and geopolitical tensions, all these findings can only verify the Chinese proverb, *"The only certainty we have is uncertainty."* In these conditions, it is necessary to react and to quickly lead a transformation of neoclassical finance toward more efficiency and more responsibility. The success of such a challenge depends on the responsiveness, agility, and efficiency of the players. New digital technologies should play a valuable role in this development. So much so that the banking supervisor of the European Central Bank considers that not all banks are well prepared for a scenario of rising rates against the backdrop of new competition from *"FinTech."* In an article published on the website of the newspaper *Les Echos* on 9 October, journalist Thibaut Madelin reports, as the ECB's Division Director, Korbinian Ibel, said when presenting the results of a stress test of the largest banks in the euro area,[17] *"Poorly modeled deposit stability could lead to significant losses in an environment of rising interest rates linked to lower transaction costs than in the past thanks to online banks… Or if Fin Tech arrives and attacks the market."* Indeed, FinTech companies can be more agile than traditional banks and thus reduce their deposits. So, are the FinTech companies, friends or foes of the banks? Even in an attempt to answer this last question, we really remain in uncertainty. Why? Journalist Sharon Wajsbrot in her article in *Les Echos* on October 18, entitled *"La création de Fintechs au plus bas,"* recalled that *"the creation of financial start-ups is slowing down in Europe and the United States. An Accenture report estimates that the revolution promised by these actors is at a standstill… After the euphoria comes the decline of regime. According to data from the Tracxn start-up analysis platform, the number of start-ups in finance fell from 32 in France in 2016 to 82 in 2015 and over 100 in 2014. The phenomenon is not hexagonal, in the United States; only 500 Fin Tech companies were born in 2016 against more than a thousand in 2015… ."* Without succumbing

[17]Of the 111 European banks tested by the institution, 60 are well equipped for a 2% point rate hike scenario. But 51 are less so and most of them have been invited by the supervisor to strengthen their own funds by next year. As a reminder, the ECB's key rate has been set at 0% since March 2016, historically low; it should evolve during 2018 leading to an increase in margins for traditional banks, but with a perverse effect on the value of their own funds.

to the prevailing pessimism or to the fascination of technology, we will try to make a precise point on the changes taking place.

Two subsections structure this section of Part II. In line with changes in the scope of responsible finance, we will deal successively with the following issues: impact investment, network data processing, artificial intelligence, FinTech, and the questioning of the banking monopoly (see section "From impact investment, to network data processing, AI, and FinTech: The challenges of the banking monopoly"). Then we will explore the recent innovations of a plethora of digitized services (see section "A plethora of digital services for responsible finance, but for what real subject?").

From impact investment to network data processing, AI, and FinTech: The challenges of the banking monopoly

The combination of social networks and digital revolution is gradually leading society to adapt to a new economic model based on collaboration in which the use and sharing of common goods play an increasing role. From there, to announce prematurely, a great changeover and the end of capitalism, there is a step not to be taken. However, there are signs that we are entering a world where we are increasingly learning to live together and interdependently beyond the markets. If capitalism is to survive for a long time to come, the beginning of its weakening lies in the fact that its theoretical foundations provide no answer to the *"indissoluble relationship between economic activity and ecological constraints… the dynamics that govern the earth's biosphere are mere externalities for economic activity."*[18]

In addition, another source of its weakening, the Internet of things invading our society (measuring pollution, fire prevention, forecasting weather conditions for agriculture, monitoring production methods and shipments, sensors in medicine implanted in the human body monitor vital functions, etc.). Capitalism is, therefore, well attacked on a second front relating to new technologies and in particular the Internet of things

[18] Excerpt from the introduction to the book by the essayist economist Jeremy Rifkin entitled *La nouvelle société du coût marginal zéro*, Babel collection livre de poche diffusée en France par Actes Sud, February 2016.

associated with big data in order to amplify communication and productivity. An alliance that can significantly reduce the marginal cost of producing and sharing many goods and services in all areas of market and nonmarket activities.

More specifically, with regard to our subject, finance, the dynamics of the alliance of networks and technologies brings proximity and the progressive effacement of intermediaries to reinforce agility and efficiency. This "other" finance could be able to satisfy the financial needs of 21st century companies, regardless of their size. However, the question remains, next to the banks or in their place? We will try to answer this delicate and sensitive question in the third subsection Banks and FinTechs: antagonisms or synergies?

As Cyrille Antignac and Bernard Attali pointed out in their book *L'investissement à haut rendement sociétal, la révolution de l'impact investing,*[19] referring to the impact investing[20]: *"The expansion of asset classes under management with social and environmental returns is under way. The surge of this type of new and socially constructive investment heralds the era of the conscientious investor. While the financialization of the economy is oriented towards the short term and unproductive speculative investment, with cyclical effects on asset values unfavorable to the stability of the world economy, societal investment with a high meaning to long-term productive investment with a high ethical value—superior to SRI—alone capable of creating long dynamics."*

To share this conviction and this analysis of the committed evolution of finance, we will therefore tackle fields as diverse as micro finance, characterized by a majority of low-value files, most often involving disintermediation, and then, at the other end, we will examine climate transition financing, requiring massive investments in the framework of more conventional products. Subsection 3 will have the opportunity to deepen the presentation of innovative engineering models based on new sources of financial disintermediation, sometimes by the digital economy. Subsection 2 will ensure the interface and the passage between the existing and the digitized future.

---

[19]Collection: les essentiels de la finance Revue Banque édition, Paris December 2016.

[20]Or impact investment, defined by JP Morgan as "investment in socially innovative and commercially competitive unlisted companies designed to produce a return on investment."

Social impact investment, decarbonization, microcredit

- In France, *impact investing*, which can be translated as "social impact investment," can concern the financing of social and solidary enterprises within the jurisdiction of the law (associations, mutual societies, cooperatives, commercial enterprises with social goals) or other enterprises with a strong social impact. Generally speaking, social impact investment can be based on conventional or nonconventional sources, ranging from traditional venture capital funds to microcredit. More recently, impact private equity funds have been developed and marketed to institutional investors. In May 2017, the AFIC Impact Club,[21] formed within the Association Française des Investisseurs pour la Croissance, indicated that its members managed €1.3 billion of investments based on the dual objective of financial performance and impact, the measurement of this impact and an active commitment to entrepreneurs. The subscribers to these funds include Caisse des Dépôts, Bpifrance, Crédit Mutuel Arkea, CNP Assurances, ERAFP, AG2R La Mondiale, Mirova, Crédit Coopératif and Natixis. The companies financed work in integration, microfinance, social real estate, renewable energy, recycling, or are located in areas served. The impact indicators published by management companies include, for example, the number of integration jobs created, number of hectares of forest preserved, number of tons of waste, water or CO_2 avoided, quantity of renewable energy produced, number of microentrepreneurs supported, minimum wage level in companies or number of visits to clinics financed, number of companies run by women, or number of people who have had access to financial services. Institutional investors are themselves launching investment funds dedicated to social impact. In 2013, Axa created a €150 million funds, and Aviva France is investing €30 million in the social economy through the Impact Investing France fund. This trend is part of a wider European movement. Major insurers such as Prudential, Zurich Insurance Group, and Legal & General have made significant commitments in terms of impact investing.

[21]About 15 management companies, members of AFIC (Association Française des Investisseurs pour la croissance, ex association du capital risque) representing more than 400 companies with a strong social impact, currently form this club within this association. AFIC Impact Club members include Alter Equity, Arkea Capital, Citizen Capital Nef, Capital Ethique, PhitrustXAnge, and ImpactInvestisseur.

In another area, and to support the transition, the change in the ESS in France in 2016, Caisse des Dépôts, in collaboration with several investors, launched the NovESS fund, which, with an initial closing of €60 million attracted investors, such as BNP Paribas, BNP Paribas Cardif, CNP, Crédit Coopératif, ERAFP, IRCANTEC, Union des mutuelles régionales (UMR), and Mutuelle Nationale Territoriale. This fund has a double objective, namely to reinforce the financial solidity of associations, cooperatives, mutual companies, commercial companies, or other ESS-oriented foundations; and to encourage the development of ESS for companies in change of scale having 6 years of activity (the amount of the possible investment is between €1 and €5 million) or companies in a growth acceleration phase having 3 years of existence (possible investment between €100,000 and €600,000). The fund targets sectors where investors have identified a significant leverage effect, allowing the change of scale and the structuring of new sectors: the health and medicosocial sector, energy transition, short circuits, or circular economy. The first investments were made at the end of 2017.

Some financial innovations for climate transition

We approach the theme of decarbonization from the angle of necessary awareness acting with some examples of actors and products essentially for the case of France. It is important to remember that without finance, there is no future for the sustainable economy. Responsible finance and its forms: solidary finance, microcredit, community savings, SRI, and so on, have been fundamental subjects for the sustainable economy for several years; environmental finance has been in *Vogue* since early 2000s.

- **Context and regulatory developments**

Several factors have led international finance to gradually integrate the elements of sustainable development and CSR into its financing practices, for example, risk analysis and due diligence have led the various financial professions to integrate new regulations into the financing of operations and to innovate, both in the products offered and in asset portfolio management methods. The challenge of climate change does not escape this evolution and is probably one of the major challenges of the 21st century. The financing of the transition to a carbon-free or rather low-carbon economy implies, after awareness raising, setting up an overall process likely to accompany this so-called "green" finance. It is no longer possible to wait and see things differently, we are an informed generation about the risks involved and the measures to be taken, probably the last to be able to act to preserve the next generation. Solidarity can save us—solidarity against the fear of the other or the temptation to withdraw. Of course we hate bad news, so we hate anticipating because it pushes us to action.

Despite an international context marked by the position of the President of the United States on the climate to withdraw his country from the Paris agreement (COP 21, December 2015), this situation has hardly affected the strategy of international investors if we believe the position of major Northern American pension funds such as the Californian funds Calpers (retirement of civil servants) or Calsters (retirement of professors) and the mobilization of new countries, China, India, in favor of the fight against global warming. On the contrary, their mobilization seems to have increased to include their management in the "2°C" trajectory in order to keep global warming below this level. European investors are even more motivated, as are their French counterparts, for whom this necessary awareness was amplified on June 30, 2017 by the regulatory obligation carried by article 173 of the law on energy transition for green growth.[22] It is now essential to increase the financial industry's contribution to these challenges in order to consolidate and perhaps promote Paris as a world leader in green and sustainable finance. It was in these terms and with this conviction that Gérard Mestrallet, Chairman of Paris Europlace and Chairman of the Board of Directors of Engie, spoke at the 3rd Annual Green Bonds Principles Conference organized by the International Capital Market Association (ICMA), held in June 2017 in Paris at the Palais Brongniart. He also said, *"More than ever, it is crucial that the financial sector strengthen its contribution to the fight against climate change. Finance for Tomorrow's 50 ClimActs[23] is a fine example of the Paris Financial Center's ambition to be a world leader in green and sustainable finance."*

The Grenelle 2 law of July 2010 paved the way by requiring ESG reporting from management companies. This law on energy transition goes further by extending the scope to institutional investors and placing particular emphasis on the fight against global warming. During this event, Paris

[22] Act No. 2015-992 of August 17, 2015 on energy transition for green growth.

[23] Since the adoption of the Paris Agreement in 2015, the Paris Financial Centre has been heavily involved in financing the transition to a low-carbon and inclusive economy. Finance for Tomorrow is the embodiment of this movement. This initiative launched in June 2017 by Paris Europlace brings together the most committed players on this issue. In the alignment of the economy and the financial system with the 2°C objective, these 50 ClimActs illustrate the dynamic undertaken to promote and disseminate best practices.

Europlace announced the launch of its new brand "Finance For Tomorrow," which aims to coordinate this mobilization of Paris market players and locally and internationally promote the excellence of the Paris financial center. With Brexit, it is, perhaps, the occasion to promote Paris in the world capital of green finance and to reinforce the link between environment and finance?

A law and a decree impose more transparency and the need to communicate on climate risk as well as to evaluate the "green" share of their investments. Indeed, the decree of this article 173, published in the official journal on December 31, 2016, requires French institutional investors (mutual insurance companies, fund managers, provident institutions…) to provide details, as of this date and as from the 2016 financial year.[24]

- The definition and implementation procedures of a personalized SRI policy (transcription of values into ESG criteria, definition of an SRI filter depending on the nature of the assets and the investment universe, procedures for applying a dialogue policy, integration of an SRI process into the investment policy, training of members of the management team, etc.).
- Defining and implementing a dialogue policy (choice of themes, i.e., climate change, gender equality, business ethics, etc.)
- Measuring the carbon footprint (setting up reporting showing the portfolio's contribution to reducing climate impacts by measuring its carbon footprint and intensity, on ESG companies and defending the greenhouse gas emissions base of portfolio companies).
- Voting rights policy (the exercise of voting rights remains a decisive vector to influence good ESG practices of companies and defend the interests of shareholders and subscribers. This involves determining the principles for exercising voting rights for the entire portfolio based on the values of the institutional investor (executive compensation, independence of directors, separation of functions, etc.).
- ESG performance evaluation (comprehensive reporting that integrates the SRI rating of the portfolio and its benchmark index as well as the ESG rating of the securities held).

[24]Many market associations have published a guide to help implement this article 173: see the websites of the FIR (FIR which has published its own guide: "Tool for better investing…"): Article 173-VI: extension of the field of the fight against climate change, www.frenchsif.org), the French Insurance Association (www.ffa-assurance.fr), the French Financial Management Association (www.afg.asso.fr) or the French Institutional Investors Association (www.af2i.org).

While at the beginning of the 21st century some large companies and institutions had taken a responsible approach to their project financing activities (e.g., in the form of charters or actions in favor of the rehabilitation of social housing), the climate emergency and COP 21 have really boosted this issue from an environmental point of view for new players on an international scale (AXA, Alliance, etc.) or on a more modest scale. There is still room for improvement in the search for more structured global policies, particularly with regard to the introduction of a common Paris carbon footprint standard. A strengthened collaboration between academic research and investors on a theme of performance/risk verification would also allow a better dissemination of these climate transition-oriented approaches. The path of shareholder commitment to the climate could also be an excellent tool for disseminating these new, more responsible practices. It is advisable to remain lucid, if these approaches are structuring, they still remain limited. In addition to the technical constraints, the search for a form of universality for indicators, and the difficulty in determining the risk associated with climate change, persists the regulatory barrier as much on the side of banks as insurers. Although under discussion, the Basel prudential standards for banks, or Solvency 2 for insurers, offer no specific advantage to investors more inclined to accompany this climate transition. In these conditions let us look at the nature of the offer and the actors. According to Philippe Dutertre, Head of SRI at AG2R La Mondiale, pilot of the SRI working group of the French Association of Institutional Investors and co-pilot of the Article 173 working group of the French Insurance Federation, in his article "Investors increasingly mobilized on climate," published in the 1418 issue of Option Finance,[25] underlines the need for a more coherent offer of funds. *"The offer of funds is similar to ready-to-wear in the world of financing the energy transition, but management companies should focus more on tailor-made solutions to meet the often different needs of investors on this subject."*

• Actors and the offer

Since 2013, the energy transition in France represents €36 billion of annual investments in energy efficiency and renewable energies, including €26 billion for retail banks. However, these figures are based on a certain uncertainty due to the absence of a green growth observatory in France; these data have been aggregated through associations, small and

[25] Page 26, Asset Management section, Option Finance, no. 1418, dated Monday, June 12, 2017.

medium-sized enterprises (VSEs, SMEs), hence the imprecision (e.g., the acquisition of a photovoltaic panel by a private individual is included in these data). Moreover, four major questions remain unanswered: (1) This new market is complex and the debates still focus too much on large investors without paying too much attention to access for the most modest or vulnerable SMEs, farmers, or individuals; (2) how to mobilize emerging countries and their population? (3) How to deal with the different financing systems between the Anglo-Saxon world, rather disintermediated, and the continental European model of the retail bank attached to proximity and the local? When will be a universalist banking model and a European finance less dominated, at international level, by the Chinese (the top five world banks are Chinese) and by the Anglo-Saxons (the top five financing and investment banks are Anglo-Saxon)? Of course, five French banks are indeed in the "Top 20" of global banks but, it is on the basis of a ranking established on the balance sheet total, for profitability, it is another matter! Alongside these important considerations, of course, but in an attempt to provide some answers to our previous questions, we sincerely believe that the dynamics have been set in motion and that the fight against global warming has become disruptive. In a dossier prepared by Option Finance No. 1418 entitled *The great debate; de-carbonization of portfolios is essential in asset management," the following is a summary of the results of this study,*[26] Bruno Fine, Chairman and Founder of Roche-Brune Asset Management, reinforces our position and emphasizes that this approach is becoming commonplace, *"From a historical perspective, we can consider that best in class management consisted in establishing a photograph and sorting the players, then classifying them. On the contrary, the commitment policy has encouraged companies to make more efforts and improve their practices. The fight against global warming goes even further because it allows us to frame a real change in society."* The revolution welcomed by institutional investors has reached a point of no return and forces them no longer to focus solely on financial profitability but to invest differently by integrating the notion of impact and sustainable profitability over the long term. To reinforce this point, the first studies show that the most virtuous companies in terms of reducing their carbon emissions would obtain the best stock market valuations. For investors, the question arises as to whether this decarbonization approach should be taken into

[26]Page 36 of the dossier, le grand débat (pp. 33–43), Option Finance, no. 1418, dated Monday, June 12, 2017.

account for all of their assets under management or whether it should be confined to dedicated funds. For our part, we believe that the question no longer arises, even if this approach only concerns a minority of investments. In future, the integration of extra-financial criteria (ESG) will fully be a part of all analyses and this problem will no longer be the prerogative of major investors, NGOs, and public authorities, even if individuals are not really willing to understand the ESG approach, often again, associated with thematic SRI funds. Nevertheless, these same individuals risk understanding more quickly the merits of investments related to the fight against global warming, water, and waste management, even if their contribution as savers is modest in the order of €5,000–€20,000 on average, sums hardly comparable to the hundreds of millions of large investors. The growing demand for assets concerned by the low-carbon issue with nearly $230 billion issued to date, this international green bond market actually weighs, in 2017, less than 0.2% of the global bond market. The dynamism of this new bond segment began in 2007. These "green" obligations aim to facilitate the energy and ecological transition by financing projects in renewable energy, green buildings, transport, water, waste, land use and so on.

Despite the lack of consolidation of the statistical data of this "green" finance where investments are mostly made in the form of bonds characterized, gradually, by their volatility, their return, their spread,[27] their risk, and their performance in the image of similar traditional products, these "green" obligations also make it possible to finance a project with a social impact. According to the official website of the Ministry of Ecological and Solidarity Transition, "A green bond is a loan (debt security) issued on the market by a company or public entity for investors to enable it to finance its projects contributing to the ecological transition (renewable energies, energy efficiency, sustainable waste and water management, sustainable land use, clean transport and adaptation to climate change), more particularly investments in infrastructure. It differs from a traditional obligation by providing detailed reporting on the investments it finances and the green nature of the projects financed." However, while they are defined in principle, no precise standard characterizes the environmental dimension of the projects financed. In 2007, the European Investment Bank

[27] A spread is the difference between the actuarial rate of a given bond and the actuarial rate of a zero coupon bond with similar characteristics. In practice, a benchmark government bond, considered risk-free, is generally used instead of the zero coupon bond.

launched its first Climate Awareness Bond, followed by the World Bank in 2008. In France, it was September 2014 before the French Development Agency issued the first green security. While the World Bank and development banks, which played a leading role in issuing this type of security, continue to ensure the liquidity of the market, the arrival of new players in France, such as large companies, local authorities, and the State, has led to the establishment of a broader investment ecosystem, such that "Paris sees itself as the capital of green finance" according to the title of Delphine Cuny's article published in the newspaper *La Tribune* on June 14, 2017. Cuny recalls some significant statistical data on green bonds for the world and national markets:

"Top 5" countries issuing "green, social, sustainability bonds" as of June 1, 2017 in billions of dollars[28]

France	China	Brazil	USA	Sweden
13,168	7,513	2,700	2,655	2,458

The French market rose from $1.86 billion in 2013 to $13.168 billion on June 1, 2017, thanks to the €7 billion issued by the French government in green bonds in January 2017. As of June 1, 2017, France was still at the top of the list of countries issuing sustainable, social, and responsible bonds, with Luxembourg remaining the leader for the listing of these "green bonds." To justify its title as green finance capital, Paris is the city with the largest number of funds specializing in green bonds. With about 15 active funds, Paris is ahead of Frankfurt and London.

In the first quarter of 2017, according to the "green bond league table," the main international subscribers of green bonds were BNP Paribas, Crédit Agricole CIB, Natexis, City Bank and Morgan Stanley.

In addition, the amounts issued in the first 5 months of 2017 are higher compared to the previous financial year. For the same referenced period, they would be €42 billion equivalent against €29 billion in 2016, despite the absence of Chinese issuance, over these first 5 months in 2017, whereas it had represented nearly 1/3 of total issuance in 2016.

[28]Attention, figures communicated on June 1, 2017 by the Bloomberg agency which include "social and sustainable" obligations. In the "green bonds" *stricto sensu*, France is second behind China internationally and first European country. China alone issued $36 billion in green bonds in 2016, 38% of the total.

For 2017, forecasters expect further volume growth to reach $120 billion worldwide.[29]

In the Commission's action plan for sustainable finance, published on March 8, 2018, a project for a European eco-label is high on the agenda to channel citizens' savings toward climate-friendly financial products. The idea of a European eco-label is simple and effective. The aim is to offer European savers, particularly more in numbers in countries such as France and Germany, an opportunity to choose a financial product with a European star logo to green their savings. As European Commission President Valdis Dombrlvskis explained while presenting the action plan to the press, "Having a European eco-label for financial products helps to highlight climate-friendly investments. It works like organic products, clothing or buildings."

Another example, in the United States, despite the election of a turbulent and unpredictable President in 2017, renewable energies such as solar and wind power have rapidly expanded in recent years. Yet, they accounted for only 17% of the country's total electricity production in 2017. The stakes are high and the obstacles to change are numerous. During the same period, GreenTech start-ups, after having been hit hard by the 2008 financial crisis, surfed on the digital wave. Technological advances related to the Internet of things, artificial intelligence, or the Blockchain promise to accelerate the energy transition, as unprecedented. Applied to the field of energy, these technologies can be summarized by the "4Ds": decarbonization, decentralization, digitalization, and democratization of renewable energies. At the forefront of green technologies in America, California has set itself the ambitious goal of producing 100% of its electricity from renewable energies by 2045. This example also shows that technology alone is not enough and that it is also crucial to bring about a change of mentality in society.

[29] On November 16, 2017, the greens bonds crossed the symbolic threshold of $100 billion since the beginning of the year. This is revealed by an analysis of the Climate Bonds Initiative which refers to the subject. Thus, in the middle of Cop 23, with the green bonds of the French State, SNCF, or Engie, the three largest issuers, the French green bonds represent €15 billion cumulated. With this performance, France ranks second among countries in terms of volume, just behind China ($16.63 billion). Behind France and in 3rd place is the United States with $14 billion. Among the major US emitters: New York MTA, which provides public transport for the big apple, Fannie Mae, a company that guarantees home loans, and Apple.

To close this section and show that the field of possibilities for promoting green obligations is huge, let us look, for example, at some innovations: two recent and one, perhaps, to come?

- The first innovation consists of setting up *financing whose remuneration is indexed to social and environmental performance*. Among corporates, this formula is gaining growing attention because, unlike a green bond, it makes it possible to develop a global strategy and not only a portfolio of projects. Banks could thus be encouraged to integrate solutions to enhance their clients' social and environmental performance into their offer. In May 2017, EDF signed a bilateral €150 million revolving credit facility agreement with ING. The rate of this credit line is indexed to EDF's sustainable development performance, according to the assessment carried out by the extra-financial rating agency Sustainalytics. Philips and Unibail-Rodamco have recently set up loans where remuneration is linked to their social and environmental performance.
- The second innovation dates from March 2017. Société General's subsidiary, Lyxor Asset Management,[30] launched *the first replication product*[31] (or tracker, meaning a product seeking to replicate a benchmark index) enabling investors to contribute to environmental protection on a nonspeculative and low-risk basis. Thus, the LYXOR Green Bond ETF seeks to replicate the evolution of the benchmark index Solactive Green Bond EUR USD IG Index composed of 113 US, Japanese, Korean, Mexican green bonds (as of March 1, 2017), denominated in euros and dollars and issued by supranational issuers, governments, public authorities, banks, and companies. Subject to currency risk, it bears an annual fee of 0.25% and is not eligible for the PEA. Its annual yield is estimated at 1.5%. The obligations

[30] For more information, we refer the reader to the management company's website: www.lyxoretf.fr

[31] A replication product or tracker, also called ETFs is an index fund that seeks to replicate the performance of a stock or index. Born in the United States in the 1990s, the first listing in France took place in January 2001. It offers individuals the performance of an equity, bond, or commodity index in all simplicity and with good liquidity without entry or exit fees, with low management fees and sometimes eligible for the PEA. It has no maturity date and may distribute dividends. Listed continuously, it offers the possibility of investing in all the stocks making up the index but through a single security that does not require the intervention of financial analysts since it reflects changes in the benchmark management tool called "passive," if it follows its base index. There are some for stocks and commodities. If the tracker does not follow its base index, it is referred to as an "asset," as in the case of leveraged pension fund trackers.

contained in this index, within the framework of collective investment schemes in securities domiciled in France or Luxembourg, are labeled green and their eligibility is defined by the Climate Bonds Initiative responsible for promoting low-carbon economies and being resilient to climate change.

- Finally, in another field, probably more difficult to achieve at a time when Europe is going through an identity crisis marked by the rise of "eurosceptic" populisms refusing political pluralism (with parties like FPÖ in Austria, SYRIZA in Greece, FIDEZ in Hungary, Party of Freedom in the Netherlands, Podemos in Spain, Alternative for Germany [AFD] in France ..., in Italy ...), where "declinism" and distrust toward institutions are on the rise, how, in this context, can we create a new sustainable economic dynamics capable of winning the support of a majority of citizens and decision-makers in order to curb the next security, financial, social, and, naturally, climate crises? This is the meaning of the question raised by Abdeldjellil Bouzidi, founder of Emena Advisory, in an article in the supplement to no 809 of Revue Banque entitled "Pour un fonds souverain vert européen."[32] The author defends the idea that this fund would act better than an "*n*th" institutional plan (such as the 2014 Junker plan, financed via the European Strategic Investment Fund) in view of Europe's multiple green investment needs. It would act *"as a vehicle for patient capitalism"*[33] and could finance itself by issuing green bonds or bonds with environmental impact in order to transform the COP 21 commitments of 2015 in Paris into concrete actions. Still according to this author, a *"green sovereign fund,"* initiated by the major European countries and possibly extended to the Scandinavian countries that are driving the energy transition, could welcome private and public players with more legibility and more capacity to attract support than a European institutional plan.

Similar to many areas mentioned above, the lack of standardization makes it difficult to harmonize and make green obligations to investors transparent. It, therefore, appears necessary for the market to be structured and strengthened by an analysis of the environmental impact of projects throughout the duration of the bond issue (currently the impact

[32] Pages 35–38 of the supplement to Bank Review No. 809 devoted to climate transition.

[33] "Patient capital: a horizon for France and Europe," works published in 2016 by, Abdeldjellil Bouzidi, within Terra Nova.

analysis is essentially ex-ante and does not take into account the real impact of the project on the environment).

Access to the bond market is difficult for small communities and for small and medium-sized private sector firms. A pooling of resources for project monitoring and implementation of detailed reporting as well as the analysis of the risks inherent in their ability to borrow would reinforce the development of the greens bonds market.

- Concerning *microcredit*, you will find, below, some elements of forms, actors, and data.

According to the annual report of the Microfinance Observatory,[34] "Microcredit is above all a tool for economic and social development, by enabling people with limited resources who have a personal project to benefit from loans that the traditional banking system denies them." It developed more than 50 years ago in emerging countries and in Bangladesh, in particular, at the initiative of the Nobel Prize winner Muhammad Yunus. It has gradually reached developed countries to accompany people in difficult times. It was at the end of the 1980s that the first microcredit programs appeared in France. A distinction should be made between personal microcredit intended mainly for professional reintegration (purchase of a vehicle to go to work, etc.) for an amount between €300 and 5,000, at a fixed rate and granted for a maximum period of 3 years; professional microcredit intended to finance the creation, purchase, or consolidation of a craft or commercial enterprise. With a maximum amount of €25,000 and a maximum of between 6 months and 4 years, the cost remains relatively high and often higher than traditional financing due to the management of files and the risks of nonreimbursement. For these two forms of loans, personal and professional, guarantees can be given by the State within the framework of the social cohesion fund.[35]

[34]The Microfinance Observatory: creation date 2009, end of annual publication of the report in 2013. Since then, the Governor of the Banque de France has chaired the Observatoire de l'inclusion bancaire, created by the Act of July 26, 2013 and regulated by the Decree of June 30, 2014. The Observatory, which brings together representatives of public bodies, associations, and banks, draws up an annual report including an analysis of indicators of banking inclusion, the practice of credit institutions (monitoring of the right to an account, the basic banking service, and the development of microcredit, etc.) and any recommendations.

[35]The Social Cohesion Fund was created by the law of January 18, 2005 and its management is entrusted to the Caisse des dépôts et consignations. Its purpose is "to guarantee loans for social purposes to natural or legal persons and loans to unemployed persons or persons holding minimum social benefits to set up their own business" (Article 80 of the

Among the actors in the microcredit system, it is important to distinguish between approved networks (banking networks approved by the Social Cohesion Fund) and accompanying networks, such as ADIE (www.adie.org), France Active (www.franceactive.org), France Initiative (www.france-initiative.org), Restaurants du cœur (www.restoducoeur.org), or Secours catholique (www.secours-catholique.org), which, under the aegis of the Caisse des depots et consignations and referenced by the latter, accompany and finance projects. In France, in 2015 75,000 personal microcredits were distributed for an average amount of €2,200; for professional microcredits, the average amount was €6,000 and €187,000 distributed. Outstanding microcredits amount to €1.3 billion. Worldwide, according to data from the Banque de France[36] and for the year 2014, 81% of beneficiaries are women, 57.3% of borrowers are of rural origin, and the outstanding amount would have reached $87.1 billion. EN 2017, outstanding microcredit would be estimated at more than $10 billion. In normal times, the percentage of so-called nonperforming loans (NPL) is between 1% and 2%. In times of crisis (strong political or environmental crises for example), it can rise to 5%. With low volatility (0.57%), the average return on microcredit is around 3%, without correlation to traditional financial markets.

Despite the foreign direct investment spread over a hundred funds to which should be added bond funds, contributions from development banks, and local savings, these volumes remain relatively low for the main international investment banks or assets managers.

In Europe, while there is a widespread recognition about the need to use digital solution to a larger degree, the ability and willingness of MFIs to do that varies greatly. Small institutions claim lack of financial resources as the main challenge in bringing technology to their organizations. The most useful digital services are those related to the automation of loan application and management of the related documentation. Small scale of operations of most MFIs in Europe is a barrier to the introduction of

---

Act). The fund is endowed by the State and a Policy Council supervises the destination of the financing granted.

[36]For more information, please refer to the Observatoire de l'inclusion bancaire's 2016 annual report and the Baromètre 2016 de la micro finance (Microfinance Barometer 2016) on the website www.banque-france.fr

FinTech solutions. The results also show that MFIs are cautious about not losing their competitive advantage of personal relationship with their clients. FinTech and digitalization solutions should be applied based on a rational calculus of costs and benefits, in line with the mission of the organization, and the needs and capabilities of the clients.

South America remains the epicenter of microfinance thanks, in part, to "dollarized" economies and its openness to foreign capital. On the other hand, for the first time in 2018, South and South-East Asia would have taken the lead in terms of investment volumes. And Africa, despite a market share of 10%–15%, is the fastest growing region.

From data processing to networking and AI

The combination of three concepts, for which we deliver a summary definition without hierarchy of importance or chronological order, has contributed to transforming our societies: big data, social networks, and AI.

- Big Data, "large data or mega data," a concept popularized about 5 years ago to reflect the fact that companies are confronted with increasingly large volumes of data to be processed which raises commercial stakes. Originally a concept attached to electronic commerce which, under the influence of geolocation practices, now it applies to a multitude of sectors of activity, including finance. Its problem is sometimes represented by 3 Vs, for Volume of the data to be processed; Speed of the collection and Variety of the data often heterogeneous; to which are added the V of Veracity (veracity or reliability of the data often falling under the declarative); and the V of Value (in the sense of the interest of the collected data and the possibility of using them). Big data refers to the explosion in the volume of digital data produced by the use of new technologies. The ultimate objective of this collection and processing of the data collected is to better know the customer and to be able to satisfy his or her needs, that is to sell him or her the products or services.

By extension and at the intersection of the storage of large amounts of data and social networks, we suggest some explanations and potentialities of *the blockchain* (chain of blocks) which can be defined as "a technology of storage and transmission of information, transparent, secure and functioning without central organ." (Definition of Blockchain Partner, the French leader in blockchain technology support). It appeared in 2008 with the digital currency bitcoin, which was developed by a person presenting himself under the pseudonym Satoshi Nakamoto. As an indication, with $45 billion, Bitcoin was the cryptocurrency with the highest market capitalization in June 2017; it preceded its competitor the Ethereum blockchain, created in 2014, which reached $36 billion in the same month. Recognized in Japan in April 2017 as a legal means of payment, its volatility was very high and its market capitalization exceeded $95 billion in October 2017. While blockchain and bitcoin were created in parallel, decentralized technology, coupled with the security these concepts provide, allow applications that are not limited to electronic payments. In addition to being used for a transfer of assets (currency, securities), the blockchain can also be used for their tracking, or even for the execution of contracts. There are two categories of blockchain: a private blockchain characterized by an organization that can modify the protocol at will, and by opposition, the public blockchain that can be consulted and used by everyone. Subject to compliance with the operating rules, in the latter case, anyone can send transactions and expect them to appear in the transaction register. Since the Ordinance of April 2016[37] on savings bonds in connection with the creation of securities issued by a company in exchange for a loan granted on a crowdfunding platform, the following text has amended Article L223-12 of the Monetary and Financial Code to define the blockchain as a *"shared electronic recording device enabling the authentication of transactions in specific securities, intended to be exchanged on participating financing platforms: minibonds."*

One possible application of the use of the blockchain in financial matters is in the transmission and representation of certain financial securities. In this respect, at the end of September 2017, the General Treasury Department published a draft order aimed at making adjustments to certain articles of the Monetary and Financial Code, namely that certain financial securities could be registered on the blockchain (negotiable debt securities, units or shares in collective investment undertakings, equity securities issued by joint-stock companies, and negotiable debt securities provided that they are not traded on a trading platform). These securities will be governed by French law when the issuer's registered office

[37] Order No. 2016-520 of April 28, 2016.

is located in France or the issue is governed by French law. The Commercial Code could also be adjusted to allow securities issued by stock companies, if the articles of association so authorize, to be registered in a shared electronic registration system. The most immediate use of the blockchain, at the risk of leading to a digital transformation of asset management, is in the problems related to the transfer of ownership of shares and the exact knowledge of fund liabilities. While increasing security and reducing transaction costs, the blockchain would also bring about disintermediation of distribution by the possibility of responding more directly to the customer via more intelligent digital platforms. Client identification and profile determination would be strengthened as a way to meet growing compliance obligations. The arrival of the PRIIPS[38] regulation and the new transparency requirements argue in favor of chaining non-erasable information carried by the blockchain. The regulator could also find extensive modes of investigation and control.

Whether the blockchain is also revolutionary, it is as it risks disrupting our entire economy because of the major fact that it eliminates the use of a "trusted third party" in the guarantee of transactions. By doing so without a regulatory authority, the blockchain supplants a whole series of banking professions, the notary, the bailiff, the insurer, central network operators (EDF, the National Institute of Industrial Property, etc.), and administrations (from land registry to civil status, etc.). Few people do not hesitate to refer "Uber uberized," an idem, to these Internet platforms (Airbnb, eBay) which live on the customer relationship and could disappear anytime. In the March 2017 issue of Capital magazine, an article in

[38]PRIIPS (Packaged Retail Investment and Insurance Products), Regulation (EU) 1286/2014 of the European Parliament and of the Council of November 26, 2014 on key disclosure documents relating to packaged retail and insurance-based investment products. This regulation aims to increase the transparency and comparability of precontractual information presented to investors. With PRIIPS and the MiFID II which aims to strengthen the market transparency and improve the investor protection. These are two structuring texts for asset managers. They shall enter into force on January 3, 2018. While the MiFID reform puts investors at the center of the stakes, it also affects the remuneration model for financial services providers, who will have to abandon their indirect remuneration mode based on the collection of retro-commission in order to switch to fee-based invoicing. In addition to the abovementioned transparency, this change in economic model is intended to increase competition in the provision of services and, in particular, by broadening the offer of low-cost index products and facilitating access to passive management. In theory, PRIIPS does not immediately concern UCITS that benefit from a transitional period until 2019; in reality, for all funds sold as part of a life insurance policy, management companies will have to respond to requests from insurers who will have to draw up a key document.

the Economy/Finance section entitled *"Difficult to understand but revolutionary, the blockchain"*[39] explains the reasons for these breaks, "Even for the most digitized among us, all this is still difficult to conceive, we must admit. A blockchain has no leader, does not depend on anyone, does not answer to any authority: it is a simple computer register managed by a program and shared in network that each one can use at will …. But, the blockchain is not a simple stationary safe, when software is associated with it, it becomes capable of doing lots of things: certifying a property, guaranteeing a procedure, transferring value, identifying rights … monetize data," and to quote a City group report of 2016 which estimated that in 10 years 2 million workstations could disappear in American and European banks! Should we remain so pessimistic? We will see in the last subsection of this second part, banks and other professions do not remain passive in the face of this technological upheaval. The following phase diagram summarizes the sequence of the steps in a blockchain purchase to show how it works.

Phase 1: Introduction of the data affected by a kind of code (called hash, this term refers to a type of file used in cryptography. It is a mathematical algorithm which makes it possible to check the size and the identical character of a file sent via a computer network), these data cannot be modified at the risk of disappearing in the event of hacking.
Phase 2: Settlement of the transaction in cryptocurrency convertible into $, €.
Phase 3: Software verifies the contractual elements of the transaction and validates them.
Phase 4: "Mining" intervention. This operation consists of assembling transactions into "blocks, " adding a header that contains the size of the block, the number of transactions it contains, the date and time, and hash controls to avoid any modification of the block, and that will serve as a unique identifier of the block. In the case of a Bitcoin settlement, the settlement will be attributed to the "minor" who was the fastest to validate the block. We do not enter, here, in the mode of remuneration of the minor who receives a commission valued in bitcoins whose methods are evolutionary. From now on, the minor (a private individual, also called a geek to refer to a person with good computer knowledge) must be equipped with computer equipment powerful enough to capture the crumbling and multitude of possible transactions.

[39] Pages 78–80, March 2017 issue of *Capital* magazine.

On the borders of blockchain, cryptocurrency,[40] and peer to peer,[41] Initial Coin Offering (ICO) is a method of fund raising, operating via the issuance of digital assets exchangeable for crypto currencies during the start-up phase of a project (definition of ICO Mentor). These digital assets are called tokens. This is why ICOs are also called "token sales." Initially, tokens are issued by the organization that created the ICO, and can be acquired by anyone during the ICO in exchange for cryptocurrency (usually Bitcoin). In a second stage, these tokens can be sold and bought on exchange platforms, at a rate depending on supply and demand. They are intended to be usable in the project financed by the ICO in question. Their value is thus supposed to depend on the service provided *in fine* by the company at the origin of the ICO, and they cannot be confused with a title of ownership of a company, such as the share. Because of the novelty of the subject, we refer the reader to the press release published by the AMF on October 26, 2017, which in the context of the launch of a consultation, evokes the main issues raised by this type of product as well as the various related legal concerns:

AMF **The AMF launches a consultation on "Initial Coin Offerings" and initiates its Unicorn program.**

Published on 26 October 2017

In the absence of specific regulations governing all new fund-raising operations based on currencies crypto and Blockchain technology, the Autorité des marchés financiers (AMF) is seeking the views of stakeholders on various possible

[40]A currency crypto, also known as crypto currency or cryptographic currency, is an electronic currency that can be used on a peer-to-peer and decentralized computer network, based on the principles of cryptography, that you can issue yourself and that allows you to settle transactions. Today, crypto currencies are alternative currencies, as they are not legal tender in all countries. This currency is activated via an encryption system. Only information whose possessor, such as a fingerprint, can allow access to the use of currency crypto. It is through this storage of information, in a network of files called block, that currency crypto is a reliable and secures system. This block records all the transactions that are made thanks to this virtual currency.

[41]Peer to peer (often abbreviated "P2P," see the section dedicated to peer to peer lending in this second part of the book) is a computer network model close to the client-server model but where each client is also a server. The terms "even," "node," and "user" are generally used to designate the entities making up a P2P network.

approaches and is launching a program to support and analyze these operations, called UNICORN(1).

For a little over a year, a new form of fundraising has emerged in the form of initial coin offerings (ICO). These programs, which are based on both the use of crypto-currencies and Blockchain technology, aim to finance specific technological projects carried out by a company or a community of developers.

During an ICO operation, participants receive tokens (commonly referred to as "tokens") issued by the project holder(s) in exchange for their investment in currency crypto or legal tender. Depending on the transactions observed, these tokens do not systematically confer the same rights (rights to use developed services, financial and/or governance rights over the project, etc.) on their subscribers.

Risky transactions reserved for an informed public

The AMF specifies that ICO's operations are intended to finance technology projects at an early stage of their development. Subscribing to these operations requires a good understanding of the nature of these projects, the underlying technology and the associated risks. This type of fundraising is by nature intended for a technophile and informed public. As the tokens issued during these operations have different characteristics specific to each operation, it is essential to be informed about the nature of the token issued, what it represents for the company issuing it and the associated risks and benefits. The AMF would also stress that OCIs present high risks:

- **Absence of specific regulations;**
- **Risks associated with information documentation;**
- **Risks of capital loss;**
- **Risks of volatility or lack of market;**
- **Risk of fraud and money laundering;**
- **Risks associated with funded projects.**

Three possible regulation tracks

As part of its innovation activities and monitoring, the AMF conducted an initial in-depth study of these transactions and their legal implications. This initial review shows that while some of the ICOs observed could fall under existing legal provisions (regulations applicable to intermediaries in various goods, to the public offering of financial securities or to alternative investment fund managers, in particular), most of these issues would remain, as the law currently stands, outside any regulations with which the AMF ensures compliance.

It is in this context, and in a forward-looking approach, that the AMF is publishing its consultation paper in which three options for framing OCI are considered:

- **Promoting a guide to good practice under constant law;**
- **Extend the scope of existing texts to include ICOs as offers of securities to the public;**
- **Propose new legislation, adapted to the ICO.**

Contributions to the consultation should be sent to the AMF until 22 December 2017, at the following address: directiondelacommunication@amf-france.org
An analysis and support program.

Considering that certain forms of ICO could in the future constitute an alternative financing method for a segment of the economy linked to Blockchain technology, the AMF is launching a programme to support and research fundraising in digital assets. Called UNICORN (for Universal Node to ICO's Research & Network), it aims to provide these project leaders with a framework for developing their operations and to ensure the protection of players and investors wishing to participate.

As part of this innovative program, the AMF will receive initiators (French and foreign entrepreneurs and their advisors) of various types of projects, which will enable it to deepen its legal and economic expertise of the transactions carried out and their implications for the traditional economy. The AMF also intends to encourage academic research on this subject and will publish an initial one-year impact analysis of these new forms of financing.
(1) Universal Node to ICO's Research & Network
Press Contact:
AMF Communications Department—Christèle Fradin—Tel: +33 (0)1 53 45 60 29 or +33 (0)1 53 45 60 28
(AMF sources)

Data processing raises many questions related to trust, law, and ethics that we cannot ignore. In the light of the recent Cambridge Analytica scandal and with the entry into force of the GDR[42] in Europe, data, its use, and possible misuse are among the issues of growing concern to the general public and economic actors. The figures published by IBM justify this concern. According to this company, 2.5 quintillion[43] bytes of data are generated every day. A number so dizzying and constantly evolving that it becomes almost impossible to quantify.

In his 2015 bestseller "Homo Deus," historian Yuval Noah Harrari describes a new ideology, "Dataism." This ideology would lead us to delegate our choices to algorithms so that they make the best and especially the most important decisions for our lives and our future, and this in our place.

[42]The new European regulation on the protection of personal data came into force on May 25, 2018. The adaption of this text should enable Europe to adapt to the new digital realities. Its objectives are: (1) To strengthen the rights of individuals, in particular by creating a right to the portability of personal data; (2) To empower data processors; (3) To give credibility to regulation through enhanced cooperation between data protection authorities (In France: the Commission Nationale Informatique et Libertés).

[43]One quintillion represents the number 1030, that is 1 000 000 000 000 000 000 000 000 000 000.

Thanks to the free flow of information, these algorithms would know us better than we know ourselves.

Can we accept this disturbing vision of a humanity that has abandoned its free choices? For our part, we believe more in a perception of the future where humanity and technology complement each other in a positive use of data (e.g., in the medical field and in helping victims,). However, we must remain cautious about commercial exploitation of any of our private data without regulation.

- Social networks (Mercator definition, Dunod Edition, mercator-publicitor.fr) online "refer to Internet sites and mobile applications that allow users to form a network of friends or relations, that promote social interactions between individuals, groups of individuals or organizations." Social networking refers to the use of networks. A social network is a group of people united by a social bond. At the end of the 1990s, social networks appeared on the Internet, bringing together people via personalized exchange services, each of whom could decide to read messages from one user or another (Facebook, created in 2004, is the best-known and most used of them). Some statistical data based on the social network usage barometer published over the past 5 years by Harris Interactive, information provided by Kantar TNS and Médiamétrie:

Number of social network users worldwide

2010	0.97 Billion
2015	2.14 Billion (2017 [estimate] = 2.8 Billion)
2020 (estimate)	• 3.5 Billion

Out of 7.5 billion inhabitants on the planet, 3.81 billion are Internet users and 2.8 billion are on social networks.

Top 5 of the world's top social networks in 2017

Name	Dare created	Number of users
Facebook	September 2006	2 Billion
Instagram	2010	700 Million
Qzone (Chinese)	2005	653 Million
Tumblr	2007	355 Million
Twiter	March 2006	328 Million

Population penetration rate by continent

North America	**66%**
Europe	54%
Asia	15%
Africa	13%

Autorité de Régulation des Communications électroniques et des Postes (ARCEP) and the Conseil Général de l'Economie regularly publish a survey on digital equipment and its use in France. For 2016 and on the basis of face-to-face interviews with 2,000 people representing the French population (12 years and over), we can extract the following data: 80% of French people have a PC; 58% a smartphone and 35% a tablet; 25% are equipped with the triptych PC, smartphone, and tablet; 14% of the French do not own any of the three devices. Concerning Internet use (fixed and mobile), access to social networks (52%) and music listening/downloading remain the two most common practices. The use of social networks largely depends on the age of Internet users. All adolescents are almost daily Internet users (94% of 18–24-year olds; 90% of managers against 68% of French). With an average of 1 h 20 min presence on social networks, the French are rather well positioned in the European ranking. While the European Union average is 76% among Internet users aged 15 and over, France is 6th with 84% (Sweden is the first with 96% followed by the Netherlands, Denmark, Luxembourg, and Finland; Great Britain is 83% and Germany 78%).

About social networks, a few observations: they constitute a vast picture with beautiful things, sometimes the comments made are misleading and would do well to remain in a sort of "dustbin." They do not represent everyone's word and can sometimes be seen as a form of justice rendered in the public square. Between the risk of suffocation of certain cases and the release of speech on all subjects, it is necessary to keep reason. It is a good thing that speech is free, but it must be done within a legal framework. It is also necessary to distinguish between denunciation and suffocation in the themes and subjects addressed. The absence of debate can hinder the search for truth and transparency. But, too much transparency can affect the desired purpose!

- AI is "the science whose purpose is to make a machine do tasks that a human accomplishes by using intelligence. This terminology appeared in 1956, we can prefer that of heuristic computing!" (Cours de Dominique Pastré à Normale Sup entitled: "L'intelligence artificielle—définitions—historique—domaines," Paris 2000, www.normalesup.org). For Pr. Pastré, "Computer science is the science of information processing, artificial intelligence is interested in all cases where this processing cannot be reduced to a simple, precise, algorithmic method. An algorithm is a sequence of ordered, well-defined operations, executable on a computer and which makes it possible to arrive at the solution in an accelerated time." Marvin Lee Minsky (1927–2016, American scientist and specialist in cognitive sciences and AI who published works such as *Perceptrons*, 1969; *The Society of Mind*, 1986; *The Emotion Machine*, etc.), one of the creators of AI, defines it as "The construction of computer programs that engage in tasks that are currently performed more satisfactorily by human beings because they require high-level mental processes such as: perceptual learning, memory organization and critical reasoning."

More simply, AI can be defined as an automated system backed by a computer and/or robot to help and simplify the work of humans. If the history of AI goes back to antiquity when myths, legends, and rumors lead man to realize his old wish to play God.

It was then initiated by the classical philosophers of the 18th century, including Liebnitz who imagined a universal language of reasoning (with his "charactereristica universalis" assimilating argumentation to a calculation), with Thomas Hobbes ("reason is nothing other than the fact of calculating"), and Descartes ("the animal machine") who explored the possibility of seeing all thought as systematic as algebra or geometry. In the XVIIIth century the automaton of Vaucanson, with the features of a duck, carries out certain functions of a living. In the 20th century the study of mathematical logic provides the bulk of the advances and its last 60 years will allow the IA spectacular progress thanks to the first computers dating from 1943. Below are a few significant steps:

- 1950: Alan Turing imagines the intelligent machine.
- 1956: AI becomes a science.
- 1957: The Perceptron is the first machine to learn.
- 1997: Chess player Kasparov is defeated by the Deep Blue machine.
- 2013: Silicon Valley giants, such as the Google, Apple, Facebook, and Amazon (GAFA), are getting their hands on AI specialists.

- 2016: The AlphaGo software beats, in Seoul, the champion of the GO game, the Korean Lee Sedol .... But, Alpha Go will not celebrate his victory, he did not even know that he was playing .... A chance for the human ...?

Alan Turing (1912–1954), a British mathematician and cryptologist, author of works (Computing Machinery and Intelligence; Pure Mathematics; Mathematical Logic ; Morphogenesis, etc.) contributed to the scientific foundation of computing, wondered, already, more than 60 years ago, what would happen if this AI took control of humans. Such a questioning justifies the fact that AI could be anxiogenic. AI has been reinforced in recent years by three major developments: (1) The Big Data we talked about and its storage capacity of a plurality of data; (2) The computing power multiplied by more than 1,000 so that a Nintendo game console today can have more computing power than NASA computers in 1969 when it landed on the moon; (3) The considerable increase in the number of data. Under these conditions, should we be afraid of the AI in view of the number of trades and jobs likely to be sacrificed? Often associated with the imagination of science fiction, AI feeds all fantasies, the end of work, the domination of machines ... AI certainly modifies the functioning of contemporary societies in depth, but it is already widely present in our daily lives (autonomous car, preventive medicine, predictive marketing, connected objects, vocal assistants, etc.). The history of humanity is marked by ruptures and for each technological revolution, breakdowns predicted the end of the world. Plato in Phaedra specifies that the arrival of writing meant the end of memory. The opposite happened and the man adapted to each event. During an interview on YouTube conducted by Patrick Poivre d'Arvor at the beginning of October 2017, the winner of the Hub Awards for the 2017 digital book, Arnaud de Lacoste, for his book, "Le seigneur des robots,"[44] declared "There is always overvaluation of the impact of a technology in the short term and undervaluation in the long term. We see the future with today's eyes," and to continue, about the evolution of trades and jobs in the hypothesis that we would have to guide a young person in his professional orientation. For the author, the jobs most at risk are those of knowledge, and to take the example of the professor, the oncologist, the surgeon where the background will be held by the machine and the diagnosis will be more and more the exchange between specialists, but to present the protocol or the treatment to the

[44] Awarded on October 10, 2017 and published by Editions Débats Publics.

patient, to analyze his behavior, it is empathy that the machine or the AI does not hold, which will again refocus the dialogue on the human dimension. You should remain optimistic and look at the bottle half full. The fears expressed above are probably unfounded. Generally speaking, two areas are anticipated as promising areas of use: on one hand, the relevance of forecasts, where the big data associated with the AI will have the capacity to access and analyze a greater variety of internal and external information, and, on the other hand, in the management of commercial performance (better mobilization of teams, more dynamic management of objectives, etc.).

In addition, the presence of virtual assistants, a kind of robot, will lead to major changes, both in management and in the organization of employee assignments. The control, audit, compliance, and reporting departments will improve their operational efficiency and also the quality of their missions by using these robots. If you think robots and algorithms will replace creativity, empathy, and human know-how, think again. The time is ripe for an abundance of man–machine synergies. With the help of the technologies associated with AI, we are moving into a new era of constant exchange and conversation, productivity, agility, proximity, and a new manifestation of trust. A trust that could gradually evolve into a new form of consensual contract between stakeholders established on a digital basis and characterized by the security, transparency, and accuracy of its data. These technological breakthroughs will offer us countless opportunities if we anticipate them and adapt. We are well in what we noted in the introduction, a situation where resistance to change is great and we are only in the early stages of what psychosociologists call the curve of change where individuals and institutions successively experience states of denial, loss of reference points, and anger before admitting their usefulness. Finance is becoming an ecosystem of advanced technologies with more efficient tools. As the pace of innovation accelerates, it is a source of creative energy and opportunity for multiple players—banking, insurance, environmental, and general economic finance. It is therefore up to us to establish a point of stage or progress of these technologies carried by actors of various sizes. This is what we will evoke, below, without claiming the exhaustiveness of the interrogations.

Similar to data, artificial intelligence also raises many legal and moral questions. We should dwell, for a moment, on these questions where trust probably remains the watchword. Consider, on one hand, the announcement of the first fatal collision of a pedestrian by an autonomous car; on the other hand, the revelation that the data of 50 million Facebook users had been used without their knowledge by a sultry political marketing company. *A priori*, no common point between these two pieces of information, yet, both highlight a major challenge for the giants of digital and AI: trust. The place of data and algorithms has continued to grow in our daily lives, often for a laudable purpose to make our lives easier. However, voices rose to underline the risks that these choices represent within the framework of a black box in an often unequal way. There are several categories of algorithms and to varying degrees from "openly malicious" in order to harm a population (e.g., the traceability of purchases made by cards issued to a population receiving social assistance), to "accidentally malicious" linked to a poor evaluation of the social fabric concerned, while passing through "Deep Learning"[45] algorithms that enrich themselves on databases that can be originally oriented.

Another area, for example, where algorithms and their possible biases can have very direct consequences for minorities and social cohesion in society is that of security. Predictive approaches have been adopted by an increasing number of municipalities in the United States, then in Europe and the results are often convincing. With a system like Predpol,[46] or its equivalents, police patrols are planned by a predictive algorithm based on past crimes. The crime reduction figures announced by the publishers of these solutions are significant, but one bias often observed is that the algorithm concentrates patrols in the neighborhoods where crime is highest. Mechanically, this concentration of means further increases the number of events in these sensitive areas and thus further amplifies the feedback loop of the algorithm (e.g., increased controls for an overrepresented African-American population).

Among "*Datateism, utopia or dystopie*" (imaginary society preventing happiness) how is responsible finance situated in our society of transitions?

---

[45] Deep learning is a short term for "learning in deep neural networks." These are automatic learning methods using deep neural networks, so it is a subarea of automatic learning (and a sub-subarea of AI in general). In deep learning, large artificial neurological networks are fed by learning algorithms and increasing amounts of data, continuously improving their ability to "think" and "learn" as they process the data. "Deep" refers to the many layers that the neurological network accumulates over time.

[46] PredPol, the leader in Predictive Policing Software, is an innovative and proven policing technology that helps law enforcement predict and prevent crime.

The evolution of AI can be compared to that of information technology, which has drastically reduced the cost of key elements of production chains. The AI concerns accounting, law, medicine, digitalization of music that has become downloadable, then forecasts, exceeding those of human performance, until facial recognition is more than 99% accurate.

There is a need for human supervision of algorithms. Faced with these biases, many voices have been raised to call on data scientists to adapt a code of ethics. In the absence of being able to impose a universal code of ethics on all data scientists on the planet, making algorithms and their decisions auditable is a path that several countries seem to want to choose. This need for transparency in algorithms raises questions. Under the pretext of our inability to formally explain all their decisions, should we abandon these algorithms? The answer is probably no, which does not exclude regulation. Moreover, we remain convinced that, as it spreads throughout companies and society, AI will become a standard, to the point of losing its competitive advantage someday.

AI can serve sustainability, the sure value of responsible finance. Sustainability is not yet unequivocally defined; everyone has their own point of view, about sustainability ratings, sustainability indices, with varying principles according to the cultural environment. By combining a multitude of different ratings and opinions expressed by analysts, managers, or investors, the sustainability of investment portfolios can be valued in a more complete and consistent manner, subject to transparency and traceability.

In our company where the company anticipates our desires (5% of purchases and a proportion which does not cease growing in the United States), is it really science fiction? Nevertheless, the reality is there. Little by little, machines learn from humans and we get to the stage where they are able to think faster than us (Google), recognize our friends or relatives (Facebook), receive orders, anticipate our needs (Amazon or Alibaba), or drive our cars (Tesla), among other things. Beyond learning from humans, machines learn by themselves. Thus, the more information we share by generating data in the system, the richer the algorithms become, and the more relevant the AI's suggestions will be in the long run. A distinction is even made between "weak" AI (that which anticipates the cognitive capacities of Man, in order to perform the predetermined tasks in an efficient and autonomous way for which it has been programmed) and "strong" AI (which would be endowed with consciousness).

But technology remains a tool that increases managers' capabilities and benefits for clients. They cannot be deterministic. Risk management is the driver of long-term investment performance and AI can be used to support and deepen the ability to identify and manage risk in investment strategies. Progress in FinTech has led to a digital revolution that seems destined to transform the asset management value chain, from fundraising to investment and operational activities.

We have already pointed out that we are living in an era of increasing inequality and decreasing share of labor income in relation to that of capital. If this trend were to continue, we should perhaps be concerned about the ethical and social consequences of material growth, which would become so rapid that humans could no longer assimilate it intellectually. If it is still difficult to take advantage of great lucidity in long-term forecasts, without predicting an existential battle between man and machine, the AI remains, however, difficult to define, because of its irreducible technical dimension. The need for legal guidance then becomes more and more pressing. It is urgent to reflect on the legal framework within which an AI can evolve. If the apprehension and regulation of current weak AIs by our positive law[47] is possible, the emergence of a strong AI would upset our reference points. The main legal avenues to be explored are probably at the level of the protection of AI creations and liability in AI, the latter not having legal personality.

A plethora of digital services for responsible finance, but for what real subject?

The world of finance is undergoing one of the most profound changes in its history. The professions of deposit banking, investment banking, markets, asset management, and corporate finance all seem to be undergoing radical transformations. It is no longer just a question of changes in practices or the arrival of new technical tools, as has been the case many

[47]The expression "positive law" refers to the body of rules of law actually in force in a state or a group of states. Positive law is written and published. Its respect is sanctioned by recourse to the courts responsible for applying it. It consists of all official legal documents: laws, decrees, administrative regulations, rules of procedure and judgments. Positive law is a living law that evolves with the times and societies. International positive law consists of all agreements and treaties in force.

times in the past. The very principles of finance are being called into question. New technologies, new players... deeply destabilizing established frameworks, and old terminology is no longer sufficient to classify these new entrants on this market. Is it possible to speak of the "uberization" of finance? The digitalization of the banking sector could bring agility, inventiveness, and reactivity, but at what price? The fall in the number of bank machines, the increasing penetration of digital banking among their customers, and the rise of online banking are the bases of a strategic reflection for retail banking. In a period when the technological component will soon no longer be a differentiating element, the real challenge for the financial industry in general, banking and insurance, will ultimately be to move from transactional utility to relational purpose. The marketing component of his model must also reinvent itself by being less in a posture at a moment of expressing a need of his client, but being more likely to accompany him throughout the stages of his life. It will then be able to concentrate on what represents its real competitive advantage: human relations and proximity. The bank advisor helped by AI as a means could, thus, be more efficient in his responses to the various life projects of his customers. The future of finance and responsible finance, in particular, will probably be more empathetic and supportive.

The world of finance is undergoing one of the most profound changes in its history. The professions of deposit banking, investment banking, markets, asset management, and corporate finance all seem to be undergoing radical transformations of varying degrees of intensity. As we have just seen, the programming interface (or application programming interface, API), the Data, the blockchain, the AI, or even the Internet of things upset our reference points. While the time is now ripe for partnerships between financial institutions and new players such as FinTech, the changes brought about in terms of organization, operation, IT systems, and skills are profound. Between cost control and the transition from transactional to relational marketing, the digital transition could open new horizons for responsible finance in its quest for meaning.

It is no longer just a question of changes in practices or the arrival of new technical tools, as has been the case many times in the past; the very principles of finance are being called into question. Backed by new technologies, new players are deeply destabilizing established models, and old terminology is no longer sufficient to classify these new entrants on this market.

The explosion of the FinTech sector brings its share of digital tools to manage finances, ensure payments, build up savings, and apply for a loan. There are solutions adapted to all situations, whether it is to save for a future purchase, to build up savings, or to manage your wealth. This subsection will, after having defined this area of FinTech, examine the possible dilemma that might oppose them to banks; to address the mapping of new payment services; to present the regulations and key data of participatory financing; and to analyze recent innovations in a plethora of digitalized services. If the aggregation of data and services, in sharing and transparency, and the grouping of partner actors, seems to be a necessary way to maintain national leadership in the financial sector, it seems useful to decipher this complex field of innovations with diverse impacts. For this, we will start from a general reflection that will lead us to progress toward increasingly specialized technological innovations.

National and international overview of the FinTech ecosystem in the service of responsible finance: Some opening remarks

At first, there was indifference, at best skepticism, and then came the fear of FinTech, and the need to react, probably, by buying up these young structures rather than dispersing investment in research and development. Finally, traditional banks, retail banks, and telephone banks (launch of Orange Bank in November 2017) have been convinced by the need to prepare to integrate these new technologies into new, often hybrid, business models ("Bank Tech" such as Kis Bank and Banque Postale combined to promote and finance innovative international projects).

The FinTech ecosystem can be defined in a banal way on the basis of the conference of November 25, 2016 of the Autorité de contrôle prudentiel et de résolution (ACPR) at the Palais Brongniart, which aimed to present the approach of the FinTech Innovation cluster of the ACPR created in June 2016. Although created at the end of the 20th century in Silicon Valley for data aggregation and banking applications, following the 2007 crisis, these start-ups grew under the impetus of former bankers and traders who embarked on entrepreneurial adventures to rethink the financial model through technological innovation. They wanted to make finance simpler, more accessible; more agile, more inventive through better quality and cheaper services; the "3 Vs" of big data: "Speed

(Vitesse)-Volume-Variety." For example, Yodlee (data aggregator), created in the United States in 1999, already has over 40 million customers and raised £500 million when it went public. FinTech terminology combines the terms "finance" and "technology," which refer to an innovative start-up that uses technology to evolve financial and banking services to make finance simpler and more accessible through better and cheaper services. FinTech is developing in all areas of finance, electronic banking, savings, and credit management (loans for individuals, corporate financing, and online payments). After having disrupted the transport, music, press, or tourism sectors, the new technologies seem now to be attacking health, insurance, and banking and financial sector (from virtual money to mobile applications via crowdfunding).

Regarding the advantages provided by FinTech, it is mainly a question of making finance more accessible and simpler through better quality and less expensive products and services. Is FinTech able to decentralize trust? Would that be a gain or a loss? Here, it will probably be easier for us to decide on the potential risks than on all the disadvantages.

FinTech is only the emerging part of a much larger process that is taking the entire economy into a new mode of operation. Worldwide, FinTech investments tripled between 2008 and 2014 to reach $5 billion in the last quarter of 2015. They exceed $20 billion in 2017 and rise to $27.4 billion in the first half of 2018 and according to a recent study by Goldman Sachs, the FinTech ecosystem could, in the near future, capture nearly $5 trillion in sales to the traditional financial sector. The wide variety of platforms with GAFA, unicorns (names of start-ups valued at over $1 billion and more than 160 in the world), start-ups, traditional banks, and neo-banks (banks backed by mobile phones) can have very different "business models" requiring a need for transparency for security reasons, as well as a good distribution of responsibilities.

Today, in an international context of innovation, in all sectors of activity, successive crises and their consequences amplify the process of change, that is, changes in benchmarks, behaviors, economic paradigms in the face of exacerbated competition, and a crisis of confidence. We must not forget the increasing loss of reference points in our society which we have already mentioned in the introduction, but which we wish to recall and underline. Indeed, we are moving from ownership to use. Consumers are now uninhibited in using services that circumvent established rules (not all social models and networks are "ethical"). The penetration and increasing use of new technologies among customers (digitization of the information system, dematerialization of contracts, electronic signature, traceability of ongoing actions, etc.), to the point of making neo-banks—still limited in their services, but very ergonomic—attractive to the eyes of consumers.

Another fact about society and changing behavior: the parables of the modern world; living fast not to die; or Time is money—the dictatorship of time is amplified by the FinTech companies that compact it. This "*short-ermism*," suffered or chosen, distracts us from our past marked by a constrained time linked to the obligations of social and professional lives that did not extend beyond the individual. From now on, we want to dominate time and FinTech is only an amplifier generating a relationship to oneself, marked by excessive consumer society, over-indebtedness, and a relationship to others by the ephemeral (social networks, broken family ...). Comments, probably, need to be qualified, but, the instantaneity ("the whole, immediately") seems well established. A new process of consumption of financial products and services is taking shape and players who do not structure offers adapted to this new situation will quickly leave the market. With this observation, we leave the purely philosophical debates to find a reality that does not exclude reflection on the themes of trust and the dictatorship of time. Will there be articulation between the greats of finance and FinTech challengers? The ideal would be to combine the energy of the latter with the financial means of the former.

To evoke the future services offered in the area of financial services, some of which are already available, it is worth recalling two facts: one on the regulatory level and the second on the profitability of banks enabling them to make possible acquisitions—the deregulation dynamics driven by Brussels and the regulators that affect the banking sphere. Is the concept of "trusted third parties" associated with the latter really threatened by FinTech, which is not only developing in the electronic payment sector? The border between FinTech and banks is narrowing and they are now inspired by each other. Should regulation provide a framework that must promote the development of FinTech at the same time by avoiding harmful excesses for consumers or savers? And without creating significant competitive biases with other players in the financial sphere? The texts, European or national, which mark out participatory financing activities or those linked to payments, clearly illustrate these questions. However, FinTech thus benefits from a more flexible regulation. Indeed, various statutes, less restrictive than the banking, insurance, or management company statutes, are accessible to them. The top 5 French banks had a 25 billion turnover in 2016, that is a return to precrisis 2007 performance in a low interest rate environment with 15% of their branches unprofitable (ECB sources). The cumulative result of the top 5 French bank is also that of JP Morgan alone.

On this question of major trends and innovations, we also refer the reader to the International Financial Risk Forum 2017—organized by the Institut Louis Bachelier (ILB), on 27 and 28 March at the Paris Chamber of Commerce. During these two days, scientific researchers, professionals, and regulators from all over the world discussed the following theme. "Retail Finance and Insurance: impact of technical innovation through majors and fintech." The main work presented was related to progress made in the fields of modeling and risks in trading and understanding financial market mechanisms. In retail banking and savings management, the workshop focused on making interest rate forecasting models more complex and efficient. Emphasis has also been placed on the wide variety of platforms with GAFA, start-ups, and banks, which can have very different business models. This implies a need for transparency for security reasons, as well as a good division of responsibilities. The debates could not avoid the theme of regulation and the question of its intensity. For our part, we believe that innovation requires a minimum of regulation in order to facilitate transparency and interaction between actors, but too much regulation without concerted action with actors would go against the intended protection of the system.

At this stage of our reflection and in the face of the abovementioned threats for a banking sector that is still struggling to find appropriate answers, two central questions need to be examined: are these FinTech companies directive or not? Do they represent opportunities or risks?

Disruption or no disruption?

Opinions remain divided. On one hand, we hear that we cannot compare the financial sector to the VTC sector, with Uber, or the hotel sector with Airbnb, because the role of banks is to transform maturities. A FinTech company is not a bank. In a bank, financing a grant to a company declared bankrupt is not lost (deposits are guaranteed up to €100,000). In a FinTech company, the lender is the final lender and compared to the previous case, it will lose its funds. Even if the maturity transformation practiced by banks is drying up, it is not the same profession. FinTech companies can challenge customer relations without replacing banks. On the other hand, FinTech developed, starting in October 2014, with the lifting of the banking monopoly that prohibited individuals from lending money. With the blockchain, disruption is approaching for the sectors, such as payment solutions, wealth management, where Tech ends have not always sought direct confrontation. The speed of the decisions, the absence of guarantee, the sometimes negative image of the banks benefit the FinTech sometimes even to pay the price of the risk!

Opportunities or risks?

Trust remains the key factor, so can FinTech companies and banks work hand in hand? Advances in technology are creating new competition where operating conditions remain favorable. Despite the low volumes, peer to peer lending, and crowdfunding credibly challenge the core banking business, the highly profitable asset management sector is linked to the spread of AI. The fact of being "rushed" has an essential virtue, that of being obliged to leave a relative comfort. And yet FinTech is an opportunity for banks. By pushing them around, this new competition allows traditional financial institutions to Modernize. By attacking banks on their own ground, FinTech companies will force them to modernize in a very short time. What would have taken 10 years will have to be done in less than 5 years. Being pushed will force banks to invest massively in digital technologies. The FinTech comes to nibble portions of the (very large) bank cake. But they need banks, their customer base, and their ability to cope with economic crises to develop. The banks' recent acquisitions in the FinTech sector demonstrate their willingness to react. For their part, the financial giants are closely observing the functioning of these light structures. Banks and FinTech do not always agree on the right way to monetize their partnerships. What are the possible economic models?

Banks and FinTech both want to cooperate via programming interfaces. But they do not agree on value sharing. This may simply involve hosting or investing in start-ups, but also more narrowly, allowing access to certain customer data, in order to create new services via dedicated programming interfaces, APIs. To draw inspiration, they need to learn to weave functional relationships with each other. In the world of finance, symbiosis seems to prevail over confrontation.

Whether they like it or not, the banks are moving into "open banking." Under pressure from financial start-ups or Internet giants who are accustoming customers to new mobile uses, major banks have understood their interest in cooperating more and more with FinTech. This may involve hosting or investing in start-ups and, more narrowly, allowing access to certain customer data to create new services. In this scenario, in addition to its role as lender, the bank thus evolve toward a function of data editor 2.0 specialized in financial services?

FinTech companies also have a major advantage over banks: they focus on the customer experience, not on the act of buying. The bank's traditional model is becoming outdated, because it no longer meets the expectations of a nomadic and hyper-connected *"consum'actor."*

Finally, other models, undoubtedly a little precursor, are of less interest for the FinTech and even lesser for the banks: they suppose that the banks develop an activity dedicated to APIs, with new consulting functionalities (zoom on certain trends, etc.) or technical support provided to partners. In this scenario, in addition to its role as lender, the bank would thus evolve towards a function of data editor 2.0 specialized in financial services.

Banks and FinTech are moving toward a business model of cohabitation. Banks envy the dynamism, technology, and sense of customer experience of FinTech, while the latter dream of having access to banks' customers. Still granular, it is a real movement of bottom which is set up. Banks are abandoning their universal character and are counting on the aggregation of third-party services via a network of partners embodied by FinTech. The objective is to move the lines of a fixed banking system to match new customer behavior and expectations.

In this new environment, what will be the involvement of the regulator and its FinTech committee ("FinTech, Innovation et Compétitivité" = FIC created within the AMF in June 2016) to simplify the life of these start-ups in transparency, security (processing big data in compliance with the Data Protection Act), and the distribution of responsibilities?

Banks are far from being as agile as FinTech in terms of customer acquisition, managing data volumes, or geographic deployment. But they have a massive clientele. And that's where cohabitation makes sense. On the FinTech companies' side, initiating partnerships with banking colossuses represents a fast path toward profitability and significant market share gains. As far as banks are concerned, they can only observe the scarcity of transaction points with their clients. Even if current transactions are still carried out via the services of traditional banks, some are diverted by tracking applications such as "Bankin" or by robot-advisors such as Yomoni. Partnering with players developing solutions that they themselves are not able to offer, because of their regulatory constraints and their structural and cultural rigidity, allows banks to renew the currently fragile link with their customers and better serve them with more appropriate offers. Fortuneo and BforBank have understood this well by developing the Linxo account aggregator under a white label. Crédit Mutuel Arkéa's verdict is without appeal, "*We do not fear their competition, our future depends on our ability to work with these players because banks that do not reinvent the way they do business will die,*" warns Anne-Laure Naveos, head of acquisitions and partnerships for the mutual group. Still granular, it is a real movement of bottom which is set up. Banks are abandoning their universal character and are counting on the aggregation of third party services via a network of partners embodied by FinTech companies. The goal is to move the lines of a fixed banking system to match new customer behavior and expectations. Because at the end, the first beneficiary will always be the customer. Banks that do not reinvent themselves are doomed to disappear.[48] The conditions for success are a collective affair for all the staff of a bank under the aegis of a "visionary" manager who can no longer be satisfied with being just a manager. For our part, we consider that we are moving toward a model of cohabitation where symbiosis seems to prevail, but for how long facing the ogres GAFA, NATU, unicorns?[49] In the meantime, the latter keep on buying several million dollars promising start-ups. This practice could prevent the development of major innovations beyond their control.

Some new competitive services: Cryptocurrency, crowdfunding, and its variations

Specialized FinTech companies have developed, mainly, in the field of payments,[50] generating a plethora of services that are difficult to seduce

[48]For a very enlightened general point of view on this theme of change, we refer the reader to Jean-Louis Beffa's book *Se transformer ou mourir*, Seuil, Paris, February 2017.

[49]In 2017, there will be 186 of them in the world, with only 18 in Europe, including only two in France (Lille-based OVH, a specialist in the Cloud, and the carpool giant Blablacar).

[50]Within the framework of thematic publications, the economic journal *Les Echos* regularly publishes sector studies. For more statistical data on the payment industry, at the international level, we refer the reader to the dossier entitled "The payment industry facing

French customers, but seek to meet needs, hitherto little or poorly covered (constitution of pools: on a personal basis for a holiday project; to offer a gift between relatives and friends on the occasion of a wedding, a birthday, retirement, etc.). Our overview of these innovations will cover topics ranging from mobile SMS, peer to peer payment, to online cashing. In addition to GAFA, banks, mobile phone operators, and smartphone manufacturers, there are many initiatives that offer new payment services to their customers or users. For example, Lyf Pay, available since May 2017, created by the merger between Wa and Fivory, the electronic wallets of Carrefour and Auchan, allows consumers to pay directly from their smartphone in their respective channels as well as at small retailers.

BNP Paribas, Crédit Mutuel, Mastercard, Oney, and Total have joined forces to reach more customers under the Lyf Pay label. With more and more mobile and connected users, the Lyf Pay application, the most advanced to date, can be downloaded on any smartphone and allows the cardholder to pay for purchases, but also to place orders online or make donations to associations. In addition to promotional offers from points of sale, the application has both a payment card and a loyalty card.

In addition, Mastercard and Visa are working on the use of connected objects as new payment media thanks to the dematerialization of the card.

Paradoxically, between political voluntarism, private initiatives, and the characteristics of banking markets, emerging countries appear to be more advanced in the adoption of these new payment methods. About 70 million Africans already use these "wallets" (here to designate wallets to designate payment systems by phone: Google Wallet allows its users to store credit cards, loyalty cards, and gift cards) attached to mobile phones via "Mobile Money." In payments and money transfers, the penetration rate of FinTech companies has already reached 40%. Thus, M-Pesa (M for mobile and Pesa for money in Swahili) in Kenya and Tanzania, created in 2007, specializes in microfinance and money transfers. Other examples, in China WeChat or Weixin, created in 2011 is a mobile text messaging application originally developed by the giant Tencent. It has become the most popular social network and a true "*Swiss Army knife*" for more than 900 million Chinese, its main competitor being Ali Pay, the oldest because

---

digital, supply mapping, deciphering competitive developments and analysis of winning strategies," Les Echos Etudes, November 2017.

it was developed in 2004 within Ant Financial, a subsidiary of Alibaba Group. In Europe, Denmark, which is observing cash payments collapse, is said to be in first place with 3 million users out of 5.6 million inhabitants. In France, according to a study by EY FinTech Adoption Index, the adoption rate of mobile payment services in France for 2016 was 27% while the European average exceeded 33%. While French people are generally satisfied (80%, according to a recent COFIDIS Retail survey for the Crédit Mutuel/CIC group) with traditional payment instruments (SEPA (Single Euro Payments Area), a European area of 34 countries in which rules and means of payment are unified), the adoption rate of the new payment methods mentioned above remains below the European average. The success of these new services depends on the combination of two factors: (1) the need for users to have a sufficiently extensive and profitable merchant network for them; (2) the ability of the operator to make its payment service profitable. Even free of charge, this service is not certain to attract French consumers. These innovations will be attractive and will satisfy the French users, if they are able to bring real new values (within the framework of the 3 "Vs," in particular: Speed, Volume, Variety).

In order to consolidate this section devoted to new payment services, the box below sets out some legal guidelines on this subject.

It should be recalled that in January 2013 France transposed the European directive known as the "Electronic Money Directive (EMD)," which was intended to accompany the development of new payment instruments on the Internet and mobile phones. On this occasion, the Monetary and Financial Code gave a definition of electronic money: "it is a monetary value that is stored in electronic form, including magnetic …." It is a digital equivalent of cash. The law of electronic money[51] is a young one, part of another that is hardly older, it takes its source in the European directive of September 16, 2009, known as DME 2, transposed in France, in the Monetary and Financial Code by a law of January 28, 2013. These new rights for payments and electronic money are to be included as an extension of the SEPA (Single Euro Payments Act) mentioned above.

[51] Concerning the foundations of these new rights and the transposition of this Directive, we refer the reader to the specialized book entitled *Droit de la monnaie électronique* by Pierre Storrer, Revue Banque edition, Paris 2014.

Three recent decrees concern our subject and more specifically: the cap on anonymous electronic money; the cap on prepaid cards; and the cap on the payment of certain claims.

Legal elements of payment entitlements and electronic money:

Concerning the capping of anonymous electronic money and the capping of prepaid cards, and despite Decree No. 2016-1523 of 10 November 2016 on the fight against the financing of terrorism, in this landscape of concern, Decree No. 2016-1985 of 30 December 2016 increases the capping of cash payments for tangible pawnbroking transactions and payments made in electronic money! Now, Article R. 561-16 of the Monetary and Financial Code if it includes the condition of exclusive acquisition of goods and services as well as the maximum stored monetary value of 250 € for capping anonymous electronic money. It modifies the ceiling which is no longer annual but monthly in the case of a rechargeable support. The maximum storage limit with a territorial limit is €250 per 30-day period. Furthermore, it is prohibited to change the electronic money medium by means of cash, except in the context of a limited circulation of this currency or for a limited acquisition of goods. Finally, anonymity falls in the event of reimbursement and withdrawal operations of an amount lowered from €1,000 to €100. These provisions are in line with the transposition of the 4th Anti-Money Laundering Directive. At the same time, an article L. 561-9-1 is created in the Monetary and Financial Code, which provides: "if there is no suspicion of money laundering or terrorist financing, persons who issue electronic money [...] are not subject to the due diligence obligations provided for in articles L. 561-5 and L. 561-5-1, subject to compliance with conditions, in particular thresholds ... ."

The maximum monetary value is set under a new article of the Monetary and Financial Code (D. 315-2) and by decree (No. 2016-1742 of 15 December 2016 for entry into force on 1 January 2017 ...):

The maximum monetary value stored in electronic form is €10,000 per calendar month; the maximum withdrawal amount is €1,000 per calendar month; the same applies to the maximum cash refund amount by means of the said medium.

Finally, for the capping of the payment of certain claims, since 1 January 2017, and in the event of a French tax domicile, or professional needs, cash and electronic money are dissociated (€1,000 for cash and €3,000 for electronic money, Art. D. 112-3 of the Monetary and Financial Code).

The following box, to close this paragraph, looks at the case of the neobanks and more specifically evokes the launch, by way of illustration, of Orange Bank on November 2, 2017 (day of the "dead," should we see a particular connotation there).

***The Orange Bank case*: the general context and justification of this strategic choice to create an online bank. What are the advantages of the mobile phone operator? On the occasion of the presentation of the Orange Group's results in March 2017, its CEO, Mr Stéphane Richard, between curiosity, speculation and fantasy, announced this creation by presenting it as the "director" of the banking sector or, even better, the "Free of the bank" by allusion to its competitor for telephony. Strengths, weaknesses and supply:**

- **Advantages**
  - **The regulatory context: since February 2017, the "Macron" law has improved conditions for banking mobility. In addition, in early 2018, the Payment Services Directive (PSD 2) requires banks to share data with their competitors ...**
  - **Experience: with more than 10 years of presence in Africa in financial services in 17 countries including Côte d'Ivoire since 2008, the Orange group already has more than 30 million customers. In Europe, Orange, together with a Commerzbank subsidiary, has developed a banking application in Poland since 2014.**
  - **The Orange network: the offer is presented in 3,700 points of sale; Orange telephone shops, Groupama and Gan agencies play a complementary role with its 27 million mobile customers. All this represents a marketing power with consistent customer databases.**
- **Weaknesses or questions**
  - **After discussions initiated with Axa Banque, then with Boursorama, a subsidiary of Société Générale, Orange finally acquired 65% of Groupama Banque's capital in October 2016. The launch initially envisaged in May 2017, then postponed to July, took place on 2 November 2017.**
  - **In appearance, in the Orange Bank project, what worries the traditional banks, the online banks and its direct competitors of the neo-banks, it is its orientation, deliberately, "low cost" which risks putting the whole market of the private individual under pressure in a context of low interest rates offering little room for manoeuvre for the profession . This "free" display for active users is particularly irritating to the banking profession. Before the end of 2017, the Crédit Agricole Group plans to react and also take advantage of its extensive sales network. Its offer would not only be accessible directly on the mobile but also via the 39 Regional Banks through their 7,000 branches, thus enabling customers wishing to pursue credit or savings offers to be welcomed by an advisor. A plus not yet possible at Orange Bank! By the end of the year, Crédit Agricole will launch a basic, low-cost commercial offer called "Eko," which will include an international payment card, a cheque book and a number of practical services, including SMS alerts, for 2 euros per month. For its part, Crédit Mutuel has chosen to compete with Orange on its own ground: it now offers the "Avantoo" package, a current account and a payment card coupled with a telephone**

subscription (unlimited mobile plan with SMS/MMS and 50 GB of Internet), billed at 10 euros per month until the end of 2017 and then at least 20 euros thereafter. As for Crédit Mutuel Arkéa, in December it will equip its new bank, named "Max," with a free bank card compatible with the Apple Pay mobile payment service.

- **With the arrival of Fintech, this world of neo-banks is ultra competitive and does not stop awakening interest. Free (under the trademark "Freebank," since 2000), SFR, La Banque Postale, BPCE will soon react, without counting the German Fintech N26 which arrived in France at the beginning of 2017 (already claims 100,000 customers) or "C-Zam," the bank account offered by Carrefour Bank which after six months of opening already claims 90,000 customers (a current account sold in a box with a MasterCard for 5 € and one euro per month).**
- **The creation of profit margins is difficult and the cost of acquiring a customer is estimated at more than 200 € (including the costs of advertising and publicity + any welcome gift). Orange Bank's target of 400,000 customers in the first year and 2 million customers in ten years remains ambitious. In addition, an annual loss of 100 million euros is expected for the first five years of the launch.**
- **The attrition rate, despite the new provisions of the Macron law, remains low (4% in the bank against 15% for mobile telephony). It is still difficult to measure the impact of the easing of mobility advocated by the Macron law because it was only implemented in February 2017!**

- **Offer: Free bank card with online opening and welcome bonus of 80 €. The credit card and account management fees are free in the event that the customer uses this payment method 3 times a month. Banking transactions are processed in real time. The credit card can be configured with the possibility of choosing its secret code or lock/unlock certain functions. Overdraft fees do not include any intervention fee in the event of an overrun and the rate of any facility is 8%. Only restriction, in case of step carried out in shop with the assistance of an adviser costs 5 € whereas it could have been made on line free of charge. Unlike online banks, Orange Bank will not require minimum income to open an account...**

Under these conditions, what lessons can we draw from this price war? If not, what are the concerns? What answer could we give to our preliminary question? What about the FinTech allies or competitors of banks, especially since the European financial authorities have been concerned about the impact of the technological and digital developments mentioned above? Indeed, in a recent document[52] the Basel Committee did not

[52]"*Sound Practices: Implications of fin Tech developments for banks and bank supervisors (Consultative Document, 49 pages).*"

hesitate to submit for consultation from August 31, 2017 to October 31, 2017, in order to assess the impact of FinTech for the financial sector and supervisors. It issues 10 recommendations on bank governance, risk control, and IT systems. For the Basel Committee, traditional players could find it difficult to resist the onslaught of FinTech. The business model of banks remains uncertain. Between 10% and 40% of retail banks' revenues and 20%–60% of their profits, in particular, will be at risk over the next 10 years. As an extension of this approach, *Les Echos* journalist, Edouard Lederer in his article,[53] published on September 4, 2017 on the newspaper's website, takes up five hypotheses on the future of the banking sector envisaged by the Basel Committee, where the darkest are not always the most improbable. Let us take these five scenarios from the most favorable to the least optimistic: (1) absolute victory of traditional banks. By relying on AI, "thanks to their knowledge of the market and their investment capacities, one possibility is for banks to improve"; (2) banks replaced by neo-banks; (3) precarious balance of cooperation in good intelligence, but, for how long?; (4) Less visible role of banks as simple financial service providers among others; (5) banks made obsolete by total disintermediation. In addition to this hierarchy from the most probable to the most unrealistic, the authors of these hypotheses do not really pronounce themselves on a more dominant scenario. In our opinion, scenarios 2 (increasing weight of new banks) and 3 (complementarities, which is the current case) seem the most credible. However, it should be noted that FinTechs are challenging the business model of traditional banks that had tried to increase their margin through higher fees or generate new fees (management or account management fees). The concern raised by the previous scenarios and the toughening of competition brought about by FinTech mean that the "low cost" parade, essentially, proposed by online banks (such as Hello bank of the BNP Paribas group, Boursorama of Société Générale, BforBank of Crédit Agricole, or Fortunéo of Crédit Mutuel Arkéa) by not charging either the bank card or account management fees for large deposits is no longer sufficient. After the originality of the Nickel account (which has more than 500,000 customers) launched in 2014 and marketed for €20 in tobacco shops, neo-banks are now settling quickly into the landscape and shaking up both traditional and online banks.

[53] Article entitled "Banks might find it hard to resist the wave of Tech ends."

Cryptocurrencies (or cryptomoney, cryptocoins): new forms of money or old recipes?

The cryptomoney revolution, which appeared with Bitcoin in 2009, claims to invent new forms of money. Today, there are nearly 2,000 cryptocurrencies, with several million followers throughout the world. How can we explain this enthusiasm, who until now remained unmoved to the warnings of those who saw a simple illusion in this revolution? We must not forget that attempts to reinvent money are not new. As sociologist Viviana Zelizer points out in her book *The Social Meaning of Money*, "Despite the common sense that a dollar is a dollar," human beings everywhere are constantly seeking to create new forms of money. Money is the main means of exchange throughout the world and has a community dimension. From Josiah Warner who opened the Cincinnati Time Store in 1827, which sold products in units of working hours, to Robert Owen who tried to establish a national fair labor exchange in 1829 in London, again on the basis of work tickets or "time money" as currency to the euro, and more recently to the initial offers of tokens[54] in the form of participative financing called ICO, all these innovations were linked to the profound desire to revolutionize society in an effort to break the inequalities. The development of alternative payment methods, both local and virtual currencies, animates the daily economic debate. Are we not on the eve of a transformation as drastic as the transition from gold to paper? Can these new forms be considered as currency in full right with regard to its three traditional functions (unit of account, value reserve, and means of exchange)? What risks do they pose to our societies?

Regulation and key data of participatory financing or crowdfunding

This new financing practice, which appeared in 2008 in France, consists of addressing Internet users to collect funds in the form of donations, loans, or equity investments in a project or a company. While grant platforms developed the most in the beginning, the new regulatory framework, initiated by the Social and Solidary Economy Act and its supplements, offer new development prospects for platforms that operate on loans or

[54]An ICO is a fundraising method that works by issuing digital assets that can be exchanged for cryptomonies.

capital investments. Participatory financing is a complementary alternative to bank financing, adapted to the local economy for VSEs, SMEs, or associations.

According to "gendarme de la profession bancaire" (acpr.banque-France.fr, the French banking regulator),[55]

"Crowdfunding works most often via the Internet and takes various forms.

- Donations with or without consideration;
- Loans with or without interest;
- Or subscriptions of securities.

In France, in order to promote the development of participatory financing in a secure environment for contributors (donors, lenders, or investors), the public authorities have adapted the regulations, by Order No. 2014-559 of May 30, 2014. A label has also been created to identify platforms that comply with the new rules introduced by Ordinance No. 2014-559 ofMay 30, 2014 and its implementing decree No. 2014-1053 of September 16, 2014. Depending on the nature of the proposed financing, participatory financing platforms may or may not have a regulated status for the exercise of their activity:

- An equity financing platform by subscription to financial securities issued by a nonlisted company must be registered with the ORIAS register as an participating investment advisor (CIP). It may also opt for the status of an investment services provider (ISP) providing the advisory service and, in this case, be accredited by the ACPR. These platforms are regulated by the AMF alone for CIPs and jointly by the AMF and the ACPR for ISPs.
- If the website offers to finance the project in the form of an interest-bearing or interest-free loan, or a donation with or without consideration, the platform must be registered with the ORIAS registry as an intermediary in participatory financing (IFP).
- The ACPR may control an IFP at any time.

Be careful. If the website collects funds on behalf of third parties in participatory financing transactions, the platform must be at least approved as a payment institution (PE) by the ACPR or be registered as a payment service provider agent."

[55]Concerning this regulatory dimension, the reader is suggested to consult the website www.legifinancepartners.com

The participatory financing platform, which collects funds on behalf of third parties in the context of such transactions, must be approved as a minimum payment institution (PE) by the ACPR or registered as a payment service provider agent (PSPA).

Whatever the financing and service model offered by participatory finance platforms, they must comply with the regulations and obligations corresponding to the activities carried out, that is fundraising, fund custody and management, public offerings, distribution of financial products. A distinction should be made between: (a) platforms based on the grant model; (b) platforms based on the loan model; and, finally, (c) platforms based on the equity investment model.

a. Since March 1, 2017, donation platforms are subject to the obligation to be registered in the single register of insurance, banking, and finance intermediaries managed by Orias as an IFP, status created by the ordinance of May 30, 2014. As an IFP, donation platforms must take out professional liability insurance. The amount of cover may not be less than €100,000 per claim and €200,000 per insurance year.

If the platform itself provides these payment services, it must be authorized as a payment institution. This authorization is issued by the ACPR, an independent administrative authority attached to the Banque de France, responsible for the authorization and supervision of banking and insurance institutions. If the platform entrusts the collection of funds to an authorized PSPA, in the form of a partnership, it must be authorized as a payment services agent. This requires registration with the ACPR.

Donation platforms benefit from a relaxation of the regulations applicable to payment institutions. They have a simplified prudential capital regime (minimum of €40,000), where the amount of payment transactions does not exceed an average of €3 million per month (average total amount made by the payment institution over the last 12 months).

Additionally, if the platform does not manage the collection of funds, by offering only a service of putting people who offer financing in touch with those who bring a project, it is not subject to the regulation of financial intermediary. When its activity corresponds to the provision of accommodation space, this may fall under the hosting providers' liability regime (Article 6. I. 2 of the Law for Confidence in the Digital Economy of June 21, 2004).

Payment institution authorization or the capacity of PSPA is not necessary for the platform to receive remuneration as an intermediary (bank charges, commissions, etc.).

b. Loan platforms, with or without interest, are subject to the obligation to be registered in the single register of insurance, banking, and finance intermediaries managed by Orias as an equity financing intermediary (IFP), status created by the order of May 30, 2014. As a PFI, lending platforms must carry professional indemnity insurance. The amount of cover cannot be less than €250,000 per claim and €500,000 per insurance year.

The participatory financing platform, which collects funds on behalf of third parties in the context of participatory financing transactions, must be approved as a minimum payment institution (PE) by the ACPR or registered as a PSPA.

The lending platforms benefit from a loosening of the regulations applicable to payment institutions. They have a simplified prudential capital regime (minimum of €40,000), where the amount of payment transactions does not exceed an average of €3 million per month (average total amount realized by the payment institution over the last 12 months). As discussed previously, for donation model platforms, payment institution authorization or PSPA status is not required for them to receive remuneration as an intermediary (bank charges, commissions, etc.).

c. For platforms falling under the equity or minibonds investment model, they must be registered in the single register of insurance, banking, and finance intermediaries managed by Orias as a CIP, a status created by the ordinance of May 30, 2014, which may offer up to €2.5 million, certain financial securities, without a prospectus approved by the AMF, and minibonds. They may also choose to opt for the status of ISP, that is, be able to provide investment services within the European Economic Area (EEA) and, in this case, be authorized by the ACPR. The latter status requires the platform to have a minimum capital of €50,000 if it receives neither funds nor securities from clients, and €125,000 if it does not.

Less than 2 years after the introduction of the regulation of the activities of participatory financing platforms, a new reform came into force in autumn 2016; the decree of October 28, 2016 introducing a new debt instrument, the minibonds, a subcategory of savings bonds. These titles, specially designed for participatory financing, have two main objectives:

1. To be simple to present and use for both investors and issuer while allowing the equity loan to be opened to legal entities and funds
2. To make it possible to keep a register of these securities thanks to "a shared electronic recording device enabling these transactions to be authenticated," in other words, a device based on "blockchain" technology

Minibonds are exclusive tools among platforms. The latter must be approved by the AMF as CIP and ISP to issue them. These statutes were created following the ordinance of May 30, 2014 on participatory financing, which gave crowdfunding its first legal status in France.

Joint stock companies (SA, SAS) and limited liability companies (SARL) whose capital is fully paid up may also issue minibonds. The company must have existed for at least 3 years, justifying a minimum of three closed accounting periods. The issue of minibonds by the same issuing company is capped at €2.5 million over 12 months.

The minibonds have been issued since October 2016 for a maximum term of 5 years with a fixed interest rate that must not exceed the wear and tear threshold. Only crowdfunding platforms holding CIP or ISP status can offer the subscription of minibonds.

Finally, regulation for public offerings of financial securities carried out through an equity financing platform that raise funds from a broad public may fall under the "public offering" regime, which requires, in particular, the publication of a prospectus subject to prior AMF approval. To avoid this formalism, the investment transaction must be qualified as a "private placement." This is the case, in particular, when the number of investors for a project is less than 150 people.

Since October 1, 2014, companies that offer financial securities to the public via equity financing platforms in the form of financial securities have benefited from a simplified procedure. No investment prospectus is required for a fundraising of less than €1 million (instead of €100,000 previously). Simplified information is sufficient. (Order of May 30, 2014 and its implementing decree of September 16, 2014).

The following statistics provide some key data on participatory financing based on the "crowdfunding barometer in France 2016" established by Financement Participatif France (FPF)[56] and KPMG as well as on

[56]FPF is an association under the French law of 1901, founded in 2012, with the objective of collective representation, promotion and defense of the rights and interests of stakeholders in participatory finance (also called crowdfunding)—particularly with regulatory

In millions of euros	2015	2016
Donations	50.1	68.6
Loans	66.3	96.6
Investments	50.3	68.6
Total	166.7	233.8

the "crowdfunding in France" dossier established by Statista for 2015 (statista.com). After doubling the funds raised between 2013 and 2014 from €33 million to €66 million, the table below shows the evolution for 2015 and 2016 by type (grants, loans, investments).

Disposition of the French to invest their savings in a crowdfunding campaign, by age group, by socio-professional category in 2015:

- ***Investing: Yes, probably 37% No, probably not 20% eventually some of their savings 40%.***
- ***By age: Yes, definitely (18–24 years) 7% Yes, definitely (35–49 years) 10% Yes, definitely (65 years and older) 2%.***
- ***By socio-professional category: Yes, certainly (craftsman or trader) 26%; Yes, certainly (liberal profession, senior manager) 6%; Yes, certainly (intermediate profession) 7%.***

Crowdfunding appears as a flexible and connected solution, closely linked to the evolution of digital technologies, promoting citizen involvement in responsible projects. The challenge today is to skillfully manage the integration of this funding practice, which not only gives greater visibility to responsible projects, but also encourages the mobilization and participation of multiple stakeholders.

Other possible areas for innovation in responsible finance: The emergence of new tools

The explosion of the FinTech sector brings its share of digital tools to help manage the finances and build savings. There are solutions adapted to all situations, whether it is to save for a future purchase, build up savings, manage your wealth, or invest. We present, below, a small selection of digital applications and innovations with regard to the plethoric offers of

authorities—to advance the financing of projects (entrepreneurial, cultural, social, humanitarian, etc.) by citizens, particularly in France.

The 1,019,488 funders in 2016 made the following average contributions to the 21,375 projects

	Donation without reward	Donation with reward	Interest-bearing loan	Noninterest-bearing loan	Bond	Minibons	Capital investments	Investments against royalties
Average number of contributions per project	47	74	329	9	182	516	112	121
Average contribution per project	62	63.4	415	66	3,622	631	6,343	309

The success rate of the projects is respectively

Donations	Loans	Investments
75%	94%	84%

digitized services while striving to privilege those related to responsible finance.

For information, at European level, initiatives have also been taken to create data sharing banks such as DEEP-De-risking Energy Efficiency Platform (a private incentive, financed in particular by the EIB, which makes it possible to pool data on green energy investments) and to list existing projects in the industrial sectors and building industry, to the development of the API, without omitting the modular financial services game. The aggregation of data, in sharing and transparency, and the grouping of partner actors, seems to be a necessary way to develop this new ecosystem. In France, however, there is no mention of "Open Bank," "green" Euro-PP (Euro Private Placement),[57] cleantech[58] financing, "peer to peer lending," and participatory financing, it is still not immune, either, to these technological intrusions. We describe some of the reflections on these five themes, keeping in mind the various omissions in view of the rapid developments observed.

- *Open Bank* or the game of modular banking services. After FinTech, blockchain, and other expressions related to the profound renewal of the banking sector that we have previously discussed, it is now Open Banking's turn to make its appearance. This term, which could be translated as "modular banking system," refers to the fact that banks share the data they have at their disposal with other banking services. Open Banking is the result of the introduction of new measures by the Competition and Market Authority (CMA) in the United Kingdom and the new European PSD 2. The aim of these

[57]Private bond placement in euros, created in France in 2012, aims to contribute to the financing of ETIs (mid-cap companies) and SMEs that do not have sufficient size to access the listed bond market.

[58]Abbreviation of clean technology, cleantech are industrial techniques and services that use natural resources, energy, water, raw materials (e.g., renewable energy, energy efficiency, ecomobility, circular economy ...) with a view to significantly improving efficiency and productivity. This approach is accompanied by a systematic reduction in induced toxicity and waste volume, and ensures the same or better performance than existing technologies.

regulations is to increase competition in financial markets and offer better services to customers by introducing more data access mechanisms. Open Banking is close to the current of open innovation and is closely linked to the concept of API. The aim of Open Banking is to separate the production and distribution of financial services. This is not a new question, but one that has arisen under the combined impetus of the trivialization of FinTech and the implementation of the PSD 2 directive, which requires payment account holders to give access to information of their accounts and initiate payments at the request of approved external bodies (such as, aggregators who are service providers in charge of providing information on accounts; initiators; or PSPAs) and mandated by customers. Thus, thanks to the API, banking applications can easily be offered to third parties and vice versa, to open its own product and service offering to external platforms—a real revolution for the banking profession used to zealously protect the access to its data.

- *"Green" Euro PPs* are to be linked to the Green Bonds theme, but here it is a question of financing SMEs that do not have access to this method of financing, so that they can also have "green" borrowing solutions at their disposal. If the "Participatory Financing for Green Growth" label (although created in April 2017) has enabled start-ups, as part of crowdfunding platforms, to inform them about the possibility of financing their renewable energy projects, by 2016, more than €11 million had been distributed to these young innovative companies in this field, according to the study on the GreenUnivers website and FPF—about 2.5 million per project (see the regulations presented in the previous subsection on crowdfunding) to associate local funders. According to www.leblogdesfinanciers.fr,

  "Euro-PP is MLT financing issued by a company (usually an ETI) or a public authority. It takes the form of an undivided loan or unlisted bonds and is the subject of a private placement. The loan is most often "arranged" by a bank from a standard contract and placed with investors by its sales teams. The arranger is remunerated by commissions. Euro-PPs, an additional source of financing, are therefore not intended to replace bank loans in their entirety, investors intervening only in addition to banks, in particular for risk reasons. Progressively, this financing formula endorses a "green" orientation under the recurrent demand of companies producing renewable energies in

partnership with SRI investors such as Mirova, which with Ackuo Energy issued €44 million within the framework of a "green" Euro-PP in 2016. Most investors are "institutional" (insurance companies, mutuals, banks, etc.). They invest alone or collectively through investment funds in the economy (FPE)."

- *Cleantech financing* consists in supporting the integration, in industrial manufacturing processes, of equipment that is more economical, less polluting, or leads to ecoefficient products, with a view to competitiveness and growth. Bpifrance[59] offers financing of this nature. According to its website (www.bpifrance.fr), eligible companies are independent SMEs[60] and/or TWAs[61] that have been in business for more than 3 years and are financially sound. The expenditures financed under this cleantech framework are intangible and tangible investments with a low pledge value, in particular those that optimize resources and processes, such as force or heat recovery equipment, improving the energy efficiency of processes, reducing polluting emissions into the air or reducing discharges into water, and reducing the consumption of inputs other than energy.
- **Peer to peer lending**
- **A**ccording to the study published by EQUINOX CONSULTING & CEPHEID CONSULTING[62] under the title, *Peer-to-peer lending, an opportunity for consumer credit players?*

The development of community Internet tools enabling users to create and distribute content (Web 2.0) has enabled the development of peer-to-peer platforms in different fields of activity: music (myspace), exchange of

[59]Bpifrance is a French financing and business development organization, created on December 31, 2012 and whose capital is held by the French State and the Caisse des Dépôts et Consignations. As a result of numerous groupings, Bpifrance supports investment. It is planned to invest around €12 billion in French companies in 2017. It operates in a context of tightening bank credit, with the objective of giving priority support to exporting SMEs and innovative companies; it also complements the offer of business angels (or "venture capitalists").

[60]According to the European definition of an SME, a company with less than 250 employees reporting either an annual turnover of less than €50 million or a balance sheet total not exceeding €43 million. It must be independent, that is, not more than 25% owned by one or more entities that are not SMEs.

[61]Up to 5,000 employees.

[62]www.equinox-cognizant.com, study from 2012.

second-hand goods (eBay), carpooling ... In the financial sector, a new type of player has emerged: online p2p lending platforms are benefiting from a favorable environment, combined with strong demand from individuals for online financial services and growing acceptance of transactions over the Internet.

Peer-to-peer lending is an emerging industry that facilitates credit sources outside the traditional banking channel by connecting consumers and small businesses directly with potential investors. Developed in England, Zopa, founded in 2005, is one of the pioneers of this form of loan. In the United States, where there are a multitude of platforms of this type which grant loans to individuals and companies, the best known is Lending Club launched by a French Renaud Laplanche.

After a thorough study of the credit application and acceptance, the loans are financed by sums lent by individuals who have opened an account on the platform. The money deposited will often be distributed among several borrowers, for small amounts, with different maturities and with visibility of the portfolio by position. Generally, the investor on the platform does not have the names of the persons to whom he lends, but, he can take note of information on his profession, the borrowed amount, the duration, and the way he reimburses. Sometimes a bank provides the back office for the platform. What are investors' motivations and potential risks? As regards the motivation, it can be supported by the amount of the remuneration close to the usual rates for the type of loan granted. Then, as the portfolio is spread over several borrowers, the lender regularly receives small amounts in repayment of its loan. These amounts are either repaid or reinvested. In Great Britain, these loans are also eligible for a tax deduction and the platforms are considered to operate more efficiently than those banks. For borrowers, the response to the request is communicated more quickly and efficiently than in a traditional bank branch. The major disadvantage of the formula, irrespective of the country, lies in the risk of nonreimbursement. In the case of the UK platform Zopa, thanks to the scoring credit set up, the default rate is estimated at 0.5% and is much lower than that of banks. This web solution of peer to peer lending is part of crowdfunding previously processed. It should simply be emphasized that not all platforms on the market are ethically or responsibly oriented and that they can sometimes be risky, fascinating, and conducive to creation and innovation. The following examples attempt to demonstrate that micro savings can easily support the solidarity projects of your choice without using your savings.

Participatory financing within the framework of responsible finance

Originally, cash back was applied only to certain bank cards. Their holders then received an amount based on the purchases made. Since the late 90s, cash back exists on the web.

You then receive a commission proportional to the purchases made on the Internet.

Similar to business providers, these platforms receive commissions from merchant sites, which they pass on in part to consumers. The principle of cash back is simple. When an Internet user makes a purchase on the site of an advertiser affiliated with a cash back site (the percentage paid by the seller to the cash back platform is around 5% of the amount of online purchases), the latter pays his customer a commission of approximately 1.5% calculated as a percentage of the validated basket. The larger your purchase, the more likely your cash back is to be consistent. This commission can allow you to anticipate future purchases, to save for your children, and you can also allocate the amount recovered to any particular activities you prefer. Even if the sums obtained prove to be small amounts, it is a way of combining the useful with the pleasant. By creating new links between consumers and brands, cash back, given the diversity of forms it can take, probably has a bright future ahead of it and should give additional meaning to purchases. Many platforms list several merchant websites and paid saving tools to guide your investment decisions In addition to optimized investment solutions at lower costs offered with the objective of democratizing savings tools, previously accessible to a certain informed clientele, several FinTech have developed to offer savings products simply and online. From €500 or €1,000 for the majority, you can subscribe various assets and contracts in order to awaken the potential of your inheritance and to optimize the evolution of your portfolio. Thanks to AI backed by new solutions, Tech's "robots-advisors" are able to advise you according to your savings project, your appetite for risk, and your interests—all accessible from your smartphone, tablet, or computer. Naturally, these new tools do not exclude supporting responsible finance products and players. Between delegated management and advised management, investors have multiple degrees of choice.

There are other forms of responsible finance expression, for example, with joint and several guarantee groups which replace the individual guarantee and introduce collective responsibility for the success or otherwise of the project with the sharing of income which partially consists of the interest being distributed in the form of a donation to joint and several bodies chosen by the saver, or even the abandonment of the partial or total remuneration (of the interest received, a dividend, a coupon, or the abandonment of management fees by the managing institution in favor of the designated joint and several bodies). The increase in individualism, overconsumption, and the dictatorship of time could have hindered the development of responsible finance. Paradoxically, this is not the case with professional and wage inequalities, including at the end of the 1990s, as in the 19th century, we are witnessing a renewal of responsible finance, for example, the Grameen Bank, created by Mohamed Yunus in 1983, in Bangladesh, essentially rural, grants loans without prior savings, on the model of credit unions. In the wake of Yunus, the whole movement of microcredit appeared; Citizen solidarity savings appeared in the mid-1980s, in Europe (CIGALES,[63] NEF, CREDAL,[64] Crédit union, Faim et développement, Triodos[65]) and in Quebec (Caisse d'économie des travailleurs, Fonds des travailleurs québécois) to fight unemployment and exclusion; Solidary finance, SRI in connection with the environmental aspect of sustainable development completes the range of financial interventions as well as impact investment, green bonds, and participatory financing of terms, which in the common language, are part of responsible finance.

The box below presents a quick zoom on some innovations presented during the "Bordeaux FinTech 2017" event held in Bordeaux on October 5 and 6, 2017. The aim of these 2 days, bringing together more than 600

[63]Cicadas or "citizen-investor network for a local solidarity economy." Cigales is primarily an investor club that brings together its members several times a year, collects their regular contributions to form a collective pool, and as its name suggests, invests in small start-up or young companies.

[64]Through its activities, Crédal puts itself at the service of people, companies, groups, and institutions with projects that respect people, the environment and/or everyone. Crédal offers a wide range of complementary services and products in investment, financing with more than 30 years of experience in accompaniment and economic animation.

[65]Triodos Bank has been financing the sustainable economy transparently since 1980. Triodos Finance B.V., a banking intermediary and exclusive agent of the Dutch company Triodos Bank N.V. founded in 1980 in the Netherlands. In France, the agency was created in 2013 and is part of the Triodos Bank group, world's leading sustainable bank.

people, 45 speakers, and 60 FinTechs, was to understand the disruptive phenomenon brought by digital technologies, to analyze its trends, and discover its players who reinvent finance. Approaching FinTech through user experience, AI, big data, blockchain, open banking, or crowdlending in different formats … such was the challenge. By 2021, nearly 3 billion people will use their connected mobiles, tablets, computers, or watches to access their banking services, according to a recent study. That is an increase of more than 50% in 5 years.

Focus on some FinTech examples that facilitate payments and the promotion of responsible finance[66]

- In addition to the oldest FinTech, "Paypal," founded in 1998, Leetchi (www.leetchi.com) is the service to collect and manage money in several countries. A French company created in 2009, 86% of whose capital is held by the Crédit Mutuel Arkéa banking group Leetchi is ideal for friends organizing a common gift for a birthday, a departure party, parties… but also for all your personal projects, associations (humanitarian, solidarity…) and many others. This platform offers free and few clicks to open a kitty on Leetchi.com. Then invite your friends to participate. Collect the money from the entries safely. When the prize pool is finished, you can spend it according to your wishes at Leetchi's partners free of charge, by requesting a transfer or by offering it directly to its recipient. In this area of new payment solutions, Leetchi claims success with 7 million users in 150 countries.
- Clezer (www.clezer.com), the young start-up winner of the Bordeaux Fintech 2017 pitch contest, proposes to develop a system allowing to divide any payment online or in store with your friends, in real time, and in complete security via a card and an application.
- Sokengo (www.sokengo.fr) is a participatory financing platform in the South West that enables associations, young companies, and individuals to finance their cultural, innovative, or solidarity projects by raising funds, developing their community target and disseminating their actions.
- Recognized for its expertise in the field of digital payment since 2001 (approved since that date), W-HA (www.w-ha.com), a 100% subsidiary of the Orange group supports retailers in their digital transformation and solves the problem of collection on behalf of third parties (from merchants to associations…). With the rise of service platforms (crowdfunding, collaborative economy…) W-HA has just launched with "API-Money" a complete white label device based on a suite of API "plug and play." In addition to security, the system makes it possible to manage a variety of uses ranging from real-time transaction tracking to customer relationship management (better knowledge of "Know Your Customer," KYC). Other solutions are also proposed by W-HA which make it possible to transform a smartphone or a tablet into a payment terminal. The operation is simple enough for the seller to enter the amount of the transaction on the terminal,

the customer validates the collection by introducing his bank card or by depositing his contactless payment device. He will receive his receipt by SMS or e-mail. It is a modern and responsive system that integrates naturally into business applications and allows mobile checkout anywhere in the store.

- Trade "differently" with BarterLink, a company specializing in resource networks. Bartering, according to BarterLink (www.barterlink.fr), is a new use of the sharing economy. Bartering, or barter, is the English word for the exchange of goods between companies. For its human, social, and environmental virtues and for the good economic sense it conveys, it enables business people to do what they do best: exchange and share. The young BarterLink network offers, in an accounting and fiscally authorized framework, an exchange of goods, services, or underused competences (machines, m2, manpower…) among the companies. For VSEs and SMEs, this network offers a simple and secure alternative to commercial transactions and traditional financing. Sharing is used as a secure way to trade without affecting the company's cash flow through a mobile application and web platform. To exchange quickly, BarterLink provides the buyer and seller, with a unit of account, an internal currency to exchange: the Link equivalent to €1. The actors have a secure account in a member area. A credit worth €6,000 is even offered for purchases even before "selling" skills or goods.
- Other examples could have been presented in the context of automated asset management consulting, where the "robot-advisor," or "robot-advisor" in French, provides portfolio management over the Internet, with little human intervention. Based on algorithms and the study of numerous data, the robot offers advice on purchases and sales to be made on different asset classes (equities, bonds, money). It can even decide to validate the transactions if the client authorizes him to do so—a way of offering low-cost services to all types of investors, including the most modest investors. (See the book referenced in footnote).[66]

In this context where disintermediation is becoming a real phenomenon for traditional banks that are increasingly subject to demanding regulation, can ethical banks still be developed? Conventional banks still play a significant role, for example, in financing projects with a negative environmental and social impact. In an article published on April 10, 2017 by the think tank Mr. Mondialisation,[67] "The list of ethical banks: why it is important to make your investments responsible," the former reports the

[66] On this theme of the FinTech revolution and for a more detailed inventory of the players, we refer the reader to the book: *THE FINTECH BOOK: The Financial Technology Handbook for Investors, Entrepreneurs and Visionaries*, by Barberis Janos & Chishti Susanne, published by Wiley, 2017.

[67] Mr. Mondialisation is an informal think tank and French-speaking citizen with an international outlook. Its objective: to stimulate free debate in the public sphere on the major global and local issues of our time and its website: mr.mondialisation@gmail.com

remarks made by Mrs. Lucie Pinson, in charge of the Private Finance campaign within the association Les amis de la terre, stating "Their responsibility in global warming is very important." Despite the opacity of the information, on several occasions, French banks have been called to order by associations because of the financial support they still provide to the fossil energy sector (participation in the financing of the Dakota Access pipeline; investments in coal-fired power stations abroad). Moreover, the article wonders whether, "Would French banks be ethical proof?" It must be emphasized that the issue of ethics goes beyond the environmental cause and the issue of human rights. Indeed, the recent financial crises have highlighted the fragility of our banks when they are involved in complex financial arrangements, the Panama papers affair for their offshore activities. Or again, in November 2015, on the eve of COP21, Mrs. Lucie Pinson reports, "the big banks had multiplied the declarations in which they claimed to disinvest in the fossil fuel sector... However, in 2016 Crédit Agricole and Société Générale were again involved in coal-fired power plant projects in Indonesia." More recently, the "Paradises papers" affair has removed confidence and reinforced the risks of damage to image or notoriety. What are the alternatives when you wish to avoid participating, via your savings, in this collective hypocrisy that Gaëtan Montier already denounces in his abovementioned book, *Ethical finance, the Great Misunderstanding*. The article above also reminds us that in order to move the lines, "in France, savings account outstandings are 10 times higher than current account outstandings, so switching savings has 10 times more impact!"

In an effort to remain objective, it should, however, be stressed that clients expect better practices from their banks caught between loss of confidence and vindictiveness on the part of politicians and civil society. To fill this image gap, banks are multiplying responsible projects and initiatives, mainly in two areas:

1. Social issues, with the implementation of more participative management practices where transactional marketing (quantitative sales monitoring) is gradually evolving toward more relational marketing (better integrating customer needs) the prevention of over-indebtedness and the development of banking inclusion.
2. The environment and the reduction of carbon borrowing (with La Nef at the top of the rankings followed by Crédit Coopératif and the Postal Bank).

Concerning, the so-called "ethical" banks, only two institutions really stand out to endorse this name in France. The NEF and Crédit Coopératif.

- In the 1970s the association of the NEF (New Fraternal Economy) participated, through the bonds of money, in an evolution of society in order to establish fraternity in the economy. The NEF, created in 1988, was first a financial cooperative offering savings and credit solutions oriented toward projects with social, ecological, and/or cultural utility. The 1984 Banking Act, which obliges all players acting as intermediaries between savers and borrowers to have the approval of the Banque de France, launched the founders of the NEF in a race for capital; they had to find 15 million francs (€2.3 million) of capital to become a bank. They finally got half of it together. The Société financière de la Nef was founded in 1988 as a cooperative under the 1947 Act. The Nef then had everything of a bank, with one exception: it was not authorized to receive and manage current accounts (chequing accounts, passbooks) but only deposits over 2 years old. It will therefore have to cope with term account resources frozen for more than 2 years in order to make suitable loans. It had to find additional income, the only margins between savings and medium-term credit not sufficient to sustain an establishment. These supplements were provided by a commercial partnership established with Crédit Coopératif which will guarantee the liquidity and solvency of the institution. Until 2015, the NEF offered its investments through its partnership with Crédit Coopératif. Thereafter, they were managed entirely by the NEF, and eventually, the passbook, the means of payment, and the current account will also be available. All this was done gradually, in 2016, it became necessary to convince, outside the circle of the militants, that an ethical bank is possible. The banking activities, authorized since April 2015, started gradually from 2016. This was achieved and now the NEF has become a full-fledged cooperative bank accredited by the ACPR. Commercially, NEF is no longer dependent on Crédit Coopératif and can open current accounts, issue bank cards, and receive deposits within 2 years. The year 2016 ended with a net loss of €1.422 million, above what had initially been forecast (approximately €1 million, the same level of losses as in 2015). Several unfavorable factors contributed to the deterioration of the result (the fall in rates, the end of commercial relations with Crédit Coopératif, the extension of its authorization, and the introduction of the first sight banking products and services, completing the offer). The NEF has nearly 38,000 member-policyholders and over €400 million in outstanding loans, for a net banking income of €8.3 million. The NEF should be approved "Entreprise Solidaire d'Utilité Sociale" (ESUS) in 2017.

- As for Crédit Coopératif,[68] it has a double lineage, the Banque coopérative des associations ouvrières (in 1893) and the Caisse centrale de crédit coopératif (1938). When they were created, these two entities were intended to finance production and consumer cooperatives. With the Banking Act of January 24, 1984, this new regulation enabled Crédit Coopératif to increase the diversification of its customers and its activities. The branch network was expanded. Caisse centrale was set up as the central body of a group of mostly cooperative credit institutions. In 1996, acquisition of BTP Banque and BTP Investissements followed by acquisition of Pommier, Finindus, Dôme (Crédifrance Factor) and Banque de l'Entreprise in 1998. Because banking regulations make it difficult for isolated medium-sized banking institutions to exist, Crédit Coopératif joined a cooperative banking group, the Banque Populaire Group. It signed a protocol with the Banque fédérale des banques populaires (BFBP), entered into its capital, and adopted the status of a société coopérative anonyme de banque populaire. The central body of Caisse centrale de Crédit Coopératif was then transferred to the BFBP. In 2009, BPCE was created, the central body resulting from the merger of BFBP and Caisse Nationale des Caisses d'Épargne (CNCE). BPCE became the central body of Crédit Coopératif which, as a popular bank, holding 1% of BPCE's capital. Crédit Coopératif is now by vocation the bank for social economy enterprises: cooperatives, mutual societies, associations, and social organizations. According to the press release of February 24, 2017, with just over €11 billion

[68] For the history of the group, we recommend reading the book by historian Michel Dreyfus: *"Financer les utopies, une histoire du Crédit Coopératif (1893–2013),"* Actes Sud 2013, with the support of the Fondation du Crédit Coopératif. To learn more about the objectives of the Fondation du Crédit Coopératif (Mécène de la culture et des initiatives sociales vers trois axes: connaître et reconnaître l'économie sociale; agir et soutenir la cohésion sociale; se mobiliser en faveur du développement durable), a cooperative corporate foundation, we refer the reader to its website: www.credit-cooperatif.coop/fondation/.

in loans outstanding at December 31, 2016, mainly devoted to companies and to the ESS sectors, Crédit Coopératif is continuing its commitment to a sustainable economy. At the end of 2016, Crédit Coopératif had 335,658 active customers, including nearly 70,000 companies and structures in the Social and Solidary Economy sector. It recorded the opening of nearly 30,000 new accounts.

These few figures highlight the very relative economic weight of our two ethical French banks. While the anchoring of these two entities in certain emerging trends mentioned above, such as the collaborative or shared economy, demonstrates the full modernity of their dynamism, they nonetheless remain very marginal. The risk would be that the cooperative model would regenerate outside cooperatives.

While we were full of hope for the cooperative and mutualist model, a recent study to which we contributed on behalf of the Caisse des Dépôts et Consignations left us somehow perplexed as to the progress that cooperative banks should have made in terms of responsible finance over their capitalist competitors. This study is entitled *Effectiveness, resilience and social and societal commitments of mutual financial institutions.*[69] Below is an extract from the conclusion on cooperative banks in a comparison with their capital-intensive peers on the basis of the years 2008 (before the crisis) and 2015. The main relevant criteria used to analyze any changes between the two referenced years relate to the proportion of *real economy* and long-term financing granted; risk control; employee participation; and governance (in particular, parity between men and women on boards). The study compares five French banks (the three cooperative groups: Crédit Agricole, BPCE and Crédit Mutuel against BNP Paribas and Société Générale) and four German banks (two cooperative banks: DZ bank, which owns Volksbank and Raiffeisenbank, as well as PSD-Banken and Sparda-Banken). It thus forms the sixth largest bank in Germany before the merger in November 2015 with the WGZ bank, grouping together 1,200 of the 1,400 German cooperative banks, facing two capitalistic: Deutsche bank and Commerzbank. In the terminology adopted for the title of the study, the concept of MFIs (Mutual Financial Institutions) also includes the study of SAMs (Mutual Insurance Companies) versus capital-intensive insurers. Concerning this research, the central question

[69]The study was completed in early 2017 in the framework of the Centre de Recherche sur la Finance Mutualiste (CREFIM) under the supervision of Esther Jeffers, Professor at the University of Picardie Jules Verne and Olivier Pastré, Professor at the University of Paris 8.

remains: "Are MFIs really mutualists?" This would only allow them to claim their specificity and thus a differentiated treatment of other private financial actors, particularly in terms of regulation. In short, is this specificity fully assumed? In conclusion of this study, we underline, "This research is worth as much, in our eyes, by the absence of conclusions … as by the empirical results to which we have arrived … . If there is an irrefutable conclusion to our research, it is the lack of statistical data on MFIs … and finally, the MFIs that communicate with the utmost parsimony on the themes … ." This being said

> *"There is no (or no longer is!) very marked difference in behavior between MFIs and non-mutualist institutions. Contrary to what existed at the origin of the mutualist movement, it is no longer possible to speak today of two alternative models … " To deal only with the case of cooperative banks and our criteria, the conclusion of this research states: "Mutual banks are more generous with a much higher level of employee profit-sharing compared to capital-intensive banks. They are less present in tax havens with the exception of Crédit Agricole. They occupy the first places when it comes to financing the real economy and long-term financing. They are also better capitalized and more prudent when it comes to risk control. Besides, in terms of gender parity, capital-intensive banks are more advanced, particularly in terms of the number of women on the board of directors. Nor do cooperative banks invest more than capital banks in Socially Responsible Investment (SRI), with the exception of Crédit Agricole, which stands out with its subsidiary Amundi."*

Prior to some general conclusions concerning this second part and at this stage of our reflections, it seems appropriate to underline the necessary mobilization of all the actors of civil society with the legislator so that they jointly commit themselves to request a more responsible inflexion of the financial sphere. The dispersed and benevolent behavior of a few actors remains insufficient to assume a transition towards more responsible finance. There will be no transition without impetus and citizen will!

Conclusion: What we must remember

To make it simple, RI is a young industry that lacks widely acknowledged and precise norms, guidelines, and definitions. So far, there is an understanding that RI is a generic term that refers to a wide range of approaches that integrate ESG criteria in the investment process. Beyond that, RI has a variety of forms. Two main approaches of RI can be identified: (1) Responsible investment as a part of the overall investment process (ESG Integration); (2) responsible investment as a product strategy (SRI Product).

The first refers to the integration of ESG criteria in the investment process. The investor understands ESG as part of his or her fiduciary duty or risk management as ESG aspects have a material impact on the economic value of portfolio holdings. These aspects have to be integrated into the financial analysis of all assets under management in order to optimize the risk-return profile of holdings and portfolios. A specific ethical motivation is possible, but not essential. In the last years, a growing number of asset managers and owners have adopted different types and scopes of these practices. Details about these practices can be found in own or third-party investment (for instance PRI statement) reports.

The second encompasses all financial products that have a specific SRI strategy. The investor understands ESG criteria as a tool to ensure that the investments he or she makes reflect his or her moral values. Consequently, he or she wants to align investment with ethics, social, or environmental purpose in order to improve the sustainable impact of investment decisions. Therefore, issuers with low ESG performance or that active in controversial sectors and/or activities are considered as problematic investments. Specific SRI products are designed for investors for whom ethical considerations play a major role in their investment strategy (e.g., church banks, foundations, etc.).

While the technology that cannot be ignored seems to be driving rapid changes in businesses, financial practices, and business models, the profusion of players, labels, and binding, even ambiguous, regulatory standards are likely to thwart the outcome of certain initiatives. Despite multiple moral incantations and numerous initiatives aimed at including extra-financial criteria in today's finance, it seems to us that the latter is still too marked by an outrageous short-sightedness and the search for margins at all costs. The reasons for the limitations to the foundation of a more responsible and faster finance, despite the many innovations presented in this second part, could come from the fact that the new products proposed, the new actors presented, would forget the technical component of this contemporary finance—a technique often erected as a standard. The challenge, then, would be precisely to regain a certain mastery of regulatory developments, for the time being, too much based on technology. The invasion of algorithms in risk measurement or performance enhancement implies a broader reflection and an analysis open to the ethical impacts sought by the contribution of techniques in the service of society. Over-reliance on AI only increases. There may be many advantages. The quality and efficiency of data processing can certainly go as far as improving regulatory compliance. But, these applications will remain promising if the associated risks are properly managed (complexity slows down assessments, risks of cyber-attacks manipulate market quotations, etc.). For the moment, the algorithms used have only been tested in periods of low volatility and they are already scaring the regulators.

With AI, will machines take power over humans? Will they end up being more cerebral and more formidable than bipeds? So many questions which are not definitively decided and from November 14 to November 17, 2017, in Nantes, the scientific community wondered, always, within the framework of the 12th days networks of teaching and research (JRES).[70] As we have indicated, AI remains difficult to control and must be monitored. Reality or fantasy? The debate remains open even within the scientific community. Thus, in the abovementioned symposium, according to Professor Jean-Gabriel Ganascia of the University of Paris VI Pierre and Marie Curie, author of the book "Mythe de la singularité, faut-il craindre l'intelligence artificielle?"[71] expert on digital humanities, to fear AI would be little justified. At the same time, the paleoanthropologist at the Collège de France, Pascal Pick, coauthor of "Qu'est ce que l'humain?"[72] (What is the human being?), emphasized, in this symposium, the human evolution and the vertiginous rise of technologies which can worry.

AI researchers and conventional economists may have very different views about the impact of new technologies. But right now, and forgetting the possibility of an existential battle between man and machine, it seems quite plausible to expect a significant pickup in productivity growth over the next years.

For the banking sphere, what are the consequences of the PSD 2, which requires them to share payment data, and the massive arrival of

---

[70]Colloquium Co-organized by the Universities of Nantes, Angers and La Rochelle.

[71]Published by Seuil, Paris 2017.

[72]Other coauthors of this book: Michel Serres and Jean-Didier Vincent, Paris 2010, publisher Le Pommier.

FinTech, a source of disruption, through the provision of a wide range of products that simplify their customers' daily lives through the user experience? These startups, which thus enter the financial products market by putting the client at the heart of the commercial act through a systematic study of the use or anticipation of the use of a product, a service, or a system, impose a cultural challenge on banks leading to reinvent their business models and their way of designing their information systems, as well as their distribution methods.

What solutions enable banks to adapt to this digital transition? Now, the threat is real and banks would have much to lose if they did not accelerate their adaptation to digital. If FinTech can still be evaluated as an acquisition target, banks need their agility and creativity. Conversely, FinTech can find, in a partnership financial support, access to data and approvals to develop. The recipes go through an amplification of digital in marketing, the use of AI for productivity gains, revisiting governance, forging partnerships via programming interfaces, integrating platform logic... so many necessary levers, but, will they be enough? Other strategies are open, coupling financial services with other services (real estate, e.g., property search, visits, preagreements on credit and services linked to moving...) specialization in a single business: asset management, equity financing...) offering white label financial services for competitors. In the scenarios we have suggested, in addition to the 5 hypotheses formulated by the Basel Committee (for the record...) offering financial services to competitors: Total victory of traditional banks; traditional banks supplanted by neo-banks; the precarious balance of cooperation between traditional banks; and FinTech becoming simple service provider in place of traditional obsolete banks we have not failed to stress that if the alliance between traditional banks and FinTech proves, temporarily, the most indispensable of ideas, it is also because the real threat lies far more in the possible role, in banking, of the GAFA than in FinTech. GAFA have the financial power, data access, technology, user experience, and agility... to meditate on

Finally, our "pregreen" list of responsible financial players, products, and systems (SRI, green bonds, green EPP, cleantech, peer to peer lending, cash back, etc.) is young, diverse, insufficiently mature, and of economic weight that does not allow this ecosystem of responsible finance, which we would like to see, to present itself as a fully alternative player in the face of modern finance. Times are changing, uncertainty remains great. Not all social networks and systems presented under the guise of leaning toward new technologies are responsible or ethical in the same way. Between a Blablacar putting drivers and passengers in contact in a collaborative spirit to participate in transport costs and an Uber seeking to impose a very profitable business model for a few people, beyond the general presuppositions which seem similar, the underlying objectives are radically different. All the social networks and all the actors of the collaborative economy do not have the same approach and the same social purpose. Let us remain confident and serene, but vigilant—according to the recent Freedom House report, which highlights the growing manipulation of social networks by states (30 countries in 2017 compared to 23 in 2016) through private opinion makers to shape online discussions or create fake news sites. Concerning the various social platforms, where Facebook probably played a major role in Russian interference in the American elections, the war of influences does not seem to be on the way out. The digitalization of our economies is not a fad, but a long-term trend that combines risk (manageable with probabilities) and uncertainty (non-manageable with probabilities) in the sense of the economic theory that is distinguished. Data will play a central role in the development of the financial sphere where yesterday's enemies (banks and FinTech) become today's friends, waiting for threats from powerful players such as GAFA. As the arrival of computer scientists was a revolution in the 1970s, that of data scientists is part of the same cultural revolution.

The bank must reinvent itself around the customer experience. It will have to shift from a quantitative-oriented business to a more accompanying business at every stage of its clients' life, while capitalizing on its most precious assets, transparency, and security in order to establish trust. To do this, we do not reinvent finance, we make it accessible. For responsible finance, in particular, how to attract more individual clients with incomprehensible jargon and nebulous product offerings? Transparency means presenting the traceability of the products of an investment. Security is explaining the nature of risk exposure and protecting data.

What we must remember

TO MAKE IT SIMPLE, responsible investment is a young industry that lacks wide acknowledgement and precise norms, guidelines, and definitions. So far, there is an understanding that responsible investment is a generic term that refers to a wide range of approaches that integrate ecological, social, and governance (ESG) criteria in the investment process. In addition to this, responsible investment has a variety of forms. Two main approaches of responsible investment can be identified: (1) as a part of the overall investment process (ESG Integration); (2) as a product strategy (SRI Product).

The first refers to the integration of ESG criteria in the investment process. The investor understands ESG as a part of his/her fiduciary duties or risk management. ESG aspects have a material impact on the economic value of portfolio holdings. These aspects have to be integrated into the financial analysis of all assets under management in order to optimize the risk-return profile of holdings and portfolios. A specific ethical motivation is possible but not essential. In the past few years, a growing number of asset managers and owners have adopted different types and scopes of these practices. Details about these practices can be found in individual or third-party investment (e.g., PRI statement) reports.

The second encompasses all financial products that have a specific socially responsible investment (SRI) strategy. The investor understands ESG criteria as a tool to ensure that the investments he/she makes reflect his/her moral values. Consequently, he/she wants to align investment with ethics and social or environmental purpose in order to improve the sustainable impact of investment decisions. Therefore, issuers with low

ESG performance or those active in controversial sectors and/or activities are considered as problematic investments. Specific SRI products are designed for investors for whom ethical considerations play a major role in their investment strategy (church banks, foundations, etc.).

While the formidable technology seems to be driving rapid changes in businesses, financial practices, and business models, the profusion of players, labels, and binding, even ambiguous, regulatory standards are likely to thwart the outcome of certain initiatives. Despite multiple moral incantations and numerous initiatives aimed at including extra financial criteria in modern finance, it seems to us that the latter is still marked by an outrageous short-sightedness and the search for margins at all costs. The reasons for the limitations to the foundation of a more responsible and faster finance, despite the many innovations, presented in this second part, could come from the fact that the new products proposed, the new actors presented, would forget the technical component of this contemporary finance—a technique often deemed a standard. The challenge, then, would be to precisely regain a certain mastery of regulatory developments, for the time being, too much based on technology. The invasion of algorithms in risk measurement or performance enhancement implies a broader reflection and an analysis open to the ethical impacts sought by the contribution of techniques in the service of society. Over-reliance on AI only increases. There can be many advantages.

The quality and efficiency of data processing can certainly go as far as improving regulatory compliance. But, these applications will only remain promising if the associated risks are properly managed (complexity slows down assessments, risks of cyber-attacks manipulate market quotations, etc.). At the moment, the algorithms used have only been tested in periods of low volatility and they are already scaring the regulators.

With AI, will machines take power over humans? Will they end up being more cerebral and more formidable than bipeds? So many questions that are not definitively decided. Artificial intelligence researchers and conventional economists may have very different views about the impact of new technologies, but right now, and forgetting the possibility of an existential battle between man and machine, it seems quite plausible to expect a significant pickup in productivity growth over the next years.

For the banking sector, what are the consequences of the PSD 2, which require them to share payment data; and the massive arrival of FinTech, a source of disruption, through the provision of a wide range of products that simplify their customers' daily lives through the user experience? These startups, which thus enter the financial products market by putting the client at the heart of the commercial act, through a systematic study of the use or anticipation of the use of a product, service, or system, impose a cultural challenge on banks leading to reinvent their business models and their way of designing their information systems, as well as their distribution methods.

What solutions enable banks to adapt to this digital transition? Now, the threat is real and banks would have much to lose if they did not accelerate their adaptation to digital. If FinTech is still evaluated as an acquisition target, banks need their agility and creativity. Conversely, FinTech can, in a partnership financial support, access data and approvals to develop. The recipes go through an amplification of digital in marketing, the use of AI for productivity gains, revisiting governance, forging partnerships via programming interfaces, integrating platform logic, and so on.

Finally, our "pregreen" list of responsible financial players, products, and systems (SRI, green bonds, green EPP, cleantech, peer to peer lending, cash back, etc.) is still young, diverse, insufficiently mature, having economic weight that does not allow this ecosystem of responsible finance, which we would like to see, to present itself as a fully alternative player in the face of modern finance.

The bank must reinvent itself around the customer experience. It will have to shift from a quantitative-oriented business to a more accompanying business at every stage of its clients' life, while capitalizing on its most precious assets, transparency, and security in order to establish trust. To do this, we do not reinvent finance, we make it accessible. In case of responsible finance, in particular, how to attract more individual clients with incomprehensible jargon and nebulous product offerings? Transparency means presenting the traceability of the products of an investment. Security means explaining the nature of risk exposure and protecting data.

Responsible finance: Utopias or realities, "from sins to works"!

"Man should put as much effort into simplifying his life as it makes it complicated."

H. Bergson, French Philosopher and Nobel Prize for Literature (1859–1941)

THE TITLE OF THIS THIRD PART underlines the recommended ways to deal with the defects or challenges ("the sins") identified in the responsible finance ("The works or commandments"). As for the quotation, it is, perhaps, a way of highlighting how far we still have to go in a world where we are better informed but less able to predict it. Between inventions and discoveries, the slightest information, the slightest rumor influences our way of seeing and thinking. Thus, is it a matter of trying not to know everything that is going to happen rather than preparing for it?

Moreover, in a world that copes with contradictions, if we accept that the transitions that are underway (energy, digital, social, etc.) will very quickly enable us to know how to do and manipulate almost everything from machines to living things, we must also consider the uncertainties in an international context. While the political and economic world is experiencing a new form of barbarism in which power relations are clearly taking over from the balances patiently forged by a few authorities, our future is being played out in the face of new players who are reluctant to be accountable to society. Thus, for the record:

- in the United States, the power of the Google, Apple, Facebook, and Amazon (GAFA) meets little resistance in the face of an unpredictable and turbulent federal state;
- Europe, far ahead in the race for innovation, favors the introduction of free competition and tries to contain the flows of migrants;
- China strives to regain the power of the middle empire.

Science and economics must regain consciousness. It could be high time to commit to developing a use of technology that is democratic, reliable, useful to citizens, and respectful of people and the environment. Societal commitment and responsible finance remain a collective challenge that cannot be anchored in our daily practices without all the players in our society acting together: citizens, companies, and the State.

In an interview[1] with L'Atelier BNP Paribas,[2] on the occasion of the publication of his latest book *Homo Humanix* (Editions Le Pommier, Paris 2017), the Belgian mathematician and philosopher Luc de Brabandère said about the computer, "I am obliged to note that the tool has become so powerful that great dangers present themselves to us. When we invented the car, it took 20 years to invent the Highway Code. But the computer is much more powerful than a car and we still do not see the code." From the birth of mathematics with numbers, 5,000 years ago, to the formulation of numbers, passing through natural philosophy (Galileo and Newton), then to encyclopedists segmenting sciences, 19th century binary computation, all of these inventions contributed, 80 years ago, to the birth of computer science, and the first fully electronic computer, electronic numerical integrator and computer (ENIAC). It is to this story that the aforementioned book and its author invite us. To specify in his interview about cybernetics could it become the perfect government by getting rid of mankind in the political decision? "No" answers Luc de

[1]Interview posted on the L'Atelier website on November 12, 2017, with the title: "Morality can be coded, ethics cannot."

[2]Created in 1978 by Jean Michel Billaut within Compagnie Bancaire, avenue Kléber in Paris, L'Atelier's vocation from the outset was to provide the various components of the company with ideas for innovation and lines of development for their businesses. Located in Paris, San Francisco, and Shanghai, L'Atelier BNP Paribas is a prospective company that has become a meeting and exchange place. This innovation watch center was quickly opened up to clients and partners of the BNP Paribas banking group as well as to any company or individual, offering them a better understanding of the challenges associated with the development of new information and communication technologies and to think about how to integrate innovations profitably into the company. Publications, conferences, incubators feed réflexions and innovations.

Brabandère by specifying, "Any software makes mistakes and a government cannot be based on imperfect software. We must therefore learn to live in uncertainty, to integrate error. And, so, to reinject ethics into our decisions. Morality is Roman, ethics is Greek. Morality can be coded, ethics cannot. As Dylan[3] said: "*You have to be honest when you're out of the law.*"

Without entering into many philosophical debates of the moral or religious order, let us recognize, however, a form of similarity with the knowledge of good and evil appearing in the Bible where the Ten Commandments would be designated as the most relevant reference point for believers, atheists, and agnostics alike. Hence with our title and the dynamics we wish, in all modesty and without claiming to be exhaustive, to impel this third part devoted to challenges and recommendations. In this search for meaning, statistical work[4] dating from 2010 has highlighted the fact that people who define themselves as atheists and/or agnostics have a better knowledge of religions than Christians. In a world marked by rising paganism and weakening of the Christian faith, a new similarity challenges us; could we not ask ourselves whether believers referring to decalogue in their moral judgments would not do so for ease, mimicry, credulity, and lack of knowledge? This reflects the image of responsible finance taken by certain protagonists as a fad in the fleeting and volatile sense because of the relative weakness of the outstanding amounts still invested, and therefore our questioning and doubt against it, myth or reality?

Gradually, under the influence of digitalization, we are in the process of moving from socially responsible investment (SRI), visualized in the 1930s, to the energy transition whose sustainable development objectives became the vector for understanding the firm's strategy at a time when the start of the next project, the emergence of the circular economy, is already appearing. SRI has long been an anecdotal, niche market. But for the past few years, investors have been in favor of responsible investments to support the most virtuous companies on a daily basis.

---

[3] Bob Dylan, born Robert Allen Zimmerman on May 24, 1941 in Duluth, Minnesota, is a singer-songwriter, musician, painter, American poet, Nobel Prize Winner for Literature in 2016.

[4] http://www.pewforum.org/2010/09/28/u-sreligious-knowledge-survey/The Pew Research Center is an American think tank known for its world religious demographic statistics. Its Head office is in Washington.

For an investor, SRI consists of taking into account "extra-financial" criteria in his or her investment choices: Environmental, Social, and Governance (ESG).

This approach can meet two objectives.

- For some investors, taking ESG risks into account ensures better long-term financial performance, and extra-financial criteria make it possible to detect new growth opportunities and minimize portfolio exposure to certain image and financial risks;
- For others, SRI is a way of favoring companies that respect values they are attached to (e.g., by favoring companies with good management of ESG issues in the supply chain).

SRI's influence has thus grown in a more demanding regulatory environment in terms of transparency and information for savers and investors, while striving to reconcile financial performance with social and environmental impact.

While responsible finance, as we have defined it in a broader sense, enjoys greater recognition, the need to take another step, namely to transform its potential through concrete actions enabling it to achieve a change of scale, remains a priority. The impact of more responsible finance on the firm's image and notoriety is recognized, as well as on its sustainability and differentiation from competitors. However, the lack of clarity on the creation of future value, acceleration of transitions, resistance to change, aversion to risks, instability of rules and laws are all constraints that mean there is still a long way to go in terms of applying investment strategies and universalize these new precepts linked to ESG, sources of innovation, and productivity gains. Between a communication tool and a real investment strategy, responsible finance has been monopolized by the media, which sometimes sees it as a response to recent crises and especially to the excesses of modern finance. Myth or reality, have we ever said! A plurality of questions remains. Is it just a passing phenomenon, or is it well anchored? In view of the attention paid to responsible finance, it remains complex and unknown because of the multiplicity of hybrid assets it conveys and also because of its lack of a universal definition. The concept is still subjective because of the different prioritization of values in different countries (priority given to the environment; society; shareholder activism, etc.). It would take consensus, or even better, consent! Far from reconciling, fully, morally, and financially, responsible finance cannot avoid performance and cannot claim to be a unique alternative model. If its importance has not stopped growing, beyond a simple phenomenon of fashion intended to give good conscience to some investors, it occupies, however, only an anecdotal part in the financing of the economy (according to the extra-financial criteria used 13%–14% in the United States, 6%–7% in France, and between 3% and 5% in the world conventional finance, that is an approximate amount of $23,000 billion for this responsible finance, according to Eurosif). In terms of performance, its defenders consider ESG filters to be risk-reducing, while its detractors consider them to be a singular limitation to diversification, which asset managers adulate so much. In fact, many recent studies (Standard & Poor's, Domini Social Index, Thomson Reuters, Nelson, etc.) have concluded that responsible finance performs close to or slightly better than traditional indices. However, the costs inherent in nonfinancial analysis, which is often more time-consuming and more complex in terms of product presentation, should be included in this performance assessment. Integrating more responsibility into finance cannot be achieved without overcoming the various constraints mentioned above.

We believe in the ability of humans to react and adapt, but it must be said that the dictatorship of short time and the speed of innovation disrupt our bearings and reinforce uncertainty despite the paradox of being better informed. It is indisputable that conventional finance has enabled the world economy to reach growth thresholds in terms of wealth and consumption never imagined which are also unevenly distributed at the same time. However, the slags of successive business crises (unemployment, inequality, loss of reference points and confidence, etc.) probably remains the most damaging, which continue to affect the image of this finance. The absence of responsibility, in a finance obsessed solely with the pursuit of profit, is one of the essential causes. For the record, here are some recent examples affecting the responsibility and trust of our finance:

- In September 2015, the international Dow Jones Sustainability index rewarded the Volkswagen group and recommended the title to the SRI funds a few weeks before the case of software supposed to measure CO_2 emissions on vehicles produced by the car manufacturer broke out.
- Already in 2012, the British bank HSBC was accused of complicity in laundering dirty money belonging to drug cartels and other entities banned from accessing the US financial system. It paid a fine of $1.9 billion. At the end of 2017, it again backslid in France. One of its subsidiaries escaped trial thanks to a new provision in the Sapin II Act, the Public Interest Judicial Convention (CJIP), which allows a

company prosecuted for corruption or tax fraud laundering to negotiate a fine, without going to trial or pleading guilty. The national financial prosecutor announced on Tuesday November 12, 2017, that HSBC Private Bank, a Swiss subsidiary of the British banking giant, had agreed to pay €300 million to escape a lawsuit for "tax fraud laundering," an unprecedented procedure and a record amount in France. A legal procedure, certainly, but, which makes us plunge into the context of the Anglo-Saxon judiciarization. This criminal agreement stems from the Anti-Corruption Act of December 9, 2016, known as the Sapin II Act, which is intended to modernize and strengthens the judicial action against cross-border financial crime. It enables the courts to obtain compensation for damage caused by corruption or tax evasion, without waiting for the outcome of a trial, in return, not for an admission of guilt but a simple admission of the facts by the suspected company. This type of transaction, hitherto foreign to French law and poorly understood in France, is also in force in the United States.

This revelation did not elicit much comment and indignation, which could be seen as an "encouragement" to continue. One member proposes to limit this procedure to fines of less than €200,000.[5]

- In France, after the 19th century and the Pereire Brothers, after the end of the 20th, and "J6M" (For Jean-Marie Messier, "Moi-même-Maître-du-Monde" or Jean-Marie Messier, Me, Myself and I, Master of the World), doubt persists in the 21st century with Patrick Drahi's Altice group boss and his acrobatic acquisitions. What are the similarities between these three significant examples? Spending entrepreneurs engaged in balancing acts including buying companies that often combine containers and content (financial and real estate or digital and entertainment) with massive debt. For Emile (1800–1875) and Isaac (1806–1880) Pereire, although the initiators of the French industrial society, bankers, and politicians with creative and overflowing genius, the bankruptcy and liquidation, in 1867, of Crédit Immobilier made Baron Jacob Mayer, known as

[5]According to the AFP on November 17, 2017, the deputy Nicolas Dupont-Aignan plans to table a bill to prohibit transactions "over 200,000 Euros" in major economic crime, protesting against a court decision that allows HSBC to avoid a trial by paying 300 million Euros.

James de Rothschild[6] (1792–1868), refuse help from the Pereire saying "The fundamental difference between a Rothschild and a Pereire is that the former would forever remain a banker with his money, while the other is basically a banker working with other people's money." For "J6M," concerns the acquisitions of Seagram (alcohols), Universal Studios and the USA Network digital package, which generated a loss of more than 14 billion for the Vivendi group in 2002 in the United States. Concerning Patrick Drahi's business, Altice had already lost more than 40% of its stock market value by autumn 2015. The promise to stop the acquisitions had somewhat restored the confidence of the financial world to an extent that in June 2017 Drahi succeeded in one of the largest IPOs of the year on Wall Street by raising $1.9 billion. However, the debt of more than $50 billion reached in the fall of 2017, combined with the decline in SFR's revenues following the loss of more than 3 million subscribers dissatisfied with the quality of services, underscores the weaknesses of a financial system driven by abundant low-interest liquidity that allows it to issue more speculative assets to satisfy investors seeking a return. Is management putting pressure on suppliers and employees enough to restore margin and confidence? That is the question for Drahi. This makes journalist Stéphane Lauer say, in an article in *Le Monde*, dated November 20, 2017, under the title, "*Le doute sur la méthode Drahi s'est installé,*" recalling Altice's slogan "*Ensemble repoussons les limites*" ("together, let's push back the limits") that "Some are convinced that Patrick Drahi has already exceeded them." For us the question remains who are the "others," the bankers, the regulators? Is it the end of a new musical or a beautiful story, as the aforementioned journalist nicknames it: "*Altice in Wonderland*?" For us, in addition to the impact of such a case in terms of image and notoriety for the world of finance, it raises questions about the quality of supervision of banks and financial institutions.[7] The latter case

[6] A traditional big money maker, innovator in risk management: personal money, information network at European level, ability to counter guarantee its financing with gold ... and founder of the French branch of the group.

[7] At a time when BNP Paribas, Crédit Agricole, and Société Générale are considered "systemic" by the Financial Stability Board, BPCE comes out of this group closely monitored by the authorities. The Financial Stability Board, the entity that coordinates the G20 countries in banking regulation, published the annual ranking of the largest banks in the world on Tuesday November 21, 2017: these so-called "systemic" institutions must, according to the regulations resulting from the financial crisis, further protect themselves to face the

illustrates the immediate danger of over-indebtedness of the private sector and governments.

In an article published in *Finance et bien commun*, no. 39, January 2011, under the title "Ethics vs Finance? An analysis of the origins, problems and future prospects of this relationship," Bruno Federico Fernández, explains the evolution of this couple, this oxymoron of "ethical finance" that we can relate to our subject. Below is a summary of his analysis. According to the author, three stages in the modern history of economic thought can be highlighted: the first where finance and ethics were united; the second where they were juxtaposed; and a third where separation was complete: (1) Adam Smith's *Theory of Moral Feelings* (1759) was revisited by the Nobel Prize Winner for Economics A. Marshall; (2) The juxtaposition with A. Marshall, professor at Cambridge University, has succeeded in separating economics from the department of moral philosophy; (3) The separation with the neo-classical Friedman and Stigler who preach that any value judgment must be completely removed from economics if it is to become a science with preaching purposes where the moral obligation would be solely to act on the basis of rational choice criteria. For Bruno Federico Fernandez:

> *Bad intentions, like the unconditional pursuit of profit, end up driving out good intentions such as gratuitousness. If trade is motivated only by price, other virtuous forms of human relationships will be excluded, which will undermine the very foundations of the market, such as willingness to cooperate and trust (Zamagni-Bruni,[8] 2007). If these acts are punishable by moral judgment (goodness, wickedness), finance cannot be ethically neutral"[...] "The current capitalistic model gives an excessive role to the market to the detriment of the state and civil society organizations.*

History shows that the exacerbation of one of these three components leads to the establishment of untenable models as was the case of communism and the welfare state. Today, the logic of "the efficient market that produces, then the State that redistributes," according to Bruno Federico Fernández, is insufficient to bring equity to society. Even corporate

---

crises. Our questioning is, how with these reinforced requirements, the financial sphere accepts this debt situation of the Altice group?

[8]Based on "Civil Economy" by Bruni (Luigino) & Zamagni (Stefano), *Civil Economy: Efficiency, Equity, Public Happiness (Frontiers of Business Ethic)"*, Oxford Bern, Peter Lang, 2007.

philanthropy is insufficient because it is assimilated to assistance that contributes little to the personal development of the most disadvantaged or to the brotherhood of civil society. We share these observations and the market, the State, and civil society must incorporate these three goals as their own: efficiency, fraternity, and equity. Financial companies need to use, in addition to the contract, reciprocity. In donation, equivalence is not given quantitatively by a price, but according to the quality of the response (In addition to the material, there is also the relational).

Responsible finance applies to all areas of finance. While it must be even better promoted among social economy actors by integrating their specificities, it is also essential for traditional and new financiers. As a funder, it seems necessary to have a complete arsenal of financing for the life cycle of companies as well as those belonging to the social and solidarity economy. Until now, however, the latter have relied almost exclusively on traditional credit or the contribution, too often reduced, of members/member-policyholders. New tools, facilitated by the ESS Law (called the Hamon Law), must be studied and made available. The concept of equity or quasi-equity should be promoted. New instruments have emerged: debt instruments (subordinated, medium- to long-term debts, short-term debt, trade finance, factoring, etc.) or dedicated instruments such as securities issues or traditional debt, loan funds, venture capital funds; schemes which can be supplemented by dedicated guarantee schemes such as regional or sectoral guarantee funds, or the mobilization of national public funds (investment for the future, access to social housing, etc.), or European funds (EIB, EIF, Council of Europe Bank, etc.).

What recommendations should be made to convince people to be sustainable, responsible, and profitable? The aim of the book is to offer a progress report on how economic and financial actors, in general, can better integrate the goals of more responsible finance into their priorities. This transition to a transparent appropriation of finance dedicated to economic development must be a necessity and must not sink into threatening "green washing." Despite the plurality of tools and rules, this responsible finance, by its approach and the traceability of its performances, appears as the only one likely to accompany the financing of the multiple transitions that reach us. Finance "*differently*" that impacts credit institutions' business models. To present and clarify our perception of the challenges and stakes of this responsible finance, we will lean our approach on the imperative obligation to act ("*Actions not words*" to use the slogan of the suffragettes which celebrated the centenary of the birth of the movement in England).

Let us also remember that in this world where we live, every one individual out of seven (more than one billion) does not have a birth certificate and official identity. Mainly located in sub-Saharan Africa and Asia, they are humans whose existence is not registered for reasons of conflict, ethnicity, and politics (e.g., many births were not registered for long in China due to one-child policy). The World Bank[9] intends to remedy this with its ID4D ("*Identification for Development*") program. Strong identification systems are critical to the success of many development programs. As part of the Sustainable Development Goals to, "provide a legal identity for all citizens by 2030, including by registering all births." The digital revolution could provide the best answer. To identify the right technologies, the World Bank's ID4D program inaugurated on October 12, 2017, a high-level expert council to "*accelerate progress towards digital identification for all.*" It has nine members from politics, global organizations, and private companies. Providing access to education, legal, health, and financial services is one of the 17 objectives of Sustainable Development stated by the United Nations. The Novethic notes, in particular, that biometric identity guarantees women's emancipation in Pakistan and that a "smart-card" acting as a bank card is accessible in Nigeria thanks to the national identity number. The "*Techfugees Global Summit,*"[10] held on October 25 and 26, 2017, in Paris, focused on these "invisibles" and ways to promote the inclusion of refugees. The summit explored, using new technologies, the key themes of a refugee's journey from departure from a country and travel, to arrival in a new environment, and social inclusion.

Between contradictions sometimes, defects and challenges, we will try to present some recommendations likely to amplify the role of this responsible finance which we call with all our wishes. After examining some major defects (*not to say "sins"*) of this responsible finance (see

---

[9]With 189 member states, staff from more than 170 countries and more than 130 branches around the world, the World Bank Group is composed of five institutions (International Bank for Reconstruction and Development; International Development Association; International Finance Corporation; Multilateral Investment Guarantee Agency; and International Centre for Settlement of Investment Disputes) working together to find sustainable solutions to reduce poverty and share prosperity. The World Bank Group is one of the main sources of financing and knowledge for developing countries (www.banquemondiale.org).

[10]The Techfugees association (Tech & refugees), created in 2015, connects NGOs and associations to refugees and supports initiatives where technology can really help people. It organized its first exhibition in October 2017 in Paris (techfugees.com).

Section 3.1), we formulate some suggestions, "the ten works or commandments" among the ones most relevant to us (see Section 3.2).

"The Sins" or major defects of responsible finance: seven diagnostic elements

Without repeating the "seven deadly sins" (greed, envy, pride, greed, laziness, and lust), we propose to the reader a nonexhaustive census which only engages the author whose omissions and assimilations you must forgive. Seven elements that we believe need to be corrected to promote the development of responsible finance both nationally and internationally. Following list is proposed successively in this section: the necessary democratization; an educational effort; improving the readability of actors and products; too many labels kill communication; search of universal terminology; access to statistical data to analyze developments; and giving priority to measuring impacts. This list does not prioritize priorities.

a. Necessary democracy

Responsible finance lies between "*ZinZins*" and militant savers, with much higher outstanding for the former, even if they themselves represent only a very small proportion of assets under management. It is necessary to recall here the simplifying difference that characterizes SRI on one hand, which is more generally the responsibility of institutional investors, and the solidarity-based finance of militant savers on the other. Even if responsible finance has a broader scope, SRI generally refers to a method of selecting companies, the majority of which are listed on the stock exchange based not only on their financial performance but also on an assessment of their ethical, social, and/or environmental behavior. Solidarity-based finance is founded on a stronger degree of commitment since the activities financed are chosen on the basis of their actual usefulness in the fight against exclusion, social cohesion, or sustainable development and which are not listed on the stock exchange. According to the 16th solidary finance barometer published in May 2018 by Finansol and La Croix, an additional €1.8 billion were deposited on solidary investments, bringing the total outstanding to €11.5 billion. This represents an 18.3% increase over the year, that is, 7.38 billion, and nearly 20% increase compared to the previous year. Growth in the second channel was just as high: outstanding bank savings reached

3.62 billion Euros, an increase of 18.7%; 548 million, that is, 9.2% more in 2017.

As for the SRI, still very little known by the French, despite the key figures for 2015 (source Novethic), SRI outstandings on the French market reached nearly € 746 billion at the end of 2015 (i.e., 2.6% of the French asset management market and still three times more than in 2007); a market that grew by 29% between 2014 and 2015. However, the institutional investors held 90% of the outstanding amounts (SRI employee savings represented 10% of the outstanding amounts).

Novethic's annual surveys quantified the French responsible investment market from 2001 to 2016, and from 2017 onward, this Caisse des Dépôts et Consignations subsidiary focuses its analysis on conviction SRI to adapt to responsible investment practices that have become more demanding. It provides us with the following latest data.

In 2017, Novethic's 123 SRI conviction funds posted a much stronger growth dynamics (+42.5% or 31.2 billion assets under management) than all 404 SRI funds distributed on the French market (+14%), accounting for nearly a quarter of total assets of more than €800 billion.

Convincing SRI offers investors' portfolios built with strong and assumed ESG bias: these are Best-in-Universe funds and environmental and social thematic funds. It is on this dynamic segment of the SRI fund market that Novethic has focused its "Indicator" analysis since 2016. Far from the logic of volume, the objective is to focus Novethic's expert analysis on an innovative and promising market dynamics. The clear increase in SRI conviction, which now represents almost a quarter of outstanding, is based on a twofold dynamics: strong inflows of €6.4 billion and good performances. Thematic funds constitute a large half of the SRI conviction offer and are predominantly environmental, even if funds on social themes are developing to a lesser extent.

It is therefore necessary to take a new step forward in order to truly irrigate the economy and change the scale. What needs to be done to increase the reach to the general public, which is a necessary part of this expected progress? Although a bit old, according to a September 2014 EIRIS-Ipsos survey, only 6% of French people know how to give a precise definition of SRI, while more than half (52%) say that social and environmental criteria are important or very important in their investment decisions. While demand is very real, almost all French banking networks offer SRI financial products. The offer does exist, but it remains little opted for. Why? And why it is not a priority for banks that is the dilemma? Despite various communication efforts, including responsible finance or solidarity savings weeks, banking marketing, banking networks, and banking training must become more involved to promote responsible finance. The latter must be an offer and not an arbitrary choice by the bank. Of course, responsible finance, more generally, is diverse and complex, and therefore more expensive in terms of information, explanations, and training than a traditional product. Supply must be further stimulated by demand, as in the case of "organic" consumer campaigns. Communication supports exist, as well as information documents, but responsible finance still does not have a clear history. The multiplicity of the innovations presented does not facilitate its diffusion toward the market of the private individuals. Even the codes and various labels are insufficient to reach the general public. Above all, they have raised awareness among institutional investors and asset managers. The documents exist, but not the story. Training and marketing departments need to deploy more campaigns than at present.

Since States are also increasingly becoming an active participant in responsible finance, it can be left to them, perhaps, to amplify public awareness on the subject. Taxation can be a lever, particularly effective and appreciated by the French, for household savings to irrigate business development. At a time when our rapidly changing economy is facing new investment needs (intangible, digital, external growth) to which banks do not always know how to provide the necessary financing and when French people's savings account for more than €2,700 billion in low-risk liquid financial investments (62% of French people's financial wealth), action should be taken to reconsider this situation. Responsible finance with its new vectors, such as blockchain and FinTech mentioned earlier, could accompany these new financing needs. Business models are evolving but the perception of financing solutions is not changing. As the economic and financial culture of savers remains relatively weak, the State and the main players in financing should do more to educate people to ensure a better dissemination of more responsible financing methods with or without twinning to traditional loans.

b. Necessary pedagogy

In addition to health, access to education is one of the first rights for all. At a time when everyone agrees that we are going through a period of economic and social change and even transitions (climate, digital), digital, in particular, affects work[11] which, under the effect of deindustrialization, is becoming bipolarized; on one hand are highly qualified jobs and, on the other, the least qualified, which are experiencing strong expansion but are poorly paid and cannot be replaced by robots. It will probably be necessary to stop protecting jobs in order to secure people as a priority. The ways of doing business are also changing, and it is important to distinguish between employment and work, where employees do not disappear. It would even be on the rise in the United States (96% of American workers would be salaried and not freelancers as preconceived ideas would suggest). Nevertheless, all these changes encourage us to reflect and rebuild knowledge in order to get out of the anxiety generated by this "platform capitalism" that threatens us.

Under these conditions, there is no reason why forms of knowledge acquisition should not be affected. However, the fundamentals of education remain: giving society the assets of its development and the individual the opportunity to control his environment and arouse his curiosity. If the Internet is changing the way we work, it is also changing the way we think. It leads to an organizational and generational break. Without aggravating the skills deficit, at a time when multiple reforms in vocational training and its financing are under way, it seems necessary for us to begin, by analyzing needs before evoking the plethoric offer; to consider, at the same time, training in technology and training in the use of this technology; to change the paradigm and to move away from the couple of diplomas/trades and toward the couple of certifications/skills integrating adaptability, reasoning, and empathy to better understand others. This requires modular training and a better correlation between the expression of needs and availability of funding.

[11]The 37th National Meetings of Crédit Coopératif, on Wednesday November 22, 2017, had "Work is capital" as their theme. If work often opens horizons for us, it can sometimes destroy us. Work builds us, it contributes to make us human. Can we still control our destiny? Work is to be accomplished in social and economic life; it is dignity more than capital. Such were the orientations of this conference which refuse to be ready to think.

Lifelong learning is becoming a necessity. While this is good news, it is also necessary to review the relevance of financing and the capacity to mobilize players and financiers while integrating the typology of companies (take into account disparities and specificities according to size: VSE/SME/ETI/GE). At a time when we are talking about redistributing financial flows to the least qualified or those seeking employment, will the most qualified not have to bear the cost of training themselves?

Here, we have not discussed the design and delivery of training (self-training, distance learning, mixed face-to-face, etc.), all factors that influence learners' motivation and the cost of teaching.

c. Necessary simplification for a better readability of actors and products

Without resorting to recent events linked to the need to simplify, let us recall that the subject, generally speaking, is not new. Montaigne was already complaining about the fact that in France there were as many laws as there were for the whole world. France—the country with 400,000 standards, the country where a law is created for each problem, —has so many laws that it is difficult to apply them. The implementing decree is often absent and, as a result, the law will not come into force. Since the 1990s, several administrative structures have been responsible for simplifying procedures, such as the Commission for the simplification of formalities, the Commission for administrative simplifications, and the Directorate General for State Modernization in 2005. During Sarkozy's presidency there was also a desire to reduce costs for companies and the State. Holland's Presidency saw the announcement of a "simplification shock" and its 450 measures concerning companies, individuals, and administration. Accessing the Élysées Palace in 2012, François Hollande promised to divide by two, and then by three, the flow of information that a TPE must send to the Administration. A Simplification Council for companies was created on January 9, 2014, from the "electronic identity card" to the "silence is acceptance" principle, according to which silence kept for 2 months by the administration is acceptance and no longer rejection of the application. Since 2014, 186 concrete measures have been implemented out of the 312 initiated. Jean-Vincent Placé was appointed to head a State Secretariat in charge of State reform and simplification, a ministry which has since been abolished. As with every political alternation, we make a clean slate of the past, the principles often remain in a state of pious wish.

Even more serious is the French-style costing of this administrative complexity. Thus, according to the OECD, the administrative burden in France represents a cost of between 3% and 4% of GDP, or between €60 and 80 billion. According to the World Economic Forum's Global Competitiveness Report (2016–2017), France ranks 115th out of 140 countries in terms of administrative "burden." According to European Commission estimates, a 25% reduction in administrative burdens on business would increase EU GDP by 0.8% in the short term and 1.4% in the longer term, saving businesses an estimated €15 billion.

The right to error was already part of the instructions given to the administrations; it is a right that cannot be opposed. However the fact of legislating is that it does not change anything to the current practices it was supposed to end. As for the simplification measures, it is a relaxation of appearance, many are referred to experiments already in progress or to be launched.

In fact, the new text on simplification, presented in November 2017 by the Minister of Action and Public Accounts, Gérald Darmanin, attacks mainly the form and not the substance. Once again, this "*n*th" reform maintains the general regulatory framework and offers, only, to substitute digital for paper and to allow citizens to challenge the decisions of civil servants. Even the right to error was already part of the instructions given to administrations; it is a non-binding right, the fact of legislating it does not change current practices. Yet simplifying procedures is certainly at least as important an issue as training and taxation, both for all administrations and for responsible finance, where too many rules, labels, and definitions make it difficult to see and read. The profusion of products, texts, and standards is "seriously" detrimental to its dissemination. We have tried to draw up a typology of the main components of this responsible finance, but we find that we only present a partial view of its fields, since the speed of inventiveness under the influence of technology is upsetting the economic and financial context.

We talked about knowledge, training, and the need to reconsider their approaches without reopening the subject, but let us not forget that economics and finance are disturbing disciplines. Their faults are to address sensitive subjects. To speak of money is to evoke the distribution of wealth and income, to speak of enterprise is to describe how goods and services are produced and placed on the market, but it is also to analyze the organization of work and the performance of the firm. The temptation is too great to talk about a better world of which we would dream of and not, sometimes, about the harsh realities linked to relocations and employment, etc. One of the explanatory factors we have here is, perhaps, the lack of knowledge of the economics and financial sphere in the France. French people are characterized by a low knowledge limited to economic indicators related to daily life (unemployment rate, price index, etc.) and even lower on macroeconomic concepts (the growth rate would only be known to a third of them, etc.). However, various attempts have been made to give the French the keys to understand the world in which they live. Two organizations, established almost simultaneously, have experienced varying fortunes in this desire to educate.

The Conseil pour la Diffusion de la Culture Économique (CODICE, Council for diffusion of an economic culture) created in October 2006 on the initiative of the Minister of the Economy, Finance and Industry, Thierry Breton, wanted to respond to this real educational need. Renewed in 2008 by Christine Lagarde, 2010 will mark the end of this council considered to be too communication-oriented.

At the same time, created in 2007, Idies, L'Institut pour le Développement de l'Information Economique et Sociale (institute for development of social and economic information) is a nonprofit association (law of 1901) whose vocation is to animate the social debate around the conditions of economic and social information necessary to the quality of a democratic life. More militant, this association is backed by partnerships such as the Economic Alternatives Review, trade unions, teachers' associations (the National Association of Economics and Management Teachers, the Association of Economic and Social Science Teachers), the Centre des Jeunes Dirigeants de l'Economie Sociale, MAIF, Crédit Coopératif.

Without counting the many debates and protests raised by the successive overhauls of economic initiation programs in secondary education and their contents, we just celebrated 50 years of the "ES" series (Economy and Social) of the general baccalaureate (high-school degree) by striving to preserve a critical view of the world in which we live. However, the Academy of Moral and Political Sciences, which has just published a report and opinion on economic and social science education, has once again been very critical of it. An opposition that is not new between the defenses of more social sensitivities on the one hand, and more liberal ones on the other. Report of Section 4 of the Academy of Social Sciences, Paris, November 2017, within the Académie des Sciences Morales et Politiques, there were criticisms such as the composition of the commission of experts dominated by representatives of the private sector; the methodology of the report was based on the exclusive analysis of textbooks; and its method of financing by the American Foundation for the Paris School of Economics.

To remain objective, let us recall that in 2008, Idies had received a grant from CODICE.

These few clarifications tend to demonstrate that the debate on the dissemination of economic and financial knowledge is still, largely, struck by ideology, which does not simplify the task for its deployment. Another example, in the area that we consider to be one of the main levers for raising awareness of long-term savings and responsible finance, is employee-share ownership, a recognized and proven factor of social cohesion via profit-sharing and incentive schemes. About 123 billion in outstanding savings as of December 31, 2016, and concerns 305,000 companies and more than 9 million private employees, it still remains poorly understood. In an article[12] in the Magazine des Professions Financières de l'économie, no. 12, dated June 2017, Claire Castanet, Director of Investor Relations at the Autorité des Marchés Financiers (AMF), points out that statistical data from a study conducted in 2016 by TNS SOFRES at the request of the AMF, *"81% of employees holding employee savings plans are convinced that employee savings plans make it possible to develop long-term savings. On the other hand, only one holder out of two considers himself capable of managing his employee savings. More than 62% believe they do not know all the characteristics of employee savings. Less than half of them are aware of the risks associated with the selected investments, and the numbers drop when it comes to arbitrage opportunities or fees. Half of the holders of employee savings plans*

[12]Title of the article, pages 78 of the magazine *"La semaine de l'épargne salariale"*, section Dossier.

surveyed believe that the information received on their investments is insufficient."

In addition to the information aspect, there is a lack of training in economics. It would probably be even more disappointing if savers continued to assess their knowledge of SME/ETI financing via flagship products such as PEE/PERCOs. Thus, from there to talk about responsible finance, green bonds, circular economy, etc., the gap must be considerable and this is without evoking the necessary fiscal simplification (knowledge of tax incentives; modulations of the social lump sum for the top-up; revisions of the rate of the social lump sum that affects these forms of savings, etc., we are aware of locking ourselves in an esoteric and technical language far reachable for the citizen) that should be associated with all these products and fields. The stability of fiscal and social rules, as in other areas, is an indispensable condition for the successful dissemination of responsible finance.

d. Too many labels

If the proliferation of labels launched both by private pharmacies and by States seems to be appreciated by professional players, it is nevertheless necessary to question whether they really constitute a godsend for the general public. For several years, various labels have already existed in European countries where the SRI market is well established. This is the case of LuxFlag in Luxembourg, the Austrian eco-label, the FNG in Germany (also present in Austria and Switzerland), or the TEEC and ISR labels in France. The problem is the heterogeneity of these different standards, which does not always make it possible to find one's way from one country to another.

The objective of striving to increase SRI subscriptions to individuals is far from being achieved. The proliferation of labels could blur communication in the market.

The AMF has, in its time, even spoken of SRI as "a "heterogeneous" concept, difficult to read and which results in too little transparency," and to demand a better overall coherence as well as important information efforts on the part of fund-management companies.

The heterogeneity of these different European labels does not always make it possible to find one's way from one country to another. In its report on sustainable finance submitted to the European Commission on January 31, the High Level Expert Group (HLEG) addresses the issue of creating a European label for SRI funds. The report suggests extending an existing label to financial products at European level, the ecolabel, which allows consumers "to identify the most environment-friendly products." This is only one part of responsible finance. The eternal question of the criteria used and the body responsible for awarding this label remains to be settled —a label with blurred outlines despite the real will to succeed and the hope that it will not be confined solely to the environment. In addition, many funds can continue to claim SRI worldwide without having obtained a label. Other countries, such as the United Kingdom, Spain or Italy, do not currently have a label.

e. **In search of universality of concepts**
Similar to the labels, the heterogeneity in the definition of concepts and selection criteria is detrimental to the dissemination of responsible finance products. Under this responsible finance generic term, we find a multitude of polymorphous, evolving, unframed, and unregulated concepts. Marked by the weight of history and sociocultural developments in different countries, partial definitions were proposed. Thus, the FIR has offered since 2013, a definition of SRI, "An investment that aims to reconcile economic performance and social and environmental impact by financing companies and public entities that contribute to sustainable development regardless of their sector of activity." As we have seen, for this placement alone, multiple approaches cohabit in various and cumulative ways (Best-inClass; Best-in-Universe [more weighted than the previous category], Exclusion, Shareholder Commitment; Climate; ESG Integration; and more recently, Impact Investing). So what about more recent concepts?

f. **In search of statistical data for relevant comparative analyses**
One of the major obstacles in the analysis and development of products is the collection of reliable statistical data. The periodicity of the reports and the various definitions of the data collection perimeters considerably hamper any comparative study. The dispersion of statistical data marked by different areas of investigation, both with national and international bodies, does not facilitate the task. Another constraint is the diversity of data collected by sector of activity, both in the areas of governance and investor behavior. The consolidation of data by sector (banking, insurance, savings, etc.) affects all comparisons. There is, probably, a work-in-progress in the field of data consolidation at the international level.

This is necessary in order to resolve the nagging question of the relationship between companies' ESG levels and financial performance, which has already been the subject of numerous studies, many of which still suffer from poverty and/or the dispersion of available data.

g. **Measuring impact: fashion or necessity?**
Investing in a context of technological transitions with the ambition of generating a positive social or environmental impact is a logic that remains difficult to evaluate. Despite of generous formulas, the evaluation of ESG criteria still poses many technical problems today. How to assess the real impact in terms of ESG performance of financial assets managed by financial market players in the context of increasingly complex regulation (e.g., different COPs, Grenelle de l'environnement, Article 173, Labels)? On a theoretical level, the question of impact is at the crossroads of different disciplines in a new field of research where the social impacts of investments are more difficult to measure than the environmental impacts (expressed in tons of CO_2 avoided, millions of liters of treated wastewater, hectares saved from deforestation, or tons of recycled waste). Indeed, for social impacts, the development of performance indicators is a work in full effervescence because, to convince, they must demonstrate their ability to move the context. Here, in the case of the measurement of social impacts, various sensitivities or perceptions subsist among the following arguments: (1) "human well-being" (measured by job creation, schooling rate, residences with renewable energy, or the number of people relocated, etc.); (2) the simple census of companies integrating sustainable themes; (3) projects that would not have seen the daylight without responsible and supportive financing.

This trial and error in definitions and concepts is normal for investments with the characteristics of a still emerging niche.

Ten recommendations ("Commandments"!)

Globalization has created an incredible amount of wealth but has also deepened multiple inequalities (in income and wealth within nations and between nations through the accumulation of capital). Uncertainties and instability characterize our economic, political, social, and institutional world. A world in mutation that generates multiple changes of landmarks and paradigms. Two examples illustrate this weakening of the context: (1) Behavior of economic actors, governance of firms, and forms of work are undergoing profound changes. Self-employment now accounts for 10% of the workforce in France, 15% in Europe, and over 30% in the United States. A constantly growing population marked, often, by a social protection inferior to that of the employee in terms of providence and retirement. At the same time, as Patrick Artus points out in the aforementioned work,[13] of which he is co-author, *"Global capitalism makes employees take more and more risks without compensation." "The risk must be remunerated, otherwise there is a dysfunction of the economy."* With this increased flexibility, the author stresses, *"The world has no unemployment problem but a problem of bad jobs"*; (2) Second source of inequality, the sharing of profits of multinationals where a significant drop in investment combined with pressure on salaries would allow an increase in the remuneration of ever more demanding shareholders.[14]

More than a revolution in corporate governance, it is about promoting a better sharing of the wealth created by all stakeholders, in order to avoid the downward spiral of social regression and the anger of employees.

In these uncertain conditions, how could responsible finance act and with what levers? If citizen contribution is essential to ensure the dissemination of responsible finance, it cannot be done, carry another form of finance, without the contribution of the State and the firm. At the same time, new tools and new approaches to responsible finance are being developed (thematic management, alternative finance, etc.) to which must be added the need to renew corporate governance, under the influence of the technological revolution. The rehabilitated company once again becomes a major player in society and its governance depends on values acceptable to its societal environment. It is then appropriate to revisit, perhaps, its status and the legal forms that protect it. This leads us to see the Company with an extended Social Object and to wonder whether mutualism is once again becoming a fully modern idea? It is this field of diverse, nonexhaustive, and nonhierarchical recommendations (not to say commandments in the biblical sense) that this last subsection proposes to present.

[13]*"What if the employees revolt?"*

[14]In the case of France, without comment from us, the latest 2018 report by the NGO OXFAM elicited many comments underlining, *"From 2009 to 2016, out of 100 Euros in profits, CAC40 companies distributed an average of 67.40 Euros in dividends to shareholders, leaving only 27.30 Euros for reinvestment and 5.30 Euros in bonuses for employees."*

a. You the State will act

We have already mentioned that, in 2017, France has accumulated €15 billion in green bonds, thanks to issues by SNCF, or ENGIE, but above all, by its €7 billion State issue at the beginning of the year. In the same spirit of responsible finance emanating from a State often cited as examples are, the largest to date, the Government Pension Fund Global Norway pending the rise of the Saudi fund of $2,000 billion (10% of investment capacity in the world), armed arm of the "*vision 2030*" plan of Riyadh. As for Norway, the Saudi fund seeks to achieve diversification and modernization of its post-oil economy through ethical management without compromise. To finance future welfare state spending, Norway traditionally sets aside all of its large public oil revenues and only allows itself to use a maximum of 4%, an arbitrary figure corresponding to their estimated return, to balance its public accounts, if not in deficit. Despite the fact that it was first funded in 1996, the fund was established in its original form in 1990. It was further split in 2006 with the creation of a specific fund to support the country's economy. In 2016, Norway's sovereign wealth fund[15] (an investment fund owned by a state), the largest in the world, has further grown, gaining 447 billion crowns (50 billion Euros) thanks, in particular, to its investments in shares, announced on Tuesday, February 28, 2017, by the Norwegian Central Bank responsible for its management. With a return of 6.9%,

[15] A sovereign fund is an investment fund owned by a state. Sovereign funds are major investors in international financial markets, with assets estimated by the Sovereign Wealth Fund Institute at nearly USD 7,500 billion in 2016. The largest have been set up to manage large commercial surpluses, notably from the sale of hydrocarbons. They make it possible to anticipate the fall in revenues from raw materials such as oil and to diversify the sources of revenue of the States concerned. This is the case for three of the largest sovereign wealth funds in existence: the Government Pension Fund (Norway), SAMA Foreign Holdings (Saudi Arabia), and the Abu Dhabi Investment Authority (United Arab Emirates), which together represent more than $2 trillion in assets. The Norwegian fund is also distinguished by very demanding ethical management rules and has its objective intergenerational solidarity, in order to enable current and future generations to benefit from oil revenues. Some sovereign wealth funds are criticized for their opacity, and lack of transparency about their objectives, when they invest in Western companies. According to the magazine "*Challenges*" (www.challenges.fr) dated January 9, 2017, "In France, we have seen a lot of work by sovereign wealth funds, particularly the one in Qatar, which have invested in major real estate transactions (Hotel Concorde Lafayette, Hôtel du Louvre, Marriott Champs-Elysées or various office buildings). France acquired its own sovereign wealth fund late in 2008: managed by Caisse des Dépôts, the FSI (Fonds Stratégique d'Investissement) was created to support the development of innovative SMEs and secure the capital of strategic companies. But the FSI was then transformed in 2012 to become the public investment bank under the name BPI France."

the fund's value reached SEK 7,510 billion (almost EUR 850 billion at the current rate) by the end of December 2016. Once again, equity investments returned the most, an 8.7%. At the end of 2016, the fund controlled 1.3% of the world's market capitalization with interests in nearly 9,000 companies. Bonds returned 4.3% and real estate 0.8%. Invested in equities (62.5% of its portfolio), bonds (34.3%), and real estate (3.2%) around the world, it has more than doubled in size in the last 5 years. Given the long-term objective of creating intergenerational savings, Norway has opted for a defensive and diversified investment profile. In 2004, the fund took a new step by setting up an Ethics Council (appointed on the proposal of the Ministry of Finance) to examine in detail the activities of the companies in which the fund invests. This measure aims to exclude all those involved in arms manufacture; tobacco production; significant or systematic human rights violations; and environmental destructions.

The second example of a sovereign wealth fund: on April 25, 2016, Crown Prince Mohammed Ben Salman Al Saud officially unveiled his ambitious reform program to the world to enable Riyadh to end its dependence on oil. On the diplomatic front, after having succeeded in obtaining from OPEC a significant drop in the price of a barrel, this plan called "Vision 2030" aims to reform the Saudi economy with a view to profound change. "We all have a sick dependence on oil in Saudi Arabia (70% of the country's income), which is dangerous," said Prince Salman. By selling 5% of Saudi Aramco, the flagship of the Saudi economy—company that is the world's leading Oil Company—it controls reserves of nearly 261 billion barrels, employs over 61,000 people, and is valued at about 2,500 billion dollars. According to Prince Salman, this sale will create a sovereign fund of $2,000 billion—a fund that will control more than 10% of the investment capacity in the world; a way to protect against any economic hazard and new oil shock.

The objective is to reduce public sectors with an increase in the private sector contribution to 65% of GDP by 2030 compared to 45% currently. If the country also wishes to develop tourism, this plan mainly makes commitments in terms of sustainable development (preservation of the environment, combating desertification, and launching a renewable energy market, etc.). In addition to the economic aspect, strong provisions must guarantee a more ethical and social management of the project (fight against corruption in the use of funds, increase in the participation of women in the labor force from 22% to 30%, reduction in the unemployment rate from 11.6% to 7%, etc.).

Norwegian and Saudi sovereign wealth funds illustrate two major points: (1) States have an essential role to play in the dissemination of more responsible finance; (2) Responsible finance is not a utopia. It needs large levers to ensure its dissemination. Two experiments to be continued without neglecting the diversification proposed by private or public greens bonds.

While there is no doubt that the State has a role to play, it is not limited to the management of funds. The State, in order to combine the new challenges of the 21st century, can go beyond the strict financial framework. It can also be, beyond the financing of technical innovations, a force for proposals in terms of experiments and social innovations by recommending solutions that go beyond traditional regulations (e.g., creation, as a matter of urgency, of ultra-social housing in a way that derogates from legislation; use of underused infrastructures during school holidays in the summer).

b. New tools you will use: like thematic management

As part of the search for the meaning to be given to asset management by both public and private savers and investors, thematic management, in vogue for over 10 years, is experiencing a renewed interest in enriching the range of funds it is likely to provide. After recalling a definition of thematic management and its main characteristics, we will look at why it appeals to long-term investors and thus to responsible finance. To meet the new needs expressed by asset management, funds are now targeting themes that cut across several sectors. It is a stock-selection process that consists of identifying global macroeconomic dynamics and exploiting them, within portfolios, via three or four major investment themes. For example, long-term themes such as health, environment, robotics, and ageing of the population are selected. Themes which, over the next 20 years, are expected to have clearly superior performance potential to multisectoral funds. The SRI dimension can, of course, be included in these selections. Another example in an article reporting on a round table between fund managers published in the magazine *Funds*, No. 107, of November 2017,[16] the Director of

[16] *Funds, "Why Thematic Management Appeals to Investors"*, November 2017, pp. 36-41.

Thematic Equity Management of CPR AM, Vafa Ahmadi, talks about his company launch, in late 2016 "a fund on the theme of disruption, with a broad ecosystem that ranges from robotics to immunology, including big data, drones ... etc." —a fund that combines performance (up 10% since its launch compared to the MSCI World Index) and responsible or ethical finance.

Neither strictly sectoral nor strictly geographical, the themes selected are suggested by the economic analysis and validated by a committee of experts whose frequency of meetings is monthly depending on the management companies. Partially free from any index reference, this committee seeks to produce active and efficient management over the long term. Moreover, there is nothing to prevent a sound asset allocation from combining ETFs (Exchange Traded Funds or trackers are instruments that combine the characteristics of a fund, such as a mutual fund, and an exchange-traded security). From a strategic point of view, the dynamics of a successful company are valued, Best-in-Class(see SRI), or "*stock picking*[17]" which consists of betting on the most promising stocks in the stock market, and the underlying trend from which the latter derives all or part of its growth. To achieve performance, assets are selected on the basis of various known and controlled methods, such as discounting future cash flows, sector comparison, and asset value valuation.

c. The correlation between ESG criteria and performance you will improve in the long term

When ethical funds were in their infancy, one of the most common assumptions was that the funds that incorporate ESG characteristics, and in particular those that are subject to strict ethical selection, necessarily had to be subject to a compromise on performance. From now on, responsible finance is by no means synonymous to lower returns. It is able to reconcile performance, risk reduction, and societalsocietal utility.

[17]According to the site www.tradingsat.com/lexique-boursier/definition-stock-picking, "*in stock picking, the manager ensures that his choice at the base (bottom) is not in clear contradiction with global market trends (up). An adept of bottom-up strategy, the manager focuses his attention on the companies' own qualities and their development prospects. Stock picking is the opposite approach to the top-down approach. In the latter, the manager chooses a market (France, United States, United Kingdom...) or a sector (pharmaceuticals, capital goods...) according to the macroeconomic and financial data at his disposal.*"

Today, investors are increasingly recognizing the potential financial importance of issues such as governance, labor management, and environmental performance. In addition, major sustainability trends such as the transition to low-carbon energy and societal impacts offer opportunities for companies to be visible on these issues and to provide solutions.

What makes sense for investors and entrepreneurs is to reconcile financial performance with environmental and societal impacts. In France, the rise of solidary funds, commonly known as "90/10 funds," is contributing to this approach. They devote up to 10% of their resources to financing solidarity projects. The rate of return is not the only criterion in the investment decision. It is necessary to integrate a series of aims within the impact objectives and to be "patient funders." Moreover, in view of the very wide dissemination of ESG criteria in investment management, including in processes that are not identified as SRI, strict rules should be laid down for the use of these criteria so that they represent a genuine instrument of differentiation and a competitive advantage.

The relationship between company ESG levels and financial performance has been the subject of numerous studies. While early research suffered particularly from poor data availability, more recent studies have the advantage of long-term data covering a wider business universe.

It is therefore necessary for investors and companies to work together to raise the bar in ESG management not only to support performance, but also to contribute positively to global sustainability goals. However, for ESG strategies, where the investment philosophy is long-term, the financial ratios are not incompatible with these criteria, however, the change in scale over time implies rethinking the valuation methods of companies. Traditional financial analysis is no longer relevant in a sustainable assessment because it does not capture all the risks. At the same time, this necessary evolution of tools must be accompanied by a change in the investors' mentalities. The education and artificial intelligence of the following "command" are likely to contribute to these developments.

d. To make emerge the possible future, the education and the intelligence you will develop

We live in a pivotal era that fascinates us as much as it frightens us. To better understand and control it, we all need education.

Encouraging sustainability and stimulating responsible finance require an educational approach.

First, it is necessary to decipher the sometimes differentiated approaches of managers and investors. For investors, the priorities can be the exclusion of certain activities (armaments, games, or tobacco, etc.), or the selection of the best players based on ESG criteria (Environment, Social, and Governance), or the direct improvement of certain situations (impact investing). It is up to private management to understand which values are particularly important for each client, the environment, social equity, education, health, etc. Given this complexity of choices, it is important to ensure that potential impacts, positive or negative, are perfectly identified and managed.

In addition to the shortcomings ("sins") noted in terms of pedagogy in the previous section, there is a need to develop specific training for responsible finance. Whatever the changes expected in teaching, professional training, and apprenticeship, our modest questions only serve to present the scope of the decisions that await the actors (learners, employers, financiers, and public authorities), included in the particular context of our theme. Corporate Social Responsibility, born out of the desire to apply ESG concepts to companies, has an important HR dimension, the stakes of which are essential to grasp in order to derive the full benefit at the risk of seeing only its regulatory, or even administrative, dimension from the subject. Secondary and higher education would do well to take up this need to integrate training in economics and responsible finance into their curricula. The HR function has a dual responsibility for the CSR approach: producing the indicators associated with its scope of activity; and promoting and leading the approach within the company and civil society to foster its cultural appropriation through training and management awareness. This global questioning represents a precious opportunity for pedagogy to rethink its priorities for action beyond the strict scope of the company. The main risk therefore consists in seeing the training dimension of the CSR approach only yet another regulatory constraint as only the legislator can produce.

Initial training must cease to be seen as the only key to lifelong employment. Apprenticeship and lifelong learning must be required at all levels of higher education. In the weekly magazine *L'Express*, January 31, 2018, Jacques Attali stated in his column, "*the governance of higher education, that of vocational training and that of continuing education are at the antipodes of each other.*" To add, if we succeed in leading their necessary change: "*we will finally have given France the means to achieve its ambitions.*"

Technology, and in particular AI, can accompany this training effort provided that this new approach also questions its regulation in the name of ethics. If AI is conceived by humans, then it necessarily becomes its mirror, with its strengths and weaknesses. It can also positively transform our education system in general and responsible finance in particular. The competences of the 21st century will be those which will put forward the human competences: creativity, sense, action, and thought. For too long, teaching has focused on learning disciplinary knowledge. To navigate these digital times, we need new compasses for educators and tools. It is at this price that the possible and controlled futures will emerge.

The AI associated with robotics amplifies cognitive abilities (processing and interpretation of images, speech, and text). Thanks to the miniaturization of sensors and the continuous increase in the speed of computers, AI makes available at low-cost volume of data that allow the development of learning techniques. Because of its versatility, AI permeates large sectors from industry to services and thereby transforms the work. In this context, it is easier to identify jobs at risk than to define those that might emerge. Should we fear this situation? In the March 2018 issue of the journal *Finance et Gestion*, entitled "*Fonction finance, quels robots pour quel avenir? The man or the robot? The man and the robot?*" Raja Chatila, researcher at the Institute of Intelligent Systems and Robotics, declared, "It will not be a question, not of aiming for economic growth through AI, but of aligning it with our values." In short, to put ethics at the heart of this approach!

In the recent work of the Unexpected Sources of Inspiration (USI) held in Paris on June 25 and 26, 2018. Sir Ken Robinson, a world reference in education, declared, "We must imperatively review our conception of intelligence: "The educational model is based on academic competence, conformity and linearity, while human life is organic. To conceive human intelligence through the prism of academic skills alone is a narrow vision."

In addition to civic education, why not teach the young ones, from primary school, a sense of solidarity and commitment in their immediate environment? As there are two values that give substance to citizenship and democracy to build a more humane society.

e. In the search of a new governance of the company you will be attached

In a general way and without retracing the history of the evolution of the concept of company, from the creation of the limited company in the middle of the 19th century to its new modes of governance today, this one is still defined by a social object. The latter was long reduced to maximizing profits in the sole interests of shareholders (Milton Friedman, Nobel Prize winner in economics states, "The sole responsibility of the firm is to make profit…") without any consideration for the environment and other stakeholders. The introduction of this notion of stakeholders was crucial to grasp the real stakes of CSR and then ESG approaches for it was indeed a question of conducting a strategic reflection by placing the company in the global perspective of its ecosystem, by integrating employees, management, social partners, shareholders, investors, suppliers, customers and consumers, local communities. Corporate social responsibility (CSR) has tried to put the company in front of its social responsibilities, but without succeeding in calling into question the weight of shareholding. In an attempt to re-found the law and a new conception of corporate governance, we suggest here some original and recent ideas presented in the framework of academic research conducted by Mines Paris Tech. aimed at rehabilitating a long-term vision as well as social and environmental ambitions in a new governance of the firm. Based on decades of findings where corporate governance, and banks are no exception, has led to restricting the horizon of management to "shortermism" and focusing management criteria on the equity and valuation of companies for the shareholder. For more than a century, this orientation toward maximizing profits in the interests of shareholders alone has hampered the search for new ways of organizational and social cohesion.

The company, on the margins of any controversy, contributes to the common good by providing goods and services useful to society, by creating employment or progress, even if sometimes, as everywhere else, some deviances could be noted that taint the reputation of the firm. Whatever the degree of responsibility, arbitration, and involvement assumed by the company and its managers with regard to human issues, the use of the extra-financial criteria presented in this book does not harm its economic performance, despite the additional costs generated. The debate, of course, is the company's social object here, but above all it is how to legislate (soft-law; hard-law; commercial code; civil code; etc.). Between principle and conscience, where should the new rules be set? Should the company suddenly carry all the virtues of society? In a point of view entitled "Enterprise and common good, let's not go too far," Robert Leblanc, President of Aon France and Chairman of the Medef Ethics Committee, declared in *Les Echos* dated February 12, 2018: *"The common good is indivisible; no actor has to appropriate the stakes he represents."* Prior to this, and in the same article, he did not hesitate to denounce the term *"stakeholders,"* widely used in this debate, considering that its reference is *"embarrassing by its plural and categorical side."*

The concepts oriented toward the "society of persons" with autonomy we propose under different declinations are not totally new, but, between enthusiasm and polemic, how do they present themselves and introduce a real break in governance?

The following concepts will be discussed in *"**Liberated enterprise**"*; *"Society with an Extended Social Purpose"*; and renewed interest in mutualism.

The concept of "**liberated enterprise**" refers to organizations that operate in a radical transformation of reporting relationships and management practices. The organization and management are reviewed in such a way as to give priority to the maximum autonomy of employees and overall performance is based solely on individual goodwill (encouraging individual responsibility by moving from leading > controlling > rewarding > sanctioning > guiding > facilitating > helping). The challenge is to eliminate, as much as possible, everything that leads individuals into the position of mere executors. The organization aims to remove any status-difference symbols. If there are no longer such relationships between principals and executors, the role of leader remains, but its mission is above all to facilitate the task of employees and eliminate what can prevent their work from being carried out effectively. The leader adopts an active support posture that listens to the needs and hesitations of the employee. The rules are minimized in the organization while promoting exchanges and results-based management. This approach is not new; it is based on theories developed since the 1960s by experts in management and motivation at work such as Douglas McGregor, Frederick Herzberg, and Tom Peters.

Another recommendation is the "*extended corporate purpose company*"[18] (SOSE), which consists of allowing any company to assign social or environmental objectives to its activity, so as to give its managers more scope for action; and whose results would no longer be evaluated solely on the basis of financial value.

But this search for social responsibility is not limited to the legal framework and associated reporting. Being socially responsible is not just about meeting legal obligations. It is for the company to define and challenge its ethics, its action, and its investment in human capital, the environment, and relations with stakeholders. Are we still in utopia? Perhaps not, if we are to believe the recent recognition of equivalent statutes in California, the "*Flexible Purpose Corporations*"[19] and the work carried out by teacher-researchers at the Ecole des Mines de Paris, Blanche Segrestin and Armand Hatchuel, through their book *Refunding the Company* published by Seuil, starting in 2012. These authors bring a new conception of the company in this book. Their work is based on the recent research

[18] Few réflexions attache to the book "*Société à Objet Social Étendu* " *Un nouveau statut pour l'entreprise*"," Under the supervision of Blanche Segrestin, Kevin Levillain, Stéphane Vernac et Armand Hatchuel, Mines Paris Tech, collection économie et gestion, Presses des Mines, 2015.

[19] This new type of company allows managers to set both financial and nonfinancial objectives without the risk of being pursued by shareholders (a kind of contribution to the development of "*social entrepreneurship*"). At the end of September 2011, California"s legislative authorities adopted the Corporate Flexibility Act of 2011 (SB 201), a law creating a new form of corporate entity: the Flexible Purpose Corporation (FPC). Until now, there have been only two types of companies in California for-profit business and tax-exempt nonprofit. The "flexible purpose corporation," according to Kevin Levillain, in an article published by the Centre de Gestion Scientifique de Mines Paris Tech in 2012: "*is a new form of for-profit corporation, recognized in California law since January 2012. Unlike a traditional company, it adds another objective to its statutes than that of profit. Such a provision protects managers who wish to exercise a social or environmental mission, without releasing them from shareholder control. With this type of company, it becomes possible to reconcile the interests of the shareholders with those of the collective forming the company and to anchor the principle of social responsibility in the very foundations of the company*".

and aims to promote enterprise as a community of innovation oriented toward a plurality of goals: wealth creation, social progress, preservation of the environment, etc. The idea behind the book is to lay the foundations for a new "contract of enterprise."

There are limits to the company's approach solely based on economic theory or business law. This slow process, driven by social actors and new, multiple, and divergent societal paradigms, is challenging financial orthodoxy and established institutions. The study of corporate governance is being renewed with the technological revolution. In this constantly changing world, the sustainable companies of tomorrow will be those that have developed a "responsible management" considering, in addition to economic and environmental aspects, the social and territorial integration dimensions, "proximity" of their activities. Pressure from stakeholders and the institutional environment are increasingly influencing funders. Between real progress, apparent compliance strategies and wait-and-see attitude, the issues are formulated in terms of transparency, new risks, and brand image. If the company could not be protected against the requirements of profitability and obtaining an "immediate" return on investment, it is in particular because in law, the notion of company does not exist. Many approaches (stakeholder theory, CSR, etc.) have tried to counter this logic of "shareholder value alone," but without the support of the law, they have so far failed. Although the law does not prohibit the consideration of ESG standards, it is unable to support them over time. Indeed, none of these approaches have been successful in preventing crises.

As a follow-up to the research work initiated and presented in the books *Refounding the Company*, *Société à Objet Social Étendu, un nouveau statut pour l'entreprise*, written by an extended team of authors, Blanche Segrestin, Kevin Levillain, Stéphane Vernac, and Armand Hatchuel, attempts are made to reject this confusion between company and society. These authors attempt to propose a new conception of the company that aims to revisit the problem of the adequacy between the law and the management of stakeholders and to reflect on new ways to achieve this. For this, they founded their research on the study of the "Flexible Purpose Corporation" of the Americans that we have just specified. Their book explains the motivations and principles of a new form of company: the "Company with Extended Social Object" allowing any company to assign to its activity social or environmental goals, so as to give more latitude of action to its leaders. And whose results would no longer be evaluated solely on the basis of financial value.

The presentation of the book recalls that "corporate governance has indeed led for several decades to restrict the management horizon and to focus management criteria on shareholder value. This has discredited, if not partly deterred, the long-term commitments and social and environmental ambitions of companies. It has also, with remarkable exceptions, seriously damaged their capacity to innovate and to think about the worlds of tomorrow. In order to reconcile business and society, the company's mission must be re-founded in law. Company law must therefore evolve to allow any company to include in its articles of association goals (territorial interest, scientific and technological progress, humanitarian and environmental objectives) that are not reducible to the interests of shareholders .... For over 10 years we have witnessed an excessive focus on short-term financial criteria in the management of our companies in France and Europe. The tradition of long-term corporate management, characteristic of Rhineland capitalism, is under pressure from globalization, accounting techniques, pension funds, and rating agencies, most of which are Anglo-Saxon-led. The drift must be stopped because it is harmful to businesses." If corporate governance is to make a real breakthrough, the saver, the citizen, and the state must also change their behaviors. The fiduciary duty to pursue the approach of short-term profit maximization associated with an investment in "impact investing" funds, for example, in order to clear one's conscience, would be a farce. If performance and impact analysis are not to be totally opposed, the rupture and the change in behavior reside within the search for maximization of a sustainable return. This is what the OSA assumes—a new challenge that we can only encourage.

For the **mutualism financial** sphere described in the first part of the book, the question now is whether it is able to adapt and respond to the technological challenges marking social and economic transformations. If mutualism preserves its "DNA" of providing, through a community of people, a collective response to an individual need that cannot be met alone (financing, prevention, health, etc.), then the modernity and sustainability of mutualism will be preserved. A parallel of this principle is found in the emergence of the collaborative economy and sharing. Mutualism is fully capable of adapting to digital and to the platforms that can irrigate this sharing. Strengthened by its values of solidarity, mutualism, in addition to the appropriation of new technologies and the need to develop its business models, must, however, focus on the following points:

It seems to us that it is under these few conditions that the mutualism sphere will be able, even better, to make itself known, to recognize itself, and thus, to cross the multiple transitions which assail our societies. Beware, however, of regional "baronies" that sometimes wish to claim a form of independence in the name of proximity (the case of Crédit Mutuel Arkéa, a bank in the West, South-West and Massif Central, in conflict with its central body, La Confédération Nationale du Crédit Mutuel, which is willing to divest itself of subsidiaries and to give up the brand for greater agility) or the appointment of managers who are highly technical but weakly imbued with mutualism values (the case of Laurent Mignon, a mutualist by adoption and former CEO of Natixis, the international bank of the listed group that succeeded François Pérol on June 1, 2018, as Chairman of the Management Board of BPCE, probably for development in Europe and the success of the digital transition).

- The emergence, over the past 15 years or so, of a mixed model (others will politely say hybrid, see "genetically modified" for the most disappointed) combining mutualism on the one hand and a vehicle on the other) has been likely to bring a certain form of trivialization. While integrating the major factors leading to changes in our societies, the redefinition of the specificities of mutualism must be more asserted for both the general public and the State, regulators, and rating agencies.
- By experimenting with innovative solutions linked to digital, mutualism must consolidate its proximity to territories in order to respond more clearly to needs that are poorly covered (including young people, strengthening social dialogue with social innovation players, promoting equity, etc.).
- Accentuate its social approaches (see also one of the following recommendations devoted to social business innovations).
- Further promote nonfinancial approaches and criteria in risk management and marketed products and services—probably a way of preserving the fundamentals or roots of mutualism.

f. Finance differently you will observe

If we have tried to show the dichotomy between conventional finance and ethical finance, is it permissible to ask ourselves the question of the existence of unethical finance? In reaction to ethical funds, investment funds called "Sin Funds" have openly claimed immorality in the United States. Thus, the "Vice Fund," the most emblematic, is created in 2002. It will change its name in July 2014 to "Barrier Fund." In October 2017, the majority of its assets in the United States totaled nearly $230 million, invested in some 40 different securities lines: Philip Morris, Lorillard, British American Tobacco, and Altria, to these big names of tobacco, the giants of the defense and armament such as Lockheed Martin and Raytheon, companies of beer such as Carlsberg A/S and Molson Coors, and some game-oriented companies were added. This fund, which counterbalances the socially responsible movement, seeks to develop in the United Kingdom, Belgium, and Hong Kong. While it invests exclusively in the tobacco, alcohol, gambling, and arms industries, these investments remain entirely in legal activities (drugs and prostitution are excluded). In a way, this is the opposite approach used by SRI to seek performance in sectors whose growth is rarely correlated with the economic situation and the bear market (economic collapse or serious economic crisis). For example, even during times of crisis, cigarette sales do not weaken. Between strategy and pure provocation, another sin fund, called Morgan Sinshares had to change its name to Morgan Funshares because the Sin Funds are now subject to regulations and changing public sensitivities. These factors contribute to reducing their attractiveness and consequently their out standings.

After this detour, it is normal to question the existence of religious finance. It seems to impose itself on spirits as a natural state carried on both sides of the Mediterranean by our Judeo-Christian and Arab-Muslim civilizations. If Catholic finance belongs to the category of ethical finance, this terminology, not commonly used, refers to dogmatic, personal, and operational dimensions. In France, if the General Union (1875–1882) ostensibly presented itself as a Catholic credit institution, and solidary finance (profane ethical finance[20] now seems to have totally replaced Christian finance. Nevertheless, with

[20]The General Union Krach is one of the first notable financial crises in France. The General Union is the name of a French Catholic bank. It was created is 1875 in Lyon

regard to the ethical principles implemented and their historically Catholic origin, a good number of actors in solidary finance can be attached to the category of Christian finance, without counting the Christian origins of certain mutual banks. The positions taken by the French Bishops' Conference sometimes lead to decisions intended to guide the management of heritage. Thus, recently, this same Conference invited about 40 Catholic organizations to commit themselves in the disinvestment of fossil energies. By 2015, an appeal had been published in the form of an article in the daily newspaper *La Croix* and was signed by many bishops to support the cause of COP 21, December 2015, in Paris. Today, some initiatives are still being taken: the first Bishops' Conference (Belgium), the first Catholic Bank of Germany, Pax Bank, as well as the most important institutions in Assisi have decided to disinvest together. In October 2017, the bishops of Belgium and a dozen Catholic institutions joined the disinvestment movement and decided to no longer finance coal, oil, and gas and turned to renewable energies for the management of their investments.

In addition, the notion of Islamic finance is more used, which is why we will briefly develop its foundations and main characteristics in relation to our subject. Islamic finance is often presented as a panacea backed by banking techniques that exclude interest rates. In reality, as a financial system in full, it has theoretical foundations backed by sharia law advocating equity and justice. Is it likely to moralize an economic activity? Inappropriate and unethical practices such as greed, corruption, and information asymmetry have characterized the behavior of financial institutions and market participants. The latter have increased their speculative operations against real investment operations in companies. In this environment of financial turbulence, Islamic finance is making progress and is of increasing interest to the international community because of its ethical-religious dimension and its anchoring in the real economy. Not only reserved for the Muslim community, this finance is based on universal ethical principles of responsibility and absence of speculation. However, it is the 1.6 billion Muslims around the world who are primarily targeted.

---

by monarchists. She went bankrupt in 1882, which later inspired Emile Zola to write his novel "*L'Argent*"

The World Bank Group and the Islamic Development Bank (IDB) published the first global report on Islamic finance[21] "*Global Report on Islamic Finance—Islamic Finance: A Catalyst for Shared Prosperity?*" This publication examines in detail the growth prospects of the sector and its ability to contribute to the reduction of global income inequalities, a better sharing of prosperity, and the achievement of sustainable development goals. After providing a panorama of Islamic finance and highlighting the main difficulties hindering its expansion, the report recommends a number of measures likely to make this sector a lever for sharing prosperity.

Islamic finance promotes a fair and equitable distribution of income and wealth. Because it is highly connected to the real economy and based on risk sharing, Islamic finance can contribute to improving the stability of the financial sector. It can also help to integrate those into the formal financial system who are currently excluded for cultural or religious reasons. Unlike traditional finance, Islamic finance is based on risk sharing and asset-based financing. In Islamic finance, bank clients hold real assets directly in the real sphere of the economy, which reduces their risk aversion. Although the sector's growth is slowing, Islamic finance assets are expected to reach $3 trillion over the next decade (75% of banking/finance assets, 40% owned by Iran, 12% by Saudi Arabia).

In 2016, with total assets exceeding $2 trillion, the Islamic finance sector faces three major challenges, according to the latest annual report of the *Islamic Finance News*: falling oil prices, rapid changes in global financial regulation, and market fragmentation. Despite single-digit growth rates versus growth rates of 10–15% over the past decade, analysts still expect more growth by 2020.

Islamic finance is a concept that has aroused and continues to arouse wide polemics, and for good reason, it has always been treated, too often, from an ideological angle.

Indeed, Islamic finance is above all an ethical finance, which privileges a system of values built on the need to avoid what is forbidden. Appeared in 1975 in Dubai, with the Dubai Islamic Bank, this finance imposes the respect of several fundamental

---

[21] Information reported on the World Bank website in early February 2017: www.banquemondiale.org/fr/news/feature/2017/02/21/new-report

religious principles in Islam: the prohibition of "riba" (interest assimilated to wear and tear), "*gharar*," and "*maysir*" (uncertainty, speculation), the financing of "*haram*" activities (alcohol, pork, pornography, etc.). Islamic finance also operates on the "Musharaka" principle that is the sharing of profits and losses between various parties, as well as the obligation to invest in the real economy through tangible assets. In theory, derivatives are therefore prohibited. In addition, councils, made up of doctors in the Islamic religion, are responsible for examining the conformity of the products proposed in each establishment. One of the main instruments is the "*Murabahah*," in order to circumvent the interest rule as practiced in conventional finance. His technique is an interest-free form of borrowing. Its principle is the bank buys the asset and then sells it to its client, in tranches, including the cost of financing in the resale price, since the notion of interest does not appear conspicuously. At the end of the contract, the bank transfers ownership of the property to its client. One of the other flagship products is the "*Ijara*," a kind of leasing. The bank acquires the property. But this time, it does not selling it to the client. It rents it out, with the possibility of buying it back at the end of the contract. Another flagship product is the "*Musharaka*," two partners invest together in a project. Both profits and losses are shared according to the capital invested by each. However, apart from Saudi Arabia, profitability remains above all the first criterion for banks that are relatively insensitive to the religious argument. Finally, there remain the "*Sukuks*," quite close to the obligations offered by conventional finance.

Despite the creation of a Master's degree at the University Paris-Dauphine, an MBA at the Faculty of Law of Strasbourg, and some associations that provide certifications, the subject, which tries to reconcile Islam, economics, and ethics, has difficulty to impose itself in France. As early as 2011, on the occasion of a conference held at the University of Evry, whose proceedings were published in the *Revue des Sciences de Gestion* (No. 255/256—May/August 2012) through an article entitled, "*Ethical finance, Islamic finance: what convergences and potentialities for development in French retail banking*," we were already drawing attention to the weight of sociocultural issues and the management of paradoxes between communitarianism and integration, on one hand, and regulatory actors' reluctance and obstacles on the other. We were already saying that Islamic investment banking had a better chance of finding its development in France (because of the efforts made by the public authorities and the main market finance players to promote Paris as the leading European financial center) than Islamic retail banking. In contrast to England, the history of the substantial presence of Muslim populations in France is explained by different economic motivations. Between the impact of the Commonwealth for the British (presence of Pakistani and Malaysian communities with long experience in Islamic finance) and the more recent arrival of a young male population not accompanied by a member of the family unit, originally, who came to work for only a few years in order to transfer a large part of his income to his country of origin and thus participate in the survival of his family in emerging nations, it will be necessary to wait for the policy of family reunification, introduced in 1974, to see the living conditions of Muslims passed from this situation of transit to a sustainable settlement of the family. From then on, it seemed difficult to ignore the identity issues underlying the concerns of 10% of the French population. We wrote, then, and this point still remains topical, "Between withdrawal into oneself through an exacerbated communitarianism and the opportunity of a better social and economic integration … it will be necessary to choose." It is also this difference in perception that distances us from the position of Great Britain. In France, according to the Ministry of the Interior in charge of religions, Muslims are estimated at a little over 6 million on the territory, a quarter of whom are practicing. Between communitarianism and integration, for a Muslim, the will to conform to his religion reinforces a determination in the act of purchase and can constitute a way of asserting his identity. Thus, in terms of consumption habits, the turnover of "*halal*" products in 2015 is equivalent to that of "*organic*" products and exceeds €6 billion. While social integration is achieved through real estate loans, it is in this area that Islamic retail banking took its first steps in France with granting, in 2010, the first Shari'ah-compliant arrangement, due to the gradual introduction of a certain tax neutrality brought about by four instructions dated August 24, 2010 (for real estate in particular, in the above-mentioned "*Murabaha*," financial income is assimilated to interest income and recorded as such). Even if Roman law is closer to Islamic law than Anglo-Saxon law, there is legal slowness to change the texts, in particular, concerning the elimination of double taxation in the field of land registration and registration fees in the context of real estate purchase/sale transactions without speculative intent; the exemption from the guarantee of latent defects in the context of sale, probably slowed down the development of this Islamic finance intended for private individuals. If we add the explanatory factors relating to the risks of reputations and the risks of uncertainty (linked to the absence of refinancing with central banks, the participatory aspect of the client associated with the losses and/or profits of the bank, and the prohibition of interest), all these facts raise questions and divergences. The development potential of Islamic finance remains largely, still, under the influence of political wishes. It is likely that Islamic finance has many assets to participate in the banking of African populations and make its contribution to the immense investment needs formulated by this continent [the recent issues of sovereign "*sukuks*" in Senegal and Côte d'Ivoire (forms of bonds) and the equity investments in banks in Africa by the Islamic Corporation for the Development of the Private Sector ("*Contrat à Impact Social*" [CIS]), a subsidiary of the IDB[22] attest to this dynamism]. A growth opportunity for Islamic finance under the following conditions: (1) the necessary harmonization of an Islamic business law; (2) the necessary information and training of the actors so that they understand the stakes. Here, too, we find the same constraints as before.

g. The circular economy you will accompany

We know that the explosion of the world population and economic growth are draining the natural resources (from now on, it is August 1st that humanity will have used all resources, a day of ecological overtaking that happens earlier and earlier each year). This is an intolerable situation because this growing production of waste is not controlled. To be convinced, it is enough to visualize the surroundings of certain large international metropolises in India, Egypt, or South America. Are we not already talking about a seventh continent

[22]The Islamic Development Bank (IDB), established in 1975, is a supra-state development bank, established to promote the economic development and social progress of its 56 countries and support Muslim communities in nonmember countries in accordance with the Islamic Shariah. Based in Jeddah (Saudi Arabia), the IDB Group also has regional offices in Almaty (Kazakhstan), Kuala Lumpur (Malaysia), Rabat (Morocco), and Dakar (Senegal). The Bank has field representatives in 12 countries: Afghanistan, Azerbaijan, Bangladesh, Guinea, Indonesia, Iran, Nigeria, Pakistan, Sierra Leone, Sudan, Uzbekistan, and Yemen.

in the oceans created by the accumulation of plastic waste? The circular economy is an opportunity to organize the production and consumption patterns of our global economy for the very long term. It is not limited to recycling, although the intelligent reuse of natural resources is an excellent way to optimize their use. The circular economy goes further. It aims to extend the life of a product or to intensify its use. From the property to the use had we retained as slogan. Sharing or rental platforms, supermarkets that start reselling second-hand equipment are all ways to encourage not to mention the use of repairs.

The circular economy is a "*mobilizing subject that allows everyone to act for the planet and is a creator of jobs that cannot be relocated: it is estimated that the sector represents a potential of 300,000 additional jobs*," the press release[23] stressed during French Prime Minister Edouard Philippe's visit to the Seb factory in Mayenne in April 2018 who presented the Government's roadmap for a 100% circular economy. The result of several months of consultation and development includes 50 measures aimed at better producing, consuming, and managing waste. It must also allow the mobilization of all to meet the objectives of the Climate Plan. Moving from a linear model, "*make, consume, throw away*," to a circular model will require the "*mobilization of all*": citizens, communities, businesses, associations, administrations, and research and development actors in all territories. The roadmap "*aims to shake up habits, to inform by showing good examples, to convince, and also to inspire.*"

For example, building and construction, with 247 million tons of waste per year, is the sector responsible for more than 70% of waste in France: "*It is therefore essential to specifically reduce this flow fed by demolition and deconstruction activities.*" It will be a question of "producing better with fewer nonrenewable resources." The roadmap also provides for tax adjustments to make waste recovery cheaper than disposal, by reducing the value-added tax (VAT) rate for recycling and increasing the general tax rates on polluting activities for land filling and incineration. By 2020, 2,000 companies will be supported to reduce their resource consumption and waste, and make savings

[23] For more information, we refer the reader to the site: www.ecologie-solidaire.gouv.fr

thanks to Ademe's[24] scheme: "*TPE & PME gagnantes sur tous les coûts*" (SMEs are winners on each cost).

- **Social business you will examine**

  France is world champion in social spending for an efficiency that does not seem to live up to its commitment. Subject to severe budgetary constraints, the State and local authorities are at pains. The development of the Social and Solidary Economy but also of SRIs testifies to an awareness of these problems. However, the projects deployed within this framework remain largely subject to "classical" logic (grants or philanthropy) that limit their innovative aspect.

  As Novethic, developed by Nobel Peace Prize winner Muhammad Yunus (creator of microcredit), points out, social business is a concept of enterprise, using the profits of the latter to produce "social" added value for the community in which it is located. The company does not pay any dividends; it reinvests its profits in its Social Business.

  In 2009, at the Davos Economic Forum, Muhammad Yunus drew up a list of the seven principles of Social Business.

  The social and solidary economy has been, and continues to be, the field of the emergence and structuring of financial practices, a little like mutualism was in the middle of the 19th century. Criticism of the traditional banking system, not inclined to take an interest in small financing and the proposal of different financing rules within new organizations, have allowed the development of the solidary finance ecosystem over the last 10 years. Loi Hamon (2014) and European (Social Business Initiative 2011) have generated the concept of social enterprise initially accompanied, by a few new players ranging from student associations to major groups in the food (Danone) and other industry (Schneider). It took some time for private sector financiers to be convinced. It took the impetus of the public authorities to set in motion, for example, in France, for holders of company mutual funds the obligation to subscribe to 90/10 funds. Brussels, following the Social Business Act, asked the European Investment Fund to create a "social" venture capital fund. In the United Kingdom, the creation of "*Big Society Capital*"

---

[24]The Agence de l'environnement et de la maîtrise de l'énergie is a French industrial and commercial public establishment created in 1991.

gave rise to "*Social Impacts Bonds*," bonds whose financial return is indexed to the success of the social impact of the funded project.

Social Business or how to combine ethics, innovation, social impact, entrepreneurship, and profitability, but a change that raises many questions of the type: toward privatization of social action? Or will social impact contracts lead to competition in social action?

Social Business is an alternative or hybrid business model, which places the positive impact on society or the environment above profit goals. An innovative and dynamic concept, its growth is accompanied by new financing methods. From micro finance, which is a solution to facilitate access to credit for the most disadvantaged populations, to financing with social impact, which is another innovation in full development. It corresponds to the investment of savings in companies with a strong social or environmental impact. This investment with an impact now represents $250 billion of outstanding worldwide and would have increased by more than 146% from 2014 to 2016. The social enterprises thus created constitute a real vector for change: they bring economically sustainable solutions to major societal problems such as hunger or malnutrition, food waste, access to drinking water, education for people who prematurely leave the education system, electricity, medical care, financial services, housing, the reception and integration of refugees, etc., financial risks that are far removed from traditional banking approaches.

The Social Impact Bond (SIB) or "CIS" in French was conceived in 2010 by British associations to finance a program for the reintegration of prisoners. Today, it is a system of financing reimbursed by the states on maturity if the social aim of the project is achieved. All SIBs now operate on this model, with a precise and measurable target impact conditioning repayment, and a social action, often innovative, which in case of success will save the states much more than the capital to be repaid. Around 40 SIBs have been implemented in the United Kingdom, Australia, the United States, Belgium, and Portugal, for amounts ranging from 400,000 to€20 million. In France, this new financial tool bears another name, the "*Contrat à Impact Social*" (CIS, in French), whose emergence and standardization was greatly encouraged by BNP Paribas by signing the first French CIS in favor of ADIE.

Impact Bonds (SIB) or Social Impact Contracts are financial bonds issued by the public sector to private actors to finance social projects, the payment of which is conditional to the success of the project. In other words, a private actor enters into a contract with a public actor, where it undertakes to finance a specific social action in exchange for a payment by the public actor of financial interests, if the results are achieved. Social impact bonds allow private actors to finance nonprofit social projects through bonds issued by public authorities, the remuneration of which depends on the results of the project (public authorities only pay for bonds if they succeed).

1. The company aims to eradicate poverty or address social problems in the areas of health, education, access to technology, or the environment. Its objective is therefore not profit maximization.
2. The company must ensure its financial and economic viability.
3. No dividend is distributed, investors only recover their investment.
4. When the invested amounts are repaid, the profits are reinvested in the business so that it can improve and grow.
5. The company must respect the environment.
6. The workforce must get market wages and better working conditions.
7. Do it with joy.

h. Banking inclusion you will amplify: from legal obligations to strengthening social cohesion

As a priority for the G20 and international financial authorities, banking inclusion issues may have different dimensions depending on the geographical areas of application. This can range from the simple possibility of opening a bank account in many countries in the Southern part of the globe to more elaborate services for the financially fragile people in developed countries. France, with a high rate of people holding a bank account (almost 96%), has not hesitated to deploy a consistent level of initiatives to promote banking inclusion. Its regulatory arsenal is placed under the authority of the Banque de France Presidency with the Banking Inclusion Observatory (OIB).[25] This body brings together the representatives of public authorities, credit

[25] For a more exhaustive overview of banking inclusion in France, we refer the reader to the latest publication, on June 8, 2018, of the latest OIB report 2017 (www.banque-france.fr/.../espace.../collecte-observatoire-de-linclusion-bancaire).

institutions and consumer, families, and anti-exclusion associations. Its work should provide data to monitor and evaluate banking practices in order to identify areas for improvement. The "*Observatoire de l'inclusion bancaire*" (OIB) was created by the Banking Separation and Regulation Act of July 26, 2013, and regulated by the Decree of June 30, 2014. It is responsible for collecting quantitative and qualitative information, defining and analyzing indicators on the conditions of access to banking services, and facilitating dialogue between the various actors involved in this field. The Observatory may make recommendations and report on good or bad practices of credit institutions. Its installation session was held on September 11, 2014.

In order to provide a reference framework, OIB has adopted the following definition of banking inclusion: "Banking inclusion is part of the process of inclusion in economic and social life. It enables a natural person to have lasting access to banking products and services adapted to his nonprofessional needs and to use them. The system is based on three socially structuring measures: (1) the right to an account; (2) a specific offer, on the one hand, of basic banking services and, on the other, a limitation of the fees charged in the event of a payment incident to these individuals in a situation of banking fragility; (3) the charter on banking inclusion and prevention of over-indebtedness which is binding on all credit, payment, and electronic money institutions and finance companies. The field of banking inclusion is evolving and will have to integrate technological and commercial developments in order to properly integrate the diversity of the needs of the people concerned. In this field, too, of financial situation of fragility and over-indebtedness, training is led to play a fundamental role with the young and the not-so-young.

i. To the dictatorship of time you will escape: from the search for sensations to the quest for meaning

Has the urgency, the dictatorship of time become the symptom of hyper modernity? An opportunity to question the management of paradoxes that assail our society without, however, providing concrete answers,

"We no longer have history, we no longer have a future, we are in the present … time is compacted. The emergency is this over activity, chosen or suffered, which affects more and more people. Urgency is the conjunction of two phenomena: the cult of speed and the cult of the moment. Is this a reality? Some contest it." Thus, Gilles Finchelstein expresses himself in his book *La dictature de l'urgence* published by Editions Fayard in

2011. For the author, urgency is the conjunction of two phenomena: the cult of speed and the cult of the moment. Is this a reality? And to refer to multiple examples of everyday life, personal and professional.

So, in everyday life, for some, everything goes faster. But, do they argue? Travel time to work increases—yet, maritime transport is developing, aircraft speed stagnates—and sometimes even decreases to save kerosene. But cycling is in, when it is not walking. Women are also getting older when their first child is born and teenagers are staying longer with their parents. Social ties are more numerous than before, easier to establish rather, but more fragile.

What about our personal lives? Food: we prepare our meals faster, we eat them faster. Fashion: ready-to-wear collections follow one another at a frantic pace—one collection per season. Information: under the effect of new technologies and competition, its content is becoming more compact, and is increasingly transmitted in real time. Transport: the development of the high-speed rail (TGV) is changing our relationship with space—we no longer measure distances in kilometers but in minutes. Health: emergency services have imposed themselves as the normal mode of entry to hospital.

What about our professional lives? Production cycles have been reduced; Work organization methods have changed and become more intense. Finance, of course, has been subject to a new rhythm. Companies are obligated to publish their results every 6 months, or even every quarter, and have been forced to achieve short-term profitability unrelated to economic reality. Laws are increasingly driven by a reaction to current events.

What are the causes and consequences of this dictatorship? Still, according to Gilles Finchelstein, three main reading grids can be schematically proposed to analyze this phenomenon:

> *"First there is a technical reading.*
>
> *The emergency is the Internet. The power of the network has accelerated the speed of History.*
>
> *There is a political reading: too many rules kill the rule .... Too many heterogeneous texts.*

There's a moral reading. Urgency is money - the disruption of the compass of our values has caused the disruption of our clocks. And in an increasingly individualistic society, money occupies a more important place in the hierarchy of values." This is Joseph Stiglitz's thesis in The Triumph of Greed

So, what reading should be preferred? Technical, political or moral? Internet, globalization or money? None of the three makes it possible to understand the changes we are experiencing. Even better, their addition is insufficient. The Internet, the market and money make system and enter in resonance to amplify even more the acceleration that we live.

What are the consequences of this new system? It has had positive effects because it has been translated into the will to live one's life to the full here and now. We have disregarded the great religions or ideologies that could lead us to always sacrifice the present for the benefit of a hope to come.

But this new system has more and more negative effects: it puts our societies under tension and leads to delegitimizing politics. It endangers future generations - if not ourselves.Global warming. Impacts on biodiversity. Threats of urban asphyxiation. These are some of the long-term risks that are known and against which we are doing too little.

In the past, the time of individuals was punctuated by the obligations of social life and work; it was a constrained time, partially, a time whose gravity was felt, but a time that did not overflow individuals. They were not trying to force time. From now on, we want to control time, to dominate it, the ultimate outcome of the capitalist logic for which "time is money" and which has resulted in an increasingly frenzied acceleration."

It is therefore a nuanced picture that must be drawn of this new relationship to time: if immediacy gives an individual the feeling of being able to free him from time, through urgency, by dealing with as many things as possible in as little time as possible, one wants to triumph over time. But if the emergency happens to overwhelm him, one is defeated. Instantaneity, on the other hand, dispenses with a fight but can, depending on the case, free it from space-time or secure it immediately. Under these conditions, it is a relationship with oneself that will be marked by excess aimed at making each moment more intense. At the same time, the relationship with others is marked by ephemerality.

Our subject is indeed at the heart of multidisciplinary debates and raises more questions than it provides answers. To complete this rapid analysis of the relationship to time, it is also possible to refer to the latest work by the sociologist and expert on social times, Jean Viard, which essentially takes up the abovementioned characteristics of our society. He evokes this revolution of time where the longer the life is, the shorter are the sequences of life. Discontinuity has become the rule and the old stability (permanent contracts, marriage, property, etc.) is transformed into adventures. The central question then is: who suffers and who chooses in this predominantly urban society driven by a digital, collaborative, and social revolution?

j. European harmonization you will support

In a period where companies seeking financing are also seeking to enhance their extra-financial responsibility to attract more investors and where environmental commitment is becoming a major issue, the Social and Solidary Economy, despite its specific governance characteristics, is not outside the general economy. The conceptualization and legibility of nonfinancial rating for both large and small companies must be achieved within a harmonious European framework. Similarly, the introduction, still at European level, of a single label focusing on impact measurement, the equivalent of Article 173 and a responsible savings plan for banking and insurance networks should be encouraged. These few simple suggestions, which can be transposed from one country to another, are likely to increase the penetration of solidarity impact products, which cannot remain dispersed and relatively confidential, for both the general public and the investors. Making an effort to harmonize subscription procedures and operating conditions with a view to gradually approximating the tax provisions linked to each product would constitute an important lever for promoting responsible finance. The one that the European States, the European Commission, and/or the European Parliament go beyond their budgetary role to offer, once, an experience of creating a solidarity product common to all 28 members (before Brexit: Brexit = expression meaning to leave Europe).

Conclusion: what we must remember

Without claiming to be an exhaustive list of the challenges, issues, and recommendations that await responsible finance, we have tried to highlight how far we still have to go in a world where we are better informed but less able to predict it. Between inventions and discoveries, the slightest information, the slightest rumor influences our way of seeing and thinking. So, it seems preferable not to try to know everything that is going to happen but to prepare for it. It is not a question of showing overwhelming optimism, but rather of being combative following awareness that responsible finance, which is still widespread, could be a chance to reexamine the end and means of modern finance, which continues to worry. A few points of reference to illustrate the reasons for these concerns are10 years after the onset of one of the biggest crises in the world, despite a renewed and high valuation of the equity markets, particularly under the impetus of the GAFAs who are racing for $1,000 billion in capitalization. This upward cycle seems to continue under the influence of the relative weight of American equities, which now represent more than 55% of the world market capitalization. Equities marked by an increasingly high price-to-earnings ratio while showing an increasing market premium compared to debt securities such as bonds (close to 1% versus 6% return for equities) the dilemma of the current economic situation that we have largely addressed with the debate on the arrival of new technologies and the impact on jobs and professions that is causing disagreement among experts between supporters of the third industrial revolution and those who predict the end of the period of stagnation.

While responsible finance, as we have defined it in a broader sense, enjoys greater recognition, the need to take another step, namely to transform its potential through concrete actions enabling it to achieve a change of scale, remains a priority. The impact of more responsible finance on the firm's image and notoriety is recognized, as well as on its sustainability and differentiation from competitors. But the lack of clarity on the creation of future value, the acceleration of transitions, resistance to change, aversion to risks, instability of rules and laws are all constraints that mean that there is still a long way to go in terms of investment strategies to apply and universalize these new precepts linked to ESG, sources of innovation, and productivity gains. Between a communication tool and a real investment strategy, responsible finance has been monopolized by the media, which sometimes sees it as a response to recent crises and especially to the excesses of modern finance.

The fiduciary duty to pursue the search of short-term profit maximization associated with an investment in "impact investing" funds, for example, in order to clear one's conscience, would be a farce. If performance and impact analysis are not to be totally opposed, the rupture and the change in behavior lie within the search for maximization of a sustainable return. There are actions to be taken. We have listed some of them: democratizing responsible finance; better training and informing its actors; and simplifying tax and regulatory procedures in order to make it easier to understand, etc.

If citizens' contribution is essential to ensure the dissemination of this responsible finance, it cannot be done, to bring a more responsible finance, without the contribution of the State and companies. At the same time, new tools and new approaches to responsible finance are being developed, along with the need to renew corporate governance under the influence of the technological revolution. The rehabilitated company once again becomes a major player in society and its governance depends on values acceptable to its societal environment. It is then appropriate to revisit, perhaps, its status and the legal forms that protect it. Other actors, such as mutualism, for example, by rediscovering its fundamentals, could be able to make its contribution to a review of finance.

While the technology that cannot be ignored seems to be driving rapid changes in businesses, financial practices and business models, the profusion of players, labels, and binding, even ambiguous, regulatory standards are likely to thwart the outcome of certain initiatives. Despite multiple moral incantations and numerous initiatives aimed at including extra-financial criteria in today's finance, it seems to us that the latter is still too marked by an outrageous "short-sightedness" and the search for margins at all costs. The reasons for the limitations in the foundation of a more responsible finance, and more quickly, in spite of the multiple innovations presented, could come from the fact that the new products proposed, the new actors presented would forget the technical component of this contemporary finance, a technique, often, set as standard. The challenge, then, would precisely be to regain a certain mastery of regulatory developments, for the time being, too much based on technology. The invasion of algorithms in risk measurement or performance enhancement implies a broader reflection and an analysis open to the ethical impacts sought by the contribution of techniques in the service of society. Over-reliance on artificial intelligence only increases with time. There may be many advantages. The quality and efficiency of data processing can certainly go as far as improving regulatory compliance. But, these applications will remain promising if the associated risks are properly managed (complexity slows down assessments, risks of cyberattacks manipulate market quotations, etc.). For the moment, the algorithms used have only been tested in periods of low volatility and they are already scaring the regulators.

With AI, will machines take power over humans? Will they end up being more cerebral and more formidable than bipeds? Legitimate questions if no regulation is set in force. Uncertainties are also reinforced by the fact that economists remain doubtful once again. Certainly, with the digital economy and new technologies, there will be losers and winners. But, our context of rapid transitions worries, though for a long time, economists considered that in case of industrial revolution and introduction of innovations, it was not worrying if people lost their jobs, because the economy was growing and new jobs would appear quickly! Except that today, despite the much sought-after flexibility, this form of postulate no longer holds true. Hidden by our mystification of growth, awareness of this phenomenon is new.

Finance must reinvent itself around the customer experience. It will have to shift from a quantitative-oriented business to a more accompanying business at every stage of its client's life, while capitalizing on its most precious assets, transparency, and security in order to establish trust. To do this, we do not reinvent finance, we make it accessible. There is a specific role for responsible finance.

While responsible finance, as we have defined it in a broader sense, enjoys greater recognition, the need to take another step, namely to transform its potential through concrete actions enabling it to achieve a change of scale, remains a priority. The impact of more responsible finance on the firm's image and notoriety is recognized, as well as on its sustainability and differentiation from competitors. But the lack of clarity on the creation of future value, the acceleration of transitions, resistance to change, aversion to risks, instability of rules and laws, are all constraints that mean that there is still a long way to go in terms of investment strategies to apply and universalize these new precepts linked to ESG, sources of innovation and productivity gains. Between a communication tool and a real investment strategy, responsible finance has been monopolized by the media, which sometimes see it as a response to recent crises and especially to the excesses of modern finance.

If the technological component will soon no longer be the only differentiating element between banks and Fintech companies, the real challenge for the financial industry will be to move from transactional utility to relational purpose. This means reconciling technological intelligence and human relationship, empathy—a technology at the service of accompanying a customer in different stages of his or her life. It is no longer just a question of changes in practices or the arrival of new technical tools, as has been the case many times in the past: the very principles of finance are being called into question. The world of finance is undergoing one of the most profound changes in its history. The professions of deposit banking, investment banking, markets, asset management, and corporate finance all seem to be undergoing radical transformations of varying intensity.

If the search for goals and search for meanings given to investments represent essential values carried by responsible finance, then only this other finance will be likely to accompany, humanly and effectively, the multiple transitions—not to say revolutions that we live to see!

"Simply serving the future!"

"There's something worse than not having succeeded: it's not having tried."
Franklin Roosevelt (1882–1945), 32nd president of the United States

IS RESPONSIBLE FINANCE NECESSARY FOR THE CAPITALIST SYSTEM AND GENERAL ECONOMY? Will it be sufficient to change its conceptual framework and content? The financial transaction is no longer judged as belonging to the realm of good or evil in itself, but is beginning to be recognized as well founded for development, insofar as it is treated in a legal framework with the concern of general interest. There is still a long way to go. As far as the interest of responsible finance is concerned, awareness now seems to be firmly entrenched in people's minds, and a real move to action is another matter. Many questions remain and it is the meaning of decoding that we have always tried to propose in this book in order to feed the reflexion.

Questions remain about the lack of transparency, the heterogeneity of evaluation methods, the validity of stock selection processes, and the explanation for the rapid expansion in the number of funds. There is some doubt among critics of ethical finance about the real "ethical" motivation of the players. Between solidarity and communication effect, the small amounts mobilized by ethical finance lead, again, to relativize their scope. Often presented as an alternative management method, is ethical finance capable of reconciling modern finance with solidarity and changing its methods? Despite the hope raised by the evolution of statistical data on both socially responsible investment (SRI) and solidarity savings, these do not yet clearly show any real advantage in purely financial management (yield, volatility, liquidity, etc.). Therefore, this is still a choice of financial strategy, but also of convictions for investors.

One obvious limitation in this responsible finance approach is the nonuniversality of the many concepts and products associated with it. The French responsible finance market is still an emerging market in search of its structure.

To conclude, while remaining on a religious metaphor and after "our seven sins and our ten commandments," we could summarize the current situation of responsible finance by this sentence: we are in the phase of evangelization, partially believing, but far from being practicing. The term "evangelization" can be used for marketing, a technique practiced in companies during the Internet boom of the late 1990s. Widely used by Apple and derived from a Greek word meaning substance "to proclaim the good news," evangelizing was about explaining to the world how the Macintosh would make life easier. Web giants have long employed technology evangelists to spread ideas about the changing world, new technologies, and new uses. Recently introduced in Europe, this new digital business aims to get in touch with teams and customers in order to set up an open society advocating the abolition of hierarchies and collaboration for the production of knowledge.

Under these conditions, the alternative of myth or reality for responsible finance still leaves a slight doubt. Will it be necessary to go through "technological evangelism,"[1] this quasi-religious veneration, to make responsible finance a major actor in the financing of the future?

Being a whistleblower is good, but here, with responsible finance, as in many areas, the central question remains that of the method, that of "how" to act. And there, the consensus is no longer appropriate. We have a lot of work ahead of us!

[1] Durand (Rémi), "Technological evangelization," Publisher FYP, 2018.

Accessibility: The principle of accessibility established by the law of February 11, 2005, aims to allow all disabled people to perform the acts of everyday life, regardless of their disability. Before January 1, 2015, some 650,000 public establishments will have to be developed to allow access to the services offered under appropriate conditions (source: www.culture.gouv.fr/handicap).

Agence de l'environnement et de la maîtrise de l'énergie (ADEME): A French public industrial and commercial establishment (EPIC) created in 1991. It is placed under the tutelage of the ministers in charge of the research, ecology, and energy, and its mission is to generate, animate, coordinate, facilitate, or carry out operations aimed at protecting the environment and controlling energy.

Association française de normalisation (AFNOR): The French Association for Standardization (abbreviated AFNOR) was created in 1926. It is the French organization that represents France at the International Organization for Standardization (ISO) and the European Committee for Standardization (CEN).

Best-in-Class: Focusing investments in companies that have historically performed better than their peers within a particular industry or sector based on analysis of environmental, social, and corporate governance (ESG) issues. Typically involves positive or negative screening, or portfolio tilting.

Bpifrance: A French organization for financing and development of companies, created in December 31, 2012, and whose capital is held by the French State and Caisse des Dépôts et Consignations.

The Carbon Disclosure Project (CDP): An association that brings together the world's largest groups and evaluates each year the consideration of climate issues in their activities and the control of their greenhouse gas (GHG) emissions (source: www.cdproject.net).

CIGALES Network: It is primarily a club of investors that meets its members several times a year, collects their regular contributions to form a collective pool, and invests in small businesses in creation or young.

Circular Economy: It designates an economic concept that fits into the framework of sustainable development (green economy, eco-design, industrial ecology, etc.). It aims to build economic growth that is not based on the depletion of natural resources, but on a reasoned use of materials and energies. The circular economy promotes the use of renewable energies and recycling is an ecological and economic model that needs to be virtuous. It aims to create innovative products, services, business models, and public policies. The circular economy is a functional economy that encourages reuse and recycling and places particular emphasis on new modes of design, production and consumption, the extension of the duration of use of products, the use rather that the possession of good, the reuse and recycling of components, and the non-use of toxic products in the manufacturing processes. The goal of the circular economy is to decouple economic growth from the depletion of natural resources by drawing inspiration from the functioning of natural ecosystems. The establishment of a circular economy is part of the energy and ecological transition approach. The production and consumption model that has prevailed since the industrial revolution is based on abundant natural resources and a linear pattern: extracted raw materials > production > consumption > waste. This model of development has accelerated "progress" and has enabled billions of people to gain some material prosperity. The foundation of the consumer society today finds its limits in the face of environmental challenges, employment, and increase in world population, which should increase by 43% between 2012 and 2100. Our levies on natural resources already far exceed biocapacity of the land, that is, its ability to regenerate renewable resources, provide nonrenewable resources, and absorb waste. Collective awareness has made it possible to take steps to reduce environmental impacts, as an essential first step. However, reducing the impact of the current development model only reduces the deadline. A more ambitious step is needed (source: www.institut-economie-circulaire.fr).

Cleantech: These are industrial techniques and services that use natural resources, energy, water, raw materials (e.g., renewable energies, energy efficiency, eco-mobility, and circular economy) in a perspective of significant improvement of the environment, efficiency, and productivity. This approach is accompanied by a systematic reduction of the induced toxicity and the volume of waste, and ensures a performance identical to or superior to existing technologies. A large and growing venture capital investment category representing a range of products, services, and processes that either directly reduce or eliminate ecological impacts or require lower resource inputs. Cleantech is an investment theme rather than an industrial sector as it may include investments in agriculture, energy, manufacturing, materials, technology, transportation, and water.

Climate Bonds Initiative: An investor-focused, not-for-profit organization that works to mobilize bond markets for climate change solutions. The aim is to reduce the cost of capital for climate-related investments by developing a large and liquid market, while providing trusted standards and certification.

Climate Principles: It brings together a set of financial institutions determined to play an active role in the fight against climate change, through their professions as advisor, lender, investor, and insurer (source: www.theclimategroup.org).

Collateralized Debt Obligation (CDO): An obligation issued by an entity (usually created by a bank) to finance the redemption of a bank's credit. In this way, loans are transformed into securities traded on the financial markets.

Common: A system that wants to be as open as possible with one or more shared resources (natural or intangible) at the center, managed collectively by a community. It establishes rules and governance in order to preserve and perpetuate this resource while having the right to use it. The commons thus question the question of property. Thus, currently we have two types of property: public property and private property. The commons are a third way to explore. Elinor Ostrom received a Nobel Prize in Economics for her work on the commons.

Conference of the Parties (COPs): COP21, COP22, and COP23: A UN conference on climate change that is held annually. The 21st conference (COP21) was held in Paris in December 2015. The conference negotiated the Paris Agreement, a landmark global treaty on the reduction of climate change. The treaty lays out a framework to limit global warming to less than 2°C compared to preindustrial levels. COP22 was held in Marrakech, November 2016, and COP 23 in Bonn, November 2017.

Corporate Governance: The system of rules, practices, and processes by which a company is directed and controlled. Corporate governance refers to all the relationships between the management of a company, its board of directors, its shareholders, and other stakeholders. It also defines the framework within which the company's objectives are set, the means to achieve them and monitor its performance (source: www.ademe.fr).

Corporate Social Responsibility (CSR): Corporate responsibility involves the search for an effective "fit" between businesses and the societies in which they operate. "Corporate responsibility" refers to the actions taken by businesses to nurture and enhance this symbiotic relationship. CSR is the integration of sustainable development by companies in their strategy, day-to-day operations, and stakeholder relations. This approach integrates the three pillars of sustainable development: the economic, social, and environmental dimensions. CSR concerns "the company's voluntary integration of environmental and social concerns into its business activities and stakeholder relations," according to the 2001 European Commission.

Credit Default Swap (CDS): Insurance contract on the repayment of a loan. The buyer pays an annual premium based on the value of the security and the seller agrees to compensate it in case of loss of value of the loan.

Crowdfunding or Cash Back: Allows the customer and the customer of a platform to collect a commission (the seller to pay a commission to the platform to which he adheres). The commission back to the client can be assigned to a solidarity project of his choice.

Decommissioning: Represents the separation of activities between retail banking and investment bank for speculative purposes on own account without exposing customers' deposits to risk.

Deregulation: The removal of regulations and control over the prices of banking services to allow a smoother flow of financial flows. She started in the United States before going to the rest of the world. Apart from the harmonization of financial systems and the removal of transfer fees, major innovations in this area are related to decompartmentalization.

Disintermediation: Characterizes the direct access of companies to financing by issuing securities rather than by indebtedness to institutional actors.

Ecolabels: These are government-initiated awards that allow consumers to identify products with a reduced impact on the environment.

Ecological Footprint: It is a tool for measuring man's impression on nature, which compares the consumption of the planet's resources with the earth's ecological capacity to regenerate them (source: www.wwf.fr).

Energy Efficiency: It characterizes processes and technologies that reduce the amount of energy required for an activity and therefore save energy.

Energy Transition Law (French)—Article 173: In August 2015, France passed the Energy Transition Law, the first of its kind in Europe, which came into full effect in June 2017. France has decided to provide a clear signal to institutional investors with this law by encouraging them to become truly engaged on the subject of RI and start considering how to better integrate ESG factors in their investments. The law reinforces the role of institutional investors in financing the transition toward a low-carbon economy and requires more awareness of long-term issues in investment decisions.

Engagement: This is the practice of shareholders entering into dialogue with management of companies to change or influence the way that company is run.

ESG: Environmental, social, and governance issues that constitute the three pillars of responsible investments. E, S, and G are the three central factors in measuring the sustainability qualities of an investment.

Extra-financial: Elements of a company's behavior that may not be immediately apparent solely from an analysis of its financial data. ESG themes are often associated with extra-financial factors.

Extra-financial Rating: This was born from the need for SRI assessments which is not solely based on the economic performance of the company, but also on its behavior toward the environment, on the respect of social values, societal commitment, and corporate governance. The extra-financial rating mainly comes from external agencies which are the specialized players. Unlike financial rating, they are paid by investors to establish these ratings and not by companies. According to Novethic, we speak of declarative notation as opposed to the rating requested by certain agencies which consists of carrying out extra financial audits at the request of the companies.

Financial Markets: Used in the plural, the term is synonymous with capital markets. Two types of markets are generally distinguished: the money market, which concerns short-term loans (up to 7 years), and the financial market in the strict sense, namely loans over 7 years and shares.

Finansol: Participating in the promotion of a more equitable economy, since 1997 the Finansol label has been distinguishing solidarity savings investments such as solidarity shareholders, booklets, or solidarity funds offered by banks, insurance companies and mutual funds, and social solidarity funds employee savings (source: Finansol website http://www.finansol.org/).

Forest Stewardship Council (FSC): It is one of the leading eco-labels certifying wood products from sustainably managed forests.

Global Impact or the United Nations Global Compact: It is an international initiative with thousands of participants in more than 100 countries committed to aligning the strategy and operation of their business with 10 universal principles, including human rights, labor standards, the environment, and the fight against corruption (source: www.pactemondial.org).

Global Reporting Initiative (GRI): It is an international initiative that brings together many companies, NGOs, and universities to develop common guidelines for companies that want to capture the economic, social, and environmental dimensions of their business (source: www.globalreporting.org).

Green Bonds: A bond that is issued to raise capital for the development of environmentally friendly projects or assets.

Green Economy: Economic activity generated by all companies helping to avoid, reduce, or eliminate environmental nuisances (waste treatment, soundproofing of buildings, production of renewable energy, etc.).

Green Washing: When a company, government, or any other groups make an unsubstantiated or misleading claim about the environmental benefits of a fund or financial instrument.

Hedge Fund: Mutual fund using the loan to achieve a variety of investments yielding returns regardless of stock market trends, which often involve playing down. They are often equated with pension funds.

High Level Expert Group (HLEG) on sustainable finance: Set up by the European Commission to develop an overarching and comprehensive EU strategy on sustainable finance as part of the Capital Markets Union.

Impacts Directs/Direct Impacts: These refer to the positive or negative, environmental, or social effects produced directly by the operation of a business (energy emissions, use of paper, etc.).

Impact Investing: It is defined by JP Morgan as an "investment in socially innovative and impact investing. Impact investing focuses on financing businesses and projects that are designed to have intentional, positive, and measurable impacts on society, while simultaneously delivering financial market returns. As the social impact is fully embedded into the business model, there need not be an inherent trade-off between impact and financial returns. Impact investing harnesses the power of capital toward solving 'real issues' facing society. It is about steering the power of capital toward 'greater utility' commercially competitive unlisted companies intended to produce a return on investment."

Indirect Impacts: These refer to the positive or negative effects, environmental or social, produced indirectly by the activity of a company (financing of a company presenting risks of pollution, of a company producing renewable energy, etc.).

Initial Coin Offering (ICO): This is a fundraising method, operating via the issue of digital assets exchangeable against crypto currencies during the start-up phase of a project (definition of ICO Mentor). These digital assets are called tokens (tokens, in French). That's why ICOs are also called "token sales."

Investissement à impact/Impact Investing: It is defined by JP Morgan as an "investment in socially innovative and commercially competitive unlisted companies intended to produce a return on investment."

ISO Standards: Thees are international standards of voluntary application intended for any type of organization whose monitoring can lead to certification. Their goal is to define and share good practices (source: www.iso.org).

ISO 14001: It defines the rules for integrating environmental concerns to enable organizations to reconcile their operating requirements with respect for the environment.

ISO 26000: It is implemented in 2010, introduces the guidelines on social responsibility and aims to encourage organizations to contribute to sustainable development.

Low-carbon Economy: An economy based on low-carbon power sources with minimal carbon emissions into the environment. It makes reference to a world where the temperature increase is contained below 2°C or 1.5°C.

Low-energy Buildings: These are buildings that achieve a very high level of energy performance, which categorizes them in class A of the "energy" label of energy performance diagnosis (EPD).

Market Terms: This is a market on which an executable contract is negotiated in the future.

Microcredit: It is the allocation of small loans to small entrepreneurs or people who are excluded from traditional lending systems. This activity is developing mainly in emerging countries but also exists in developed countries.

Microfinance: These services provide financial services tailored to people excluded from the financial system. They are a means of fighting poverty, especially in emerging countries.

Mr. "Mondialisation": This is an informal think tank and Francophone citizen with an international focus. Its objective is to fuel free debate in the public sphere around the major global and local issues of our time and its website is mr.mondialisation@gmail.com

Negative Screening/Disinvestment: An investment approach that excludes some companies or sectors from the investment universe based on criteria relating to their policies, actions, products, or services. Negative screening is a strategy of avoiding investing in companies whose products and business practices are harmful to individuals, communities, or the environment. It is a common mistake to assume that SRI "screening" is simply exclusionary, or only involves negative screens. In reality, SRI screens are being used more frequently to identify and invest in companies that are leaders in adopting clean technologies, managing environmental impacts, and integrating exceptional social and governance practices (see "Positive Screening" below).

New Economic Regulations Act (NRE): This obliges French listed companies since 2001 to include a section in their annual report on how do they take the social and environmental consequences of their activity into account.

New Economic Regulations Act (NRE): It is a law which obliges French listed companies since 2001 to include in their annual report a section on how they take into account the social and environmental consequences of their activity.

Novethic: Media and research center, Novethic fosters global understanding of the economy and its transition to a more responsible business model. The research center supports the implementation of best practices in sustainable finance and trains decision-makers, managers, and operational staff within corporations and financial institutions. Novethic is a pioneer in certification in Europe. It has years of experience in the labelling market. Since 2009, it has created and promoted a label scheme that indicates the sustainable and environmental quality of financial products. Novethic offers two types of labels: ESG labels and Green labels. It offers high-quality training to investment professionals to deepen their knowledge of sustainable and ESG issues. These training include Master Classes, which offer investors thorough training courses built on the experiences of their peers, and The Sustainable Investment Training Course, which trains financial advisors to integrate ESG and ethics factors in their investment advice. It is funded by the European Commission in accordance to the Leonardo Program. Novethic publishes research reports about the latest responsible investment trends, for instance figures on responsible investment market. In depth, it analyses the sustainable impact the investment process or climate commitment of investors might have. Novethic describes exhaustively the mobilization of investors to tackle climate change. It has developed CarbonRisk, a tool to easily identify the investment risks associated to climate change. Regularly, it updates reports about this unique market development (source: http://www.novethic.fr/novethic/v3/qui-sommes-nous.jsp).

Observatory of the Banking Inclusion: It is created by the law of July 26, 2013, and regulated by the decree of June 30, 2014. The Observatory which brings together representatives of public organizations, associations, and banks draws up an annual report including an analysis of indicators of banking inclusion, the practice of credit institutions (monitoring of the right to the account, the basic banking service and the evolution of microcredit ...) and possible recommendations.

Open Bank: this term, which could be translated as "modular banking system," refers to the fact that banks share the data they have at their disposal with other banking services.

Pan European Forest Certification (PEFC): This is an organization that certifies products whose timber has been harvested from European forests, maintained according to the rules of sustainable forest management, particularly in terms of replanting plant species.

Peer-to-Peer Lending: This is an emerging industry that facilitates credit sources outside the traditional banking circuit by connecting consumers and small businesses directly with potential investors.

Pôle Finance Innovation: It is created and certified in 2007, by Christine Lagarde, Minister of the Economy, Finance and Employment, is the main institution bringing together the FinTech ecosystem and innovation in the finance sector.

Principles for Responsible Investment (PRI): The UN-supported Principles for Responsible Investment (PRI) initiative was launched in 2006. The world's leading proponent of responsible investment, PRI is an independent organization bringing together and supporting an international network of investors to put the six Principles for Responsible Investment into practice.

Principles of Ecuador: These are a set of guidelines that requires a detailed analysis of each new project funding of more than $10 million to meet the World Bank's social and environmental standards.

PRIIPS: (for Packaged Retail Investment and Insurance Products), Regulation (EU) 1286/2014 of the European Parliament and of the Council of November 26, 2014, on key information documents relating to packaged retail and insurance-based investment products. This regulation aims to increase the transparency and comparability of pre-contractual information presented to investors.

Renewable Energy: Energy is renewable when it is produced through natural processes (sunlight, wind, waterfall, etc.). Renewable energies do not emit GHGs, unlike fossil fuels (source: www.ademe.fr).

Replication Product or Tracker: It is also called Exchange Trade Funds (ETF), is an index fund that seeks to replicate the performance of a value or index.

Securitization: Transformation of receivables into securities made by the sellers to a company created for this purpose, which finances the purchase of the receivables by sellingby selling securities. Securitization allows a bank to transfer credit risks to other agents.

Shadow Finance (Shadow Banking): It includes all companies that provide banking services (credit, wealth management, etc.) but are not regulated as such. These include hedge funds, crowd funding platforms, and wealth management companies.

Shareholder and Responsible Democracy: It is a formulation of English origin meaning that listed companies must allow their shareholders to decide on the remuneration levels of their managers. In France, although privileging the self-regulation recommended by the code of ethics of governance defined jointly by the AFEP (French Association of Private Enterprises) and Medef (Movement of Companies of France), in 2014, the leaders of the CAC 40 were subject to the system of "Say on Pay" which introduces the concept of consultation on their remuneration.

Social Cohesion Fund: This was created by the law of January 18, 2005, and its management is entrusted to the Caisse des Dépôts et Consignations. Its purpose is to guarantee for social purposes loans to natural or legal persons and loans to the unemployed or holders of social minima setting up their business" (Article 80 of the law). The fund is funded by the state and an orientation council oversees the destination of the funding granted.

Social Networks (definition of Mercator, Dunod Edition: mercator-publicitor.fr website): *"designate websites and mobile applications that allow users to build a network of friends or relationships, which promote social interactions between individuals groups of individuals or organizations."*

Solidary Company of Social Utility (In French: "Entreprise Solidaire dUtilité Sociale" = ESUS): In order to obtain this ESUS approval, companies must act in one or more areas of the social and solidarity economy and meet many criteria (the average of the 5 highest salaries does not exceed 7 times the SMIC; high cannot exceed 10 times the SMIC, leaders are elected by employees or members, at least 30% of employees have contracts for integration or professionalization, or are recognized workers with disabilities ...).

Solidary Economy: It favors social and environmental actions in relation to commercial and financial objectives: micro finance (solidarity credits), savings or solidarity investment, fair trade, integration companies are part of it (source: www.ademe.fr).

Spread: It is the difference between the actuarial rate of a given bond and the actuarial rate of a zero coupon bond with similar characteristics. In practice, instead of the zero-coupon bond, a benchmark government bond, considered risk-free, is generally used.

SRI: Socially Responsible Investment is above all an investment whose objective is to create value, and is characterized by the consideration of ESG criteria in the choices of the saver. SRI refers to various approaches to integrating sustainable development into financial management. It consists in taking into account so-called "extra-financial" criteria, that is to say ESG criteria in their choice of investment (source: www.novethic.fr).

Stakeholders: Designate the individuals and/or organizations that an organization can impact through its business. They may be internal or external stakeholders, public or private (employees, shareholders, customers, suppliers, NGOs, public authorities, local authorities, consumer associations, etc.).

Sustainable Development: This is a model of development that refers to "the ability to meet the needs of present generations without compromising the ability of future generations to meet their own needs" (Brundtland Report, 1987). It integrates three dimensions: economic (efficiency, profitability), social (working conditions, human rights), and environmental (consumption, polluting emissions) (source: www.ademe.fr).

Sustainable Purchases: A sustainable purchasing policy involves taking environmental and social criteria into account in purchasing process decisions. It aims at the acquisition of environmentally friendly products, social laws and ethics, but also the incentive of providers and suppliers to engage in this process (source: www.ademe.fr).

The United Nations Environment Program (UNEP): This is an organization established in 1972 to coordinate United Nations activities in the field of the environment, to assist countries in the implementation of environmental policies and encourage sustainable development (source: www.unep.org).

Triodos Bank: This has been financially supporting the sustainable economy since 1980. Triodos Finance B.V., an intermediary in banking operations and sole agent of the Dutch company Triodos Bank N.V. was founded in 1980 in the Netherlands. In France, the representation was created in 2013 and is part of the Triodos Bank group, the world's leading sustainable bank.

United Nations Development Program (UNDP): UNDP is the United Nations' global development program. It works across 170 countries and territories, helping to achieve the eradication of poverty, and the reduction of inequalities and exclusion.

United Nations Environment Program (UNEP): UNEP was set up in 1972 as an agency of the United Nations to assist developing countries in implementing environmentally sound policies and practices. Today, UNEP is the leading global environmental authority, setting the global environmental agenda within the United Nations system.

UN Global Compact: An initiative to encourage businesses worldwide to adopt sustainable and socially responsible policies and report on their implementation. The UN Global Compact supports companies to

- do business responsibly by aligning their strategies and operations with Ten Principles on human rights, labor, environment, and anti-corruption; and
- take strategic actions to advance broader societal goals, such as the UN Sustainable Development Goals, with an emphasis on collaboration and innovation.

UN Environmental Program Finance: Initiative (UNEP FI): An initiative led by the UN that seeks to encourage the implementation of sustainability principles in financial institutions through the incorporation of ESG factors in risk analyses.

Accenture Report, *Fintech: Has the Revolution Aborted*? 2017

Aglietta (M.) & Rebérioux (A.), *Drift of Financial Capitalism*, Albin Michel, Paris, 2004

Allouche (D.) & Prigent (I.), *Financial Markets without Faith nor Law?*, PUF, 2016

AMF, *AMF Report on Socially Responsible Investment (SRI) in Collective Management*, November 2015

Antignac (C.) & Attali (B.) "High-Yield Societal Investment, the Revolution of Impact Investing", *Essentials of Banking and Finance*, Revue Bank Editions, Publisher Bank Review, 2016

Banking on Climate Change, Report Published at the End of March 2018 by Several NGOs, Oxfam, Greenpeace, Rainforest

Banque de France, For an Analysis of the Financial Crisis of 2007 and the Following Years: "Documents and debates" of the Banque de France: The number 2 published in February 2009 and the number 3 published in January 2010

Barberis (J.) & Christi (S.), *The FINTECH Book, The Financial Technology Handbook for Investors, Entrepreneurs and Visionaries*, Wiley, 2017

Basel Committee, "Sound Practices: Implications of Fintech Developments for Banks and Bank Supervisors", Consultative Document, August 2017, 49 pp.

Beffa (J.L.), *To Transform or Die*, Seuil, Paris, February 2017

Bouzidi (A.), *Patient Capital: A Horizon for France and Europe* Work published in 2016 within Terra Nova

Bruckner (P.), *The Wisdom of Money*, Essay Grasset, Paris, 2016

Capron (M.) & Quairel-Lanoizelée (F.), *The Company in Society, a Political Issue*, Textbooks Collection, Great Landmarks, La découverte edition, Paris, January, 2015

Capital Review, An article in the section Economy Finance, under the title "Difficult to Understand but Revolutionary, the Blockchain", March 2017, pp. 78–80

Castanet (C.), "Week of Employee Savings", *Magazine of the Financial Professions and the Economy*, Dossier, no. 12, June 2017, pp. 7–8

Chanteau (J.P.), Coriat (B.), Labrousse (A.), & Orsi (F.), "Introduction", *Regulatory Review*, 2nd Semester, Autumn, 2013

Chanteau (J.P.) & Labrousse (A.), "Elinor Ostrom's Methodological Institutionalism: Some Issues and Controversies", *Regulatory Review, Capitalism, Institutions, Powers* [Online], p. 14, 2013

Coriat (B.), *The Return of the Commons, the Crisis of the Ideology Owner*, LLL editions: The links that liberate 2015

Davis (K.) & Bolstrom (R.L.), *Business and Its Environment*, McGraw-Hill, New York, 1966

De Brabandère (L.), *Homo Informatix*, le Pommier Edition, Paris, September 2017

De Lacoste (A.), *The Lord of Robots*, Public debate editions, Paris, October 2017

Demaria (C.), *Sustainable Development and Finance*, Maxima, Paris, 2004

Deschodt (E.), *History of the Mont-de-piety*, edition of the search for noon, November 1993

"Devoted to the Climate Transition", *Bank Review*, Supplement no. 809, pp. 35-38

Dreyfus (M.), *Financing Utopias, a History of Crédit Coopératif (1893–2013)*, with the support of the Crédit Coopératif Foundation, Actes Sud, 2013

Dughera (J.), "Solidarity Finance: History and Relevance", *The Encyclopedia of Sustainable Development*, no. 103, des Récollets Editions, November 2009

Eliet (G.), "The New Business Ethics, Point of View", *Les Echos*, July 16–17, 2004, p. 13

Fernandez (B.F.), "Ethics vs Finance? An Analysis of the Origins, Problems and Future Prospects of this Relationship", *Review: Finance & the Commons*, no. 39, 2011

Festinger (L.), *A Theory of Cognitive Dissonance*, 1957

"Financing a Sustainable European Economy", Final Report 2018, High-Level Expert Group on Sustainable Finance, UE, January 2018

Frederick (W.C.), "The Growing Concern Over Business Responsibility", *California Management Review*, 1960, pp. 54–61

Freeman (R.E.), *Strategic Management: Stakeholder Approach*, Pitman, Boston,1984

Frontezac (S.), "Towards a Generalization of the Compliance Programs", Letter no. 50 of the French Association of Government of the Enterprise (AFGE), 3rd quarter 2017

Ganascia (J.G.), *Myth of Singularity, Is It Necessary to Fear Artificial Intelligence?*, Seuil Editions, Paris, 2017

Gendron (C.), "Social Issues and Representations of the Company", *Review of the Semiannual Mauss*, 2000 p. 15

Guérin (I.), Labie (M.), & Servet (J.M.), *The Crises of Microcredit*, Zed Books, London, 2002

Igalens (J.) & Joras (M.), *Corporate Social Responsibility, Understanding, Writing the Annual Report*, Personal Collection /ANDP, Paris, 2002

Jeffers (E.) & Pastré (O.), (Under the direction of): "Efficiency, Resilience and Social and Societal Commitments of Mutual Financial Institutions". Study returned at the beginning of 2017 and carried out within the framework of the Center for Research on Mutual Finance (CREFIM) for the group Caisse des Dépôts et Consignations

Le Goff (J.), *The Exchange and Life, Economy and Religion in the Middle Ages*, Plural Collection, Hachette Literatures, 2004

Le Net (M.), Editorial of the journal "Ethical Company", no. 16, April 2002

Lederer (E.), "Banks may Have Trouble Resisting the Wave of Fintech", *Les Echos*, September 4, 2017

Les Echos, Economic Newspaper, "The Payment Industry in the Face of Digital, Mapping of Supply, Decryption of Competitive Developments and Analysis of Winning Strategies", *Les Echos Etudes*, November 2017

Lewis (A.) & Mackenzie (C.), "Morals, Money, Ethical Investing and Economic Psychology", *Human Relations*, vol. 53, no. 2, 2000, pp. 179–191

Lobez (F.) & Vilanova (L.), *Bank Micro Economics, Finance Collection*, Presses Universitaires de France, Paris, 2006

Luther (R.G.), Matako (J.), & Corner (D. C.), "The Investment Performance of UK Ethical Unit Trusts", *Accounting, Auditing and Accountability Journal*, vol. 5, no. 4, 1992, pp. 57–70

Luyendijk (J.), *Diving in Murky Water — An Explosive Investigation among Bankers*, Plon Publishing, Paris, 2016, under the translation of De Plunkett L.

Mc Guire (J. W.), *Business and Society*, McGraw-Hill, New York, 1963

Mortier (G.), *Ethical Finance: The Big Misunderstanding*, FYP editions, Paris, April 2013

Moussé (J.), *Business Ethics: Freedom, Responsibility, the Decision-Maker Facing the Ethical Question*, Dunod, 2001

Neuviale (A.) & Voyenne (D.), *Participatory Finance for Business,* Economica, Paris, 2016

Neuviale (A.) & Voyenne (D.), *Option Finance*, no. 1418, June 12, 2017, two articles: Page 26, Asset Management section: "Investors More and More Mobilized by the Climate". Page 36 of the dossier, the big debate (pp. 33--43): "The De-carbonization of Portfolios Is Essential in Asset Management"

Orléan (A.), *Power of Finance*, Odile Jacob, Paris, 1999

Ostrom (E.), *Governing the Commons: The Evolution of Institutions for Collective Action*, Cambridge University Press, Cambridge, 1990

Paranque (B.) & Perez (R.), *Finance Differently? Critical Réflexions and Perspectives on Modern Finance*, Collective work, Septentrions Presse Universitaire, 2016

Pastré (O.) & Vigier (M.), *Capitalism Disoriented,* Ed. La Découverte, 2003

Patten (D.) et al "The Market Reaction to Social Responsibility Disclosures: The Case of the Sullivan Principles Signings", *Accounting, Organizations and Society*, vol. 15, no. 6, 1990, pp. 575–587

Perez (R.), *Corporate Governance*, Landmark collection, La Découverte Edition, 2003

Pick (P.), Serres (M.), & Vincent (J. D.), *Qu'est ce que l'humain*, éditeur Le Pommier, Paris, 2010

Postel (N.) & Sobel (R.), Collective work published under the direction of: *The critical Dictionary of CSR*, in a chapter devoted to the NRE (New Economic Regulation) law, Presses Universitaires du Septentrion, 2013, pp. 294–298

Report of the French Committee on Investment with Social Impact, President, Hugues Sibille, Reporter, Cyrille Langendorff, State Representatives, Claude Leroy Themeze (MEF), Nadia Voisin (MAEDI), September 2014

Ricœur (P.), "Ethics and Morals", *Journal of the Catholic Institute of Paris*, vol. 1, no. 34, April–June 1990, 131

Rifkin (J.), *The New Zero Marginal Cost Society*, Actes Stud, Paris, February 2016

Roux (M.), *Management of Retail Banking*, Eska Editions, Paris, March 2017

Roux (M.), *Strategy and Governance of Mutual Financial Institutions*, Revue Bank Editions, Paris, September 2015

Roux (M.), "University Point of View: Could Confidence and Growth Be Reborn?", Letter no. 44 of the French Association of Corporate Governance, April 2016

Savall (H.), Péron (M.), Zardet (V.), & Bonnet (M.), *Socially Responsible Capitalism Exists*, Management in Freedom Collection, EMS Editions, Paris 2017

Schumpeter (J.), *Theory of Economic Evolution*, Dalloz, Paris, 1935

Segrestin (B.) & Hatchuel (A.), *Refund the Company*, Seuil Editions, Paris, 2012

Segrestin (B.), Levillain (K.), Vernac (S.), & Hatchuel (A.), *The Company with Extended Social Object: A New Status for the Company*, Economy/Management Collection, Presses des Mines, Paris, 2015

Senard (J. D.) & Notat (N.), Report: "The Company, Object of Collective Interest", 2018

Storrer (P.), "Electronic Money Law", *Bank Publishing Review*, Paris, 2014

Teoh (S.), Welch (I.), & Wazzan (C. P.), "The Effect of Socially Activist Investment Policies on the Financial Markets: Evidence from the South Africa Boycott", *Journal of Business*, vol. 72, no. 1, 1999, pp. 35–89

Valérian (F.), *Crisis in the Governance, Business Ethics and Searched Profit*, Eska Editions, 2011

Vidal (F.), Finance: the illusion of security, "How to Know if Finance Is No Longer a Weapon of Mass Destruction? How to Be Sure That the Next Financial Crisis Will Not Bring the World Economy Back into Turmoil?". *Les Echos*, web site: heading; debates, August 7, 2017

Walton (C.C.), *Corporate Social Responsibilities*, Wadsworth, Belmont, CA, 1967